Messages from Heaven and Other Miracles

Chicken Soup for the Soul: Messages from Heaven and Other Miracles
101 Stories of Angels, Answered Prayers and Love That Doesn't Die
Amy Newmark

Published by Chicken Soup for the Soul, LLC www.chickensoup.com
Copyright ©2019 by Chicken Soup for the Soul, LLC. All Rights Reserved.

The publisher gratefully acknowledges the many publishers and individuals who granted Chicken Soup for the Soul permission to reprint the cited material.

Front cover image of rainbow courtesy of iStockphoto.com/rakoptonLPN (©rakoptonLPN)
Front cover image of tree courtesy of iStockphoto.com/Zerbor (©Zerbor)
Back cover and Interior photo artwork courtesy of iStockphoto.com/baona (©baona)
Photo of Amy Newmark courtesy of Susan Morrow at SwickPix

Cover and Interior by Daniel Zaccari

Distributed to the booktrade by Simon & Schuster. SAN: 200-2442

Publisher's Cataloging-In-Publication Data
(Prepared by The Donohue Group, Inc.)

Names: Newmark, Amy, compiler.
Title: Chicken soup for the soul : messages from heaven and other
    miracles : 101 stories of angels, answered prayers and love that
    doesn't die / [compiled by] Amy Newmark.
Other Titles: Messages from heaven and other miracles : 101 stories of
    angels, answered prayers and love that doesn't die
Description: [Cos Cob, Connecticut] : Chicken Soup for the Soul, LLC,
    [2019]
Identifiers: ISBN 9781611599855 | ISBN 9781611592856 (ebook)
Subjects: LCSH: Miracles--Literary collections. | Miracles--Anecdotes. |
    Angels--Literary collections. | Angels--Anecdotes. | Prayers--Literary
    collections. | Prayers--Anecdotes. | LCGFT: Anecdotes.
Classification: LCC BL487 .C453 2019 (print) | LCC BL487 (ebook) | DDC
    202.117/02--dc23

Library of Congress Control Number: 2018960683

PRINTED IN THE UNITED STATES OF AMERICA
on acid∞free paper

25 24 23 22 21 20 19   01 02 03 04 05 06 07 08 09 10 11

Messages from Heaven and Other Miracles

101 Stories of Angels, Answered Prayers and Love That Doesn't Die

Amy Newmark

CSS

Chicken Soup for the Soul, LLC
Cos Cob, CT

Changing the world one story at a time®
www.chickensoup.com

Table of Contents

❶
~Saying Goodbye~

❷
~Love That Doesn't Die~

❸

~Finding Faith~

❹

~Signs from Above~

❺

~Heavenly Reassurance~

❻

~Answered Prayers~

❼

~Finding Peace~

8

~Heavenly Guidance~

9

~Angels Among Us~

10

~How Did That Happen?~

Saying Goodbye

Love's Farewell

No language can express the power and beauty and
heroism of a mother's love.
~Edwin Chapin

Putting the blood-pressure cuff back in the metal basket on the wall, I looked down at my patient. I brushed some hair back from her forehead and watched her still figure. "Julie, it looks to me like you're leaving us tonight. I'm going to step out of the room and call your family, but I'll be right back."

The fluorescent glare of the hall lights assaulted me as I left her dimly lit hospital room. She was directly across from the nurses' station, a spot we reserved for our sickest patients. I stepped quietly behind the desk and pulled out her chart to locate her emergency contact numbers. As charge nurse of the oncology floor, I had assigned Julie to myself this evening, even though I suspected I was assigning myself a broken heart.

"Hi, David, it's Linda at the hospital."

"How's Julie? Is she okay?"

Listening to the panic in her husband's voice, I tucked away my own emotion for now. "David, she's resting comfortably, but I think you should come. I just checked on her, and I don't think she's going to be with us much longer."

After reassuring David a few more times that Julie was not suffering, and making sure he wasn't driving alone to the hospital, I returned to her room as promised. The months of treatment had made her frail.

She looked like a child lying there rather than a woman my age. I thought about my toddler and preschooler at home. They were probably splashing every inch of the bathroom at that moment, soaking our dog and their daddy as he attempted to give them a bath. I missed some precious moments when I was at work, but I had the next couple of days off. I would be with my children tomorrow. Julie was not likely to see her toddler and preschooler tomorrow or ever again.

Pulling a chair up to her bedside, I took a seat and held her hand. "It's Linda. I'm back, and David is on his way."

Julie couldn't open her eyes or speak, but as long as her heart was beating, she could listen. "Your first hospital admission seems like yesterday, but I guess it was six months ago now. When I saw your diagnosis of lung cancer, well, I don't want to say I blamed you, but there was a certain reassurance there. I thought smoking was where we differed. When you told me you had never smoked, I was so angry. I wanted desperately to blame someone or something for what was happening to you. You, though, handled it with grace and peace."

As I teetered on the edge of losing a friend rather than a patient, the door burst open. David was in the lead followed by parents, in-laws, aunts and uncles. When young people die, it is a very different situation than it is for elderly patients. They have not outlived any of the people who love them.

Standing, I steered David toward the chair. "Just talk to her and hold her hand. Let her know you're here," I said softly.

Rounding the foot of the bed, I guided her relatives out of my way until I was standing directly opposite from David. I picked up Julie's other hand, but held it by the wrist. Now that she had her family with her, I resumed my role as nurse. My hand-holding was pulse-checking in disguise.

Soft sobs and murmured voices filled the room, but for the most part, I only heard Julie's breathing. She was having long periods of apnea, meaning she just didn't breathe at times. As one of those periods of apnea lengthened, I could no longer feel her thready pulse in the hand I continued to hold. Instead of whipping out my stethoscope to listen for a heartbeat, I stayed still. I glanced at my watch to note a probable time of death, but otherwise remained where I was. I had no desire to rush David or his family into this new reality—life without Julie. Besides, they would notice soon enough.

Her erratic breathing gradually quieted the room. All eyes and hearts were fixated on her, watching this young woman slip away. Finally, her mother asked, "Is she…"

Before the question could be completed, Julie gasped for air. Letting go of her hand briefly, I repositioned my index finger on her wrist, searching for and finding a pulse. This time, though, it was stronger. As her breathing became regular once more, there was a collective sigh in the room. By the end of my shift, her condition was stable, and most of her relatives had returned home.

My two days off passed at the speed of light, and I was soon back at the nurses' station. Just as I arrived, Julie had one of our aides roll her wheelchair over to me. While she normally appeared fragile, her body ravaged equally by the disease and the treatment, she glowed that day. Her smile and her spirit had not been dimmed by her physical struggle.

"Linda, they said you were coming back today, and I was hoping to see you. I've been discharged! David has gone to pull the car around."

"Oh, Julie, I'm so happy you're going home," I said. "And I want to apologize for scaring David and your entire family the other night. It's just that I really thought…"

"No, please don't apologize. That's actually the reason I was hoping to see you before I left. I need to tell you what really happened."

I had crouched down so we were face to face, and I found myself once again holding her hand. On some level, I think I needed reassurance that she was really here.

Taking a deep breath, she looked into my eyes. "The other night," she began, and then she paused. "The other night, when I died, I went to heaven."

"I couldn't feel a pulse," I whispered.

"And you shouldn't feel bad about calling David. How could you possibly have known I'd come back?" she said with an impish grin. "Anyway, when I got there, I asked for just a little more time. That sounds crazy, both that I died and that I asked to come back, but I promise it's the truth. The reason I wanted to come back was because I had one little bit of unfinished business here. I've been given just enough time to take care of it."

"What?"

"My girls are so young. We both know they won't remember me."

I started to object, but I knew she was right.

"That's okay. I understand," she said, patting my hand. "But when they are older, even if David gives them the most wonderful stepmom in the world, they will probably wonder about me. I'm not going to be here for any of their special moments, so I'm going to write letters. Sixteenth birthdays, graduations, weddings, whatever—I need to write down what I would say to them."

Tears streamed down my face as I nodded in reply.

"I won't be with them, but my love will be."

—Linda Kinnamon—

Menga's Sign

Mother love is the fuel that enables a normal human
being to do the impossible.
~Marion C. Garretty

Mom was looking very tired. Her long battle with diabetes was nearing its end, as her kidneys were starting to shut down. I spent as much time as I could with her in those final months, and I told my children to cherish every moment with her.

My daughter, Cheyanne, had a special bond with my mom, probably because I was a single mom for many years. From the time Cheyanne was young, my mom took care of her when she was sick and I had to go to work. They would spend weekends together, we went on vacations together, and my daughter even had a special name for her — Menga. We didn't know where the name came from, but she was called that by all of my daughter's friends, and by my son, born eight years later.

After hearing that Menga didn't have much time, Cheyanne, now in her twenties, went to visit her every chance she got. I didn't know much about their conversations during those visits, but after my mom passed, I learned they had spoken about her impending passing.

Eventually, Mom passed away. It was hard, but at least she wasn't in pain anymore. My daughter offered to go with me to the funeral home to make the arrangements. Afterward, we sat in the car, and Cheyanne told me about one of the conversations she had with Mom. She said, "I told Menga that after she passed away, she needed to send me a sign that she is okay, and it needs to be big. Otherwise, I will miss it and not realize it's really her." She said Menga gave a little laugh and promised she would try.

The funeral was a blur. The gravesite poems and prayers were also a blur. Family and friends walked by in tears, offering condolences. Then, out of the blue, a relative who I didn't recognize handed me something. She said, "I made this for you and your family in memory of Aunt LaDon."

I said, "Oh, thank you so much. It's beautiful."

Taking a better look, I realized she had handed me a tile. I elbowed my daughter sitting next to me and said, "Look what someone gave me. Isn't it beautiful?"

My daughter looked at the tile and gasped out loud.

I said, "What's wrong?"

She said, "Look at it!"

I looked again. My mind was still a blur. It showed an etching of a feather, with other feathers turning into birds and flying away. The phrase "Your Wings Were Ready, But My Heart Was Not" was engraved on it. I said, "I know. Isn't it pretty?"

She said, "Mom, look!" As she turned her leg to show me her calf, I quickly realized that the engraved feather on the tile matched the feather tattoo my daughter had put on her leg a year earlier. We both started crying. Yes, her Menga let her know, in a big way, that she was okay.

— Vicky Webster Pealer —

Samantha

For death is no more than a turning of
us over from time to eternity.
~William Penn

When our son Michael was four years old, my husband Jim would take him along on his bicycle, strapped securely into a child seat. On one occasion, Michael began complaining loudly that his dad was sitting too far back on the bike and "squashing Sam." This happened several times, and we concluded that "Sam" must simply be Michael's imaginary friend. So Jim decided to play along and ask Michael a few more questions.

"How old is Sam?"

"Sam is five."

One day, Jim asked, "How is Sam today? Does he like riding on the bike?"

Michael replied rather indignantly (as if his dad should know), "Sam's not a boy! She's a girl. And she's not my friend. She's my sister!"

Jim and I were both stunned and incredibly moved by this revelation, for we knew something that we had never shared with Michael, assuming he would be too young to understand. Before he was born, we had lost a child early in pregnancy. Had it been a girl, we were going to name her Samantha, and she would have been a year older than Michael.

A few months afterward, Michael seemed to stop seeing Sam, but he always remembered her. A couple of years later, we heard someone ask him if he was an only child, and he replied, "No, I have a sister."

In 2014, the year that Michael turned twenty-one, Jim was diagnosed with an aggressive brain tumour just before his fifty-eighth birthday. He bravely endured nine gruelling months of treatment, but nothing worked. Then he developed tumours on his spine, which meant he was bedridden in hospital.

At his bedside about a month before he died, I noticed his spirits seemed to be uplifted by something, and I asked him if anything had happened. He shared with me an amazing vision he had experienced earlier that day.

He had seen a young woman who greeted him with the words, "I've waited a long time to meet you, Dad." Somehow, he knew this was Samantha. She had taken him into a room where a lot of people were present. He had known some of them in this life, but they had died. Others, he did not recognize, but he still knew he had some deep connection with them because Samantha was introducing him to each one.

This vision lessened his fears about death considerably; it was as if he knew all these people would be waiting to greet him. I could only marvel at what he told me, and I thanked God for the comfort it had obviously brought him.

Six days before Jim's death, he was moved into a local hospice. He was unable to say more than a few words during this time and was largely in a semi-conscious state. He looked so worn and haggard that staff were surprised by the contrasting picture of the handsome, smiling Jim I placed by his bedside. He had been through so much, and I could not wish his suffering to be prolonged any longer. But the day before he died, in the middle of one of the worst times of my life, I was "surprised by joy." I had the following experience — one I felt I could only put in words through poetic prose.

The Day Before
The day before you left, dear,
Your face in slumber changed:
You looked so young and carefree,

No longer strained by pain.
A smile kept playing on your lips,
Like I'd never seen before.
You raised your arms as if to greet
Some visitors at the door.
You had seen our unborn daughter
In a vision that you'd had —
When you'd heard her whisper softly:
"I've waited to meet you, Dad."
Although I felt like weeping,
Your smiles made me laugh instead!
Were angels — or lost loved ones —
Now gathering 'round your bed?
I couldn't see what you could see
So I prayed that I might feel
Some semblance of their presence
And know your joy was real.
Then at once it overwhelmed me:
A love far beyond this world —
And a fleeting sense my darling boy
Was with our darling girl.
The day before you left, dear,
Did your spirit just take flight?
Then its shell, no longer needed,
Simply shut down in the night.

— Deacon Sylvie Phillips —

Knowing

*Everything science has taught me — and continues
to teach me — strengthens my belief in the continuity
of our spiritual existence after death.
Nothing disappears without a trace.*
~Wernher von Braun

I had been up since 6:00, going through my notes one last time before my exam. By 9:30, I was satisfied that I had done all I could to prepare. I had forty-five minutes before I had to leave for campus, so I headed off to my bedroom and flopped backwards onto the bed.

Almost instantly, I felt myself being pulled downward, awake but not really present. I was being drawn into a deeply meditative state, unlike anything I had ever experienced before.

I felt myself standing. Then my dad was there, facing me. I could feel his presence and see him as if he were real. His thick, wavy, salt-and-pepper hair was in need of a haircut. His blue eyes were staring at me, his expression solemn.

Suddenly, I realized I was crying. I could feel giant teardrops streaming down my cheeks. I was crying but I didn't know why.

I looked at my dad and could tell that he knew. I could see the wisdom within his eyes. He reached out his hand to comfort me and wipe away my tears, but it didn't help. I only cried harder. Neither of us spoke. Instead, he leaned forward and placed a kiss upon my tear-stained cheek. When I felt his lips touch my skin, I awoke with a start.

I was shaken, uncertain of what had just happened, unsure of where I was or the time. When I thought about the time, I remembered my exam. Had I missed it? I looked over at my alarm clock in a panic. It was 10:10. Forty minutes had passed since I lay down. I had to go.

I jumped up to leave the room, but I stopped when I reached the door. I realized that I felt as if I really had been crying — harder than I had ever cried before. I put my hand up to my cheek to see if there were tears. There were none, but I could still feel Dad's kiss upon my right cheek.

I wanted to call him but there was no time. I gathered up what I needed and headed off. As I walked, I pondered what had just happened. It had felt so real. If it was a dream, did it mean anything? If so, what? Why had I been crying so hard?

I didn't have any answers, but I had to stop thinking about it and refocus on the exam I was about to take.

After the exam, I was busy with my other classes and coursework, as well as spending time with friends. I didn't think about the dream again that day.

The next morning, I was preparing for class when the phone rang. It was my mom. She never called this early. She said that she was on her way to see me and asked me to wait for her. I told her I was about to leave for class, but she asked me to wait. "It is important," she said. My blood ran cold.

I waited for what seemed like hours, sitting at the kitchen table, pressing myself into the corner of the room as if to brace myself for what was to come. I watched the white flakes falling outside my window. It was the first snowfall of the season. Forty minutes had passed when a vehicle pulled up and parked: a gold minivan. Mom's minivan was white. I let out my breath, unaware I had been holding it, and then I saw my two brothers climb out, followed by Mom and our minister.

I buzzed them into the building and waited for the news. Mom burst through my door and blurted out, "Your dad died."

I heard a voice ask, "What happened?" Then I realized it was mine.

"He was struck by a train last night and killed instantly."

I looked down and saw the VCR clock flash 10:10, and then I

remembered the "dream" and the fact that it didn't really feel like a dream, but more like a meditation. It felt real. And then I realized that Dad's spirit knew what was going to happen, and he had come to say goodbye.

Because of that visit on the morning before his death, I know a part of him is still here with me. It doesn't happen very often anymore, but every now and then I feel a kiss on my right cheek, and I smile, knowing it is him.

—Ange May—

Tele-Gram

Grandmother. The true power behind the power.
~Lisa Birnbach

When I think of a truly amazing woman, I think of my grandma — or, as I liked to call her, "Gram." Gram Gerty had this beautiful, warm spirit. She epitomized a Jewish grandma because she never believed anyone could possibly be full. She also looked fabulous, always dressed to the nines. No one ever believed she was her age. She wore big clip-on earrings, but that was the only thing inauthentic about her.

She was the perfect combination of kind but tough. She was forced out of Austria at age thirteen because of the Nazis, so she learned early on how to be a true survivor. When her husband died young, she took over and ran his business on her own. She always said to me, "Kelli, there are ups and downs in life, probably more downs. But you have to focus on the ups."

In November 2013, Gram died at the age of ninety-two. We had a very special relationship and the night she died, although I didn't know she was dying, I had a dream about her.

She and my family were all eating dinner together, something that was important to my grandma. She looked good in my dream, and I remember feeling so happy that she had apparently "recovered" because she had struggled in her final years. My grandma valued her independence, and when she no longer had that, it affected her mentally and physically. In the dream, I was happy she was finally at peace. I said, "Grandma, you look so well. I'm so glad you're okay." And she said, "Yeah, I'm fine."

I was awakened by a call from my dad around 6:00 a.m. He told me that my grandma had passed and I said, "Dad, that is so strange. I had a dream about Gram last night." I told him about the dream and he paused for a moment and then said, "Kelli, I had almost the exact same dream." He described the same scenario I did — that we were sitting around the dinner table eating, and my grandma looked well. She told him she was "fine."

Later that morning, I called my older brother to tell him the sad news. The first words out of his mouth? "That's so weird because I had a dream last night that we were all eating around the table, and she looked good. She told me she was fine."

We couldn't believe it. Nothing like this had ever happened to us before. We never had the same dream. And in all of our dreams, my grandma looked the same — happy and healthy — and she made sure to tell each of us she was fine.

— Kelli Miller —

Safely Arrived

The love between a mother and daughter
knows no distance.
~Author Unknown

From a young age, I loved my mother's stories. She spoke of her childhood during the Great Depression, how it affected her family, and how she worked in a knitting mill as a young teen to help out. She talked about her early twenties, when she and her best friends would go dancing to the sounds of the big bands.

My favorite story was about how she and my father first met while he was visiting her hometown on leave from the Army. It was love at first sight for them! They were married when she was twenty years old, just before he had to ship out for World War II. I relished hearing her tales of visiting my dad when he was stationed at a base stateside, first in Florida and later in Oklahoma. She recalled how she wanted to do her part to support our country during the war while my father was overseas, so she became a real-life Rosie the Riveter, working in an arsenal in upstate Watervliet, New York.

When I was a young girl, I'd come home every day after school to a wonderful snack Mom had prepared for me. She would always sit down and ask me about my day. After my father passed away when I was fourteen, our long chats helped us get through some of the darkest days of grief.

Those cherished talks became a staple of our relationship over the years, and even when I was married and no longer living at home, those phone calls continued, with our good-night call taking place between ten and eleven each evening. It always ended with "love ya."

After the birth of my daughter, we dubbed ourselves the "Three Musketeers" because we three were always together! What a joy to see that special bond I had with my mother now being enjoyed by my daughter. One of my favorite photos of my daughter was taken when she was a little girl, right after her nightly bath. She had been clad in her fuzzy robe, wet hair wrapped up in towel, and legs propped up on the arm of a chair as she happily chatted away on the phone with my mother. One year, Mom even gave my daughter a Christmas "granddaughter" ornament of a little mouse reclining in a chair with a telephone receiver to its ear, symbolizing their nightly chats!

When she was ninety-four, Mom had a bad fall that resulted in her moving to a nursing rehabilitation facility. Mom had always called me on my house phone, so when she first went into the rehab facility, I forwarded my calls to my cell phone to be sure I would never miss one. Our good-night calls continued for a couple of months at our usual time of 10:00–11:00 p.m. with news of how her day went, what she ate, which resident was going home, and what time I'd visit the next day. When she became too weak to dial herself, she'd ask the nurse's aide to call me. Those good-night calls were so important to both of us that we had to keep up our lifetime tradition.

Then one day, Mom became too weak to speak, and our nightly calls came to an end. When I knew the end was near, I whispered to her to say "hello" to my dad, and to please send me a sign when she arrived in heaven so that I knew she was there. She passed early that morning and, through tears, I cancelled the call forwarding to my cell, knowing I would never again hear her special ringtone or her gentle and cheerful voice on the other end of the line.

The rest of that day was a blur. The following morning, I noticed the message light blinking on our home answering machine. I thought it odd, as I had just cancelled call forwarding the day before, and I did not recall hearing the phone ring that night. I clicked the Play button, and the recording said: "Call, Sunday, 10:29 p.m.," followed by two bursts of static, then a hang up. Chills ran up my arms as my heart leapt in my chest. I checked the Caller ID. No incoming calls were listed at all! Tears spilled down my cheeks; I knew it was my mom giving me a sign she knew I would understand — a phone call at our usual time — saying her final "good night, love ya" to me, and letting me know she had arrived safely in heaven.

"Thank you so much for calling me from heaven, Momma," I whispered through tears. "Love ya, too. Forever and always."

— Dorothy Wills-Raftery —

Together Again

Earth has no sorrow that heaven cannot heal.
~Sir Thomas More

My ninety-one-year-old father was in hospice, and my sister Judy and I were at his bedside every day. One day he was so pale and still that I wondered if he was in a coma. I laid my head on the pillow next to his and began to say the Lord's Prayer. "Our Father, who art in heaven…"

Dad began making sounds along with my words and I realized he was praying along with me. A week prior, he had professed his faith in God after decades of considering himself faithless.

I drew a chair next to his bed and sat quietly holding his hand. I stayed later than usual that day, reluctant to go home. I was sure the nurse was going to call me during the night to tell me Dad had died, but the phone didn't ring. I slept until the alarm went off at 7:00 a.m.

As I dressed to leave my house that morning, I looked out my bedroom window. An overcast sky and generally gloomy day reflected how I was feeling. Storm clouds were building in dark, layered formations across the sky.

Arriving at the center around 9:00 a.m., I walked the long hallway to Dad's room, greeting staff and residents along the way.

I paused in the doorway. Judy was already there, sitting next to the bed and holding Dad's hand. Dim light from the only window in the room was diminishing as the dark storm clouds enveloped the building.

I hugged Judy and asked her if he was responsive. She shook her head. The sky outside the window had taken on a deep purple hue, a prelude to a frightening but spectacular show. In minutes, an intense wind began to howl, and driving rain pelted the window. Lightning flashed repeatedly.

Dad's breathing slowed. My daughter Margie and my granddaughter Emily arrived. Three generations of women counted the seconds between breaths. A sense of peacefulness enveloped us as Margie read the Twenty-Third Psalm aloud. It had comforted Dad a couple of days earlier.

The end was near. Each of us dabbed at the tears trickling down our cheeks. We watched as Dad's facial features relaxed.

There was a startling crack of thunder, accompanied by a flash of lightning. We all flinched, but Dad remained still.

Suddenly, his eyebrows lifted, as if he saw something pleasing. I wondered if he was seeing Mom at that moment. Our quietly devout mother had died twelve months earlier, and since then the only thing Dad talked about was wanting to be with Mom. They had been inseparable during their seventy-one years of marriage.

A low, deep rumble of thunder shook the windows in the care center. Our legs could feel the vibrations in the floor of the darkened room. The lights in the building flickered.

One corner of Dad's mouth curled upward as Margie spoke the words, "Yea, though I walk through the valley of the shadow of death, I will fear no evil...."

With that, Dad exhaled for the final time.

The storm outside began to subside. Amazingly, beams of late afternoon sun sliced through a section of the dark clouds, creating a staircase of light that touched the ground outside Dad's window.

Speechless at the sight, I felt God had created a miracle and sent us the sign we needed. Mom and Dad were together again.

—Nancy Emmick Panko—

My Man and the Sea

*There are things that we don't want to happen but have
to accept, things we don't want to know but have
to learn, and people we can't live without
but have to let go.*
~Author Unknown

I will be forever grateful that my husband Bob had minimal physical pain throughout his thirteen months of chemo, radiation, and surgery. His passing was peaceful, with his family present.

Knowing his final wishes, I declined the sales pitch for a fancy urn at the crematorium and handed over a coffee can for his ashes. Specifically, a Folgers coffee can. Coffee had been Bob's lifesaver in many ways. It was vital during long shifts throughout his twenty years of service in the United States Navy. Coffee also helped him maintain thirty-five years of sobriety, for which we were both extremely thankful.

Bob wanted to take advantage of the Navy benefit of having his ashes scattered at sea from a Navy ship, so I started working on that. But I ran into a snag.

I learned his ashes would eventually be put aboard a deploying Navy vessel, and then somewhere, at some time, he'd have his burial at sea. I was sure the service, an honor offered only by the Navy, would be a lovely ceremony. However, no family or friends would be present. That seemed incredibly sad. The paperwork from the Navy instructed me to complete their forms and return them — with Bob's ashes.

I'm sorry, but I was not going to mail my husband! Months later, the Folgers can still sat on Bob's dresser, draped with a white satin cloth a friend had decorated with the American and Navy flags.

While at a family function, I mentioned my quandary. I wanted to comply with his wishes, but I didn't want to send him off with an impersonal ceremony we wouldn't be allowed to attend.

"Hey, we toured an aircraft carrier that's a permanent museum at the San Diego Navy Pier when visiting California," my niece Heather said. "You could scatter the ashes yourself." She paused, trying to recall the ship's name. "Oh, yeah, the *Midway*."

I was stunned. The *USS Midway* had been Bob's first ship and our first duty station together — in San Diego! How serendipitous that my niece had been on the ship recently, and then present when I mentioned my dilemma. What if I took a small portion of ashes to the place our married life started? Then, when I was ready, I could personally deliver the remainder to the Naval Station Norfolk. The plan would return him to two of the three oceans in which he'd served. Would it be irreverent to scatter him, with part of him over here, and part of him over there? I decided he would be okay with that.

Despite some lingering qualms about deviating from Bob's orders, I called Alice, one of my oldest and dearest friends. Our families met while stationed in Rota, Spain, over forty years before. She frequently went to San Diego to visit her son, Jeff. I shared my idea for the trip out west, including the target date of January fifteenth, which would have been Bob's sixty-seventh birthday. She was totally onboard with the idea.

The next question was how to discreetly disperse the ashes. I couldn't just throw them into the air. A strong wind might blow him back on the ship or, worse, onto museum visitors. Not good! I needed the perfect vessel that would stay intact until it hit the water, but then immediately disintegrate before it floated to shore within reach of children, dogs, or shell hunters. I strolled through a craft store seeking inspiration, and I settled on tissue paper.

San Diego had changed since 1969, but it still holds a special place in my heart. The night before going to the ship, I put a few pebbles on a small sheet of red tissue paper. After adding a small sampling of ashes, I folded it into a small square, and then wrapped it in the white paper, shrouding it with the red tissue.

Jeff had been quite close to Bob and decided to come with us to the ship for our ceremony. My first step aboard brought a wave of memories. Once again, I was awed by the massive size of the aircraft carrier. Hours later, we were still touring several decks and soaking in the impressive history of vital missions the great vessel had carried out when we heard an announcement that the museum would be closing soon.

I still hadn't located a quiet, secluded place for our purpose. (Later I learned there was no perfect place because the *Midway* does not allow disbursing of ashes. I hadn't thought such a small tribute would be a problem. And there had been no signs warning against anything going overboard, even my teabag's worth of cremains. But I highly recommend checking the laws so a tribute doesn't become a legal problem.)

Once we found what we thought was the perfect location, the three of us stood alone at the rail. I took the precious packet from my purse, said a few words, and held Bob close for a few moments. "I love you," I said, holding what felt like an awfully tiny package to be so full of meaning to me. I let the parcel fly from the palm of my hand, and a small part of him returned to the sea. Tears followed, and my loving companions gathered me in their arms as our emotions flooded over the three of us.

Another closing announcement forced us to let go of each other. It was then I noticed my precious package still floating atop the water, as a curious seagull flew straight for it. Thankfully, my shriek sent the scavenger soaring away as a corner of the red rectangle tilted downward and slowly disappeared below the surface. Still working to mask my tears and flushed face, we headed toward the hanger bay where an enlistment ceremony was underway. A new generation was taking the helm to protect our shores. A museum employee appeared in the doorway and strongly urged us to leave. Turning to go, I glanced back for one last goodbye. Grabbing Alice's arm, I gasped, "Look!"

Her eyes followed my pointing finger. A red ring of seaweed

rocked gently as it floated directly over the spot where the packet had landed, forming a perfect wreath. I heard in my heart the reassuring phrase that Bob had said so many times during nearly forty-six years. "Ya done good, Wifey."

— Barbara Bennett —

A Mysterious Comfort

*The most beautiful thing we can experience
is the mysterious.*
~Albert Einstein

I was twelve years old when I watched my grandmother die in my father's arms. Dad was sobbing, "Mama, Mama, please don't die!" There I stood at the foot of her bed, dry-eyed, unblinking, holding her feet in those awful black stockings.

I had never seen a grown man cry, let alone someone die. Little did I realize that what I was about to witness would stay tucked deep in my soul for the next thirty years, never to be put into writing — until now. It was like Scarlett O'Hara saying, "I'll think about that tomorrow."

My paternal grandmother lived with us. To me, she was just this old world presence in our home and, as a typical preteen, I felt guilty and selfish for being so resentful. Grandma was from Denmark and spoke broken English. To a twelve-year-old, she was ancient, gloomy, and sort of scary.

As the only girl in a family of boys, certain chores were assigned to me in the care of our grandmother, such as brushing and braiding her waist-length hair. She didn't care about hygiene and rarely allowed my mother to wash her hair. Consequently, my grooming duties were far from pleasant.

On the day she died, my father and I were alone in our two-story house. I remember hearing the horrible thumping sound as Grandma fell down the stairs, probably from a stroke or heart attack. I was right behind my father as he picked up her frail body and gently laid her on her bed. Grandma's eyes were open, and I could hear the rattling sound as her breathing slowed to a stop.

Then, just as she drew her last breath, I stared with amazement as a very thin wisp of what looked like smoke rose up from somewhere between her heart and her head.

I never spoke of what I saw the day my grandmother died. It was way too mysterious, and I did not want to be called a crazy kid.

Fast-forward thirty years to the day I signed up for a class in becoming a hospice volunteer. The class was taught at a large Los Angeles hospital by an oncology nurse named Cathy. I knew intuitively that I had been led to Cathy, who would be a mentor in this thing called Death and Dying. I had been delivering Meals on Wheels for a few years, and hospice felt like my next calling. I attended every class and took copious notes.

One day, Cathy explained a phenomenon she referred to simply and matter-of-factly as The Silver Cord. "If you're lucky," she said to our class, "and you are right there as a patient makes her or his transition, you might see a wisp of what looks like smoke arise from the body at the moment of death. What you are witnessing is the soul, or the spirit, leaving the body."

Oh, my God, I thought, as my mind flashed back to my grandmother's death so long ago. I sat there in that class of potential hospice volunteers feeling absolutely stunned.

I now know, personally, that certain specific conditions have to be exactly right if I am to see The Silver Cord at the moment of someone's death. Most importantly, I cannot be emotionally attached to the dying person, I cannot be crying, and I cannot blink. Other than my grandmother, I have only seen this phenomenon two other times, because usually I am at the bedside of friends and hospice patients who have become dear to me.

Knowing for sure there truly is "life after death" — that the soul, or spirit, rises up — is a profound comfort to me.

— Bobbie Jensen Lippman —

Family Matters

So what is true for life itself is no less true for the
universe: knowing where you came from is no less
important than knowing where you are going.
~Neil deGrasse Tyson

I knocked on the door and then tried the knob without waiting for a response. "Debbie, it's Linda," I called out, stepping inside the living room.

"I'm in the bedroom with Gary. Come on back."

Closing the door behind me, I headed down the hallway that had become so familiar over the past two months. Family photos lined the walls, smiling faces framed in gold. There had been good times and bad times in this small brick house. Now was definitely one of the bad times for this family.

Stepping into the bedroom, I found Debbie right where I expected. She was sitting in the chair beside Gary's hospital bed. His eyes were closed, and he appeared undisturbed by my entrance or the fact that Debbie had called out to me while seated right next to him.

"I came as soon as I could. Our team administrator didn't give me much information, just that you had called about a change in Gary's condition and wanted to see me. How long since he's been awake?" I asked.

"Last night," Debbie answered as she gently stroked his hand. "He wasn't very hungry, just tired. He fell asleep before six and hasn't woken up this morning."

Being a hospice nurse is a privilege. It's an honor to help patients and families with their end-of-life journey. But while I do my best to prepare them for this day, it is never easy. "I'll check him out," I said, grabbing my stethoscope.

Debbie kissed her husband's forehead, and then she stepped out of the room. I listened to his heart and lungs, and checked his vital signs, but Gary remained unresponsive. After finishing my assessment, I went back down the hall in search of Debbie. I found her on the phone in the kitchen, already calling family members.

She hung up the phone and wiped her eyes. "What do you think I should feed him for breakfast?"

"Debbie, I'm sorry," I said, seating myself across the table from her. "We've discussed what would happen when this day arrived, but it's time to go over it again. Gary isn't waking up. We can't feed him or give him anything to drink. He would only choke. His body is shutting down. Hunger and thirst go away. Hearing and smell stay, though. Just be there for him. Hold his hand. Talk to him. If you want, set a strong cup of coffee beside his bed where he can smell it."

"I know. You told me it would happen, but it still came as a surprise. I've cooked for Gary and our family practically all my life. It just doesn't feel right."

Together, we walked back to the bedroom. Gary looked peaceful as I began explaining to Debbie the next steps in the process.

"Mom! What's going on? How's Dad?" A large man filled the bedroom doorway, tears in his eyes.

"You must be Jeff," I said, stepping forward to guide him into the room.

"Son?"

At the sound of Gary's voice, Debbie and I turned in unison. Looking back at us, Gary smiled.

"Oh, sweetheart!" Debbie cried as she flung herself forward, wrapping him in a hug. "We thought you were dying!"

"I'm still here," Gary said as he patted Debbie on the back. "What are you doing off work in the middle of the day?" he asked, looking at Jeff.

"Mom called and told me this might be it, so I rushed over," Jeff replied, wiping his face with the back of his hand.

"I called hospice this morning when you didn't wake up, Gary, and Linda came over. She thought this was the beginning of the end, too. She told me I couldn't feed you," Debbie said.

"Speaking of food, I'm starving!"

"Well, you didn't eat dinner last night or breakfast this morning, so I'm not surprised," Debbie said, casting an accusatory glance my way.

"What I'd love is a steak dinner," Gary continued. "I guess that's not possible, but boy it sounds good."

"Coming right up!" Debbie proclaimed. "Jeff, I have some rib-eye steaks in the freezer. If I thaw one in the microwave, will you grill it?"

"Sure, Mom," Jeff said, following her out of the room.

"Gary, I'm going to stay for a bit if you and Debbie don't mind," I said, taking a seat in a rocking chair near the bed. My mind was replaying the morning's events. What had I missed? How could Gary be awake now when he had been knocking on death's door a few minutes ago?

The quickest steak dinner ever created arrived moments later. Jeff carried the tray into the bedroom with Debbie following on his heels. "I microwaved the potato, but that shouldn't hurt a thing," Debbie beamed. "It's full of butter, sour cream and cheddar, just the way you like it."

"Set it down there." Gary motioned to the over-bed table that hospice had provided.

I moved out of the way, allowing Jeff and Debbie to be on either side of Gary. When he didn't pick up his fork or knife, Debbie began cutting the meat for him. Both Jeff and Debbie offered to feed him, but he refused. After a few more minutes, Gary nodded in the direction of the tray.

"You can take that anytime you want, but it was by far the best steak I've ever smelled."

"You're not even going to taste it?" Debbie asked.

"I'm afraid not, but it really smelled good," Gary said, reaching to hold Debbie's hand. "I need to tell you something, though. I've been doing some visiting. When you couldn't wake me up, it's because I wasn't all here. It's hard to explain, but I've been with Ashley."

"Ashley? But honey, she died in that car accident when she was sixteen," Debbie whispered.

"I know, but she's waiting for me on the other side. She's doing just fine. Little Emmie is right there with her."

"Emmie?" I asked.

"Emmie was Jeff's youngest, but she drowned in a backyard pool when she was only two. Ashley belongs to our oldest child, Rob. You haven't met him yet," Gary said, looking in my direction. Turning back to face Debbie, he continued. "I'm going to be absolutely fine there with Ashley and Emmie. I just thought I should come back and tell you where I'm going."

"Oh, Gary," Debbie sobbed, laying her head on his shoulder.

"One more thing," Gary added. "You won't be joining me there for a very long time, Deb. You will be staying here with our kids and the rest of the grandchildren while I'm with Ashley and Emmie."

Gary's last two days held no more surprises. Debbie spent most of her time at his bedside, talking to him or bringing him food or coffee so he could enjoy the smell. When he peacefully took his last breath, Debbie kissed him goodbye.

"I can't be upset," she said. "Gary took away the fear of the unknown when he came back to tell me where he was going. It's our grand-daughters' time to be with him."

— Linda Kinnamon —

Chapter
2

Love That Doesn't Die

The Beauty of Rubber Bands

The love game is never called off
on account of darkness.
~Tom Masson

We saw it at the same time. It was a sunny, blue-sky day in June, and my daughter Jamie and I were wearing beautiful dresses and walking on a small, paved path on a golf course. We were just a few feet behind a photographer, my new husband Nick, and Nick's two daughters. We were heading to an old, stone bridge for more wedding photos when Jamie and I saw the big, thick rubber band in our path. We stopped, looked at each other, and smiled.

I tucked that rubber band into my bouquet, and we moved on to take more photos and celebrate the joining of our families. It had been twelve years since her daddy had died, and I had waited for just the right partner. I had no doubts about the new adventure we were beginning. Still, that rubber band made my heart swell with happiness. I knew Mike was giving us the thumbs-up, letting his girls know it was okay to move forward.

My late husband Mike used to have a job in which he encountered hundreds of rubber bands a day. What did he do with them? He shoved them in his jeans pockets and brought them home. At first, he just emptied his pockets and left piles of rubber bands on the counter when he walked in the door after work. Then, after much complaining from me, he started putting the rubber bands in brown paper bags and saving them.

"What," I used to ask him, "do you need all those rubber bands for?"

"You never know," he used to say.

I gave up the battle and accepted the fact that our closets would be filled with brown paper sacks stuffed with thick rubber bands.

Just two years into our marriage, when our daughter was not even a year old, Mike was diagnosed with cancer and unable to work as much. The bags of rubber bands dwindled. When he died, I actually missed those rubber bands — even the piles on my counters and in his jeans pockets. Eventually, I put the bags away, far out of sight. I couldn't bear to see them anymore, but I couldn't bear to throw them out, either.

About three months after Mike died, I found a big, thick rubber band just like the kind he had brought home from work so many times. The rubber band was lying on my bathroom counter, but there was absolutely no reason for it to be there. It made me think of Mike and smile, and I laughed out loud for the first time in a long while.

A few weeks later, I found a rubber band hanging from the knob of the cabinet above the stove. I was flabbergasted. I had no idea how it had gotten there. I still don't.

Since then, rubber bands have popped up in my path in the most unusual places. In a clothes hamper. On my mom's dining-room table. On my desk at school after summer vacation. On the deck of a cruise ship in the Caribbean. On a street in New York City.

I found the New York City rubber band a few years after Mike died when I was crossing a busy street in Times Square with two colleagues. We were there for a conference, but had been in the hotel watching the Ohio State/Michigan football game. I'm a die-hard Buckeyes fan, even though I had married a rabid Wolverines fan. Ohio State was losing, and I couldn't stand to watch anymore, so my friends and I left the hotel. When I jumped with glee over the discovery of the wet, dirty rubber band smack-dab in the middle of the crosswalk, my friends thought I was nuts. I explained why finding that rubber band was so thrilling to me, saying that I thought Mike left it so I would know he was watching over me in New York City. My friend Kara commented with a laugh: "Yeah... or maybe he's rubbing it in that his team is beating your team!"

To anyone else, rubber bands are second only to duct tape in the myriad ways in which they can be utilized. They are useful. They are practical. They hold things together. To me, rubber bands are beautiful. They are magical. They held the pieces of my broken heart together until it was healed enough to love again. And now, rubber bands remind me that even though people die, love never does.

—Julie Rine Holderbaum—

12

Butterfly Angel

Awaken to the universe's simple gift of the butterfly.
Watch with fascination and joy as a jeweled treasure
glides by and gently touches your soul.
~K. D'Angelo

My mom loved butterflies, and they were thick in Kentucky the summer after she died. Orange and black monarchs fluttered around me while I clipped and shaped the flowers and bushes that attracted them. I was fifty-seven years old—a wife, mother and grandmother—but I felt like a child, one who needed my momma. I wondered if my life would ever be the same again.

With each passing day, though, the pain eased, and I was finally able to move forward with life as I knew it: family, work, and everyday routines. My husband and I spent most weekends at our home on Nolin Lake in south-central Kentucky. We considered it a get-away from the stresses of our careers. Owning a second home also created responsibilities, but we didn't mind doing the cleaning, cooking, and yard work when fewer things competed for our time. We enjoyed the change of pace. I actually appreciated the outdoors and the effort required to beautify our property. I especially enjoyed maintaining the landscape plants along our semi-circular driveway. Working outside in the sunshine enabled me to clear my head while I mourned for my mom.

I had inherited my mother's love for one of nature's most beautiful creatures, and I became accustomed to regular visits from my many butterfly friends, never forgetting my mother's passion. While trimming plants and pulling weeds as I normally did during the summertime, the orange butterflies entertained me. They never seemed to notice my intrusion into their space.

One day, a single black-and-white striped butterfly appeared. I looked around for others like it, but it was alone. I paused to admire its unique appearance. Then, to my amazement, it soared over to me and landed on my arm. I stood still, not wanting to disturb it.

"Where did you come from, special one?" I asked out loud as if I expected a reply. It remained on my arm for what seemed like minutes, but I was certain it could only have been seconds before it flew away. The monarch butterflies continued their own activity with no regard for that unlikely visitor.

Later in the day, I mentioned my experience with the solitary black-and-white butterfly to my husband. He was not nearly as fascinated with the unusual encounter, so I dropped the subject. But when we boarded our pontoon boat for a long twilight cruise, a black-and-white butterfly flew inside the canopy and again landed upon my arm. I held my breath. As we pulled away from the dock, my new friend took flight and retreated back into the lakeside foliage where it came from.

I knew then that my experience was not happenstance. I began to believe in my heart that Mom was sending me a sign. Of course, she would choose a beloved butterfly as her signal, knowing that I would react lovingly to her presence. I pondered that premise carefully, but chose to keep it private. Nevertheless, it gave me peace.

All summer long, I looked forward to my visits with "Mom" as my black-and-white butterfly angel greeted me at our home on the lake — always alone, but among the many common monarchs.

"Hi, Mom," I'd say as I gave her my undivided attention. And when "she" flew away, I'd respond, "See you next time." And I was confident I would.

As the summer came to an end and the weekends at the lake became less frequent, my butterfly reunions ended. I shared my butterfly story with family and friends. They replied politely with positive comments, but I could tell they didn't really believe in my special butterfly. How could I blame them? I couldn't adequately describe the joy and comfort my butterfly angel brought me.

Three years later, my father passed away. Heartbroken, my sisters, brother and I took on the difficult task of cleaning out our parents' home to prepare it for sale. Each of us discovered items that were meaningful or sentimental to us. One such discovery for me was Mom's book about butterflies. I knew I had to have it, and none of my siblings objected. I took it to my lake house.

My new book was full of pictures of the various butterfly species. I learned that the orange butterflies that kept me company during my lonely summer — although very similar in appearance to the monarch — were most likely the viceroy, Kentucky's state butterfly. And if my research was correct, the black-and-white butterfly sent from my mother was named the zebra swallowtail for its zebra coloring and long tails on its hind wings like a swallow's. My newfound knowledge about my butterfly friends — simply knowing their names — somehow added another degree of insight into my acceptance of the special gift my mother gave to me.

Nine years after my mother died, I paid a visit to the cemetery. I stood quietly before the double tombstone engraved with my parents' names. Two zebra swallowtails came to rest gracefully upon the stone. Stillness overcame me as I again realized their significance. And when they took flight, one of them completely encircled me before "she" flew away.

— Pam Carter —

13

Grandpa's Mushrooms

I am… a mushroom on whom the dew of heaven
drops now and then.
~John Ford, The Broken Heart

I spent many happy childhood summers at my grandparents' small cottage in the country, but the summer I turned ten was different. Grandpa had died that winter, and it was just Grandma and me now. The cottage felt empty. Even my parents' arrival for a long weekend visit could not shake the sadness around us. We all missed Grandpa.

Late Saturday morning, I walked into the kitchen where Grandma was making lunch for everyone. The spicy and sweet scent of frying onions filled the air. Grandma added a little oil in the pan, and then put in chopped potatoes. Fried potatoes with mushrooms and onions was Grandpa's favorite dish, and the three of us often went to the forest to pick mushrooms. This summer, with Grandpa gone, Grandma did not feel like looking for mushrooms.

"It smells good," I said.

"No mushrooms. Sorry," Grandma said.

I hugged Grandma. "I like potatoes with onions."

"The salad is ready, too," she said. "Let's go get your parents."

My parents were in the yard inspecting a rotten tree stump next to Grandma's strawberry patch.

"The stump needs to go," Dad said. "Who knows what critters may make it their home. Before we know it, we'll be fighting some trunk rats that attack strawberry plants." He inspected the stump, pushed and pulled it a bit, and kicked it to test how strong it still was. "We need to take it out."

"It would be pretty hard to do," Mom said. "Look how massive this thing is. What was it? A birch? A pine? It's so rotten, I can't even tell."

Dad looked at the stump again. "It's already crumbling by itself, so it won't be hard to take out. What do you think?" He turned to Grandma.

"It was a birch tree," Grandma said and turned to me.

"Your grandpa and I planted it years ago, long before all of you were born."

"I remember it," Dad said. "It was nice." He paused, and then looked at Grandma. "I miss him, too, but he would have wanted this stump removed. Why keep something that's no longer useful?"

"Let's keep it," Grandma said. "Pulling it out might damage the strawberries. The old roots stretch far underground."

"I can do it carefully, and your strawberries will only thank me for ridding them of this monstrosity," Dad said.

"Call me silly," Grandma said, "but I feel like this stump connects me to Grandpa. It was the tree we planted after we got married, and I really want to keep it."

A sudden rain put a stop to our discussion, and we went inside to have our lunch of potatoes fried with onions.

The rain continued the rest of the night and well into the next day. By late afternoon, the sun came out. We walked outside to enjoy the nice weather.

Grandma stopped by the tree stump. "It looks different," she said and put on her glasses.

I ran up to the stump and looked. I couldn't believe what I saw. The whole stump was covered with little brown mushrooms. They grew from the cracks in the wood, right from the rot.

Grandma leaned in and snapped off one little mushroom. She inspected it, broke off the hat, and crushed it between her fingers. She smelled it and then took off her glasses, looked at us, and smiled.

"What are they?" I asked.

"The scientific term is Armillaria. Grandpa always called them honey mushrooms. They were his favorite. The best wild mushrooms there are, he always said."

"Can we pick them?" I asked.

"We sure can," Grandma said. "Bring our mushroom knives and the basket. And tell your dad that the stump stays."

I ran back into the house, grabbed the basket and the mushroom knives, and raced back out. Making sure to cut the mushrooms off carefully to preserve the spores, Grandma and I filled our whole basket in minutes.

"What are these mushrooms called again?" Mom asked.

"Armillaria, or honey mushrooms," Grandma said.

"Can I call them Grandpa's mushrooms?" I said.

"Good idea," Grandma said. "Grandpa would like it."

That night, we ate fried mushrooms for dinner. For the rest of the summer, Grandpa's mushrooms kept coming back after each rain, and we ate a lot of mushrooms, just like when Grandpa was there.

—Julia Gousseva—

14

Lily White

Flowers grow out of dark moments.
~Corita Kent

My father was an avid and gifted gardener. His back yard was an oasis of green in the heart of the city, with a pond filled with water plants, a half-dozen raised beds full of grasses, mosses and flowers, and a bustling population of toads and songbirds. But the most impressive, and most beautiful, were the lilies.

He loved his daylilies, and he had dozens of different variations and species—from the Black Phantom, a deep purple flower that flowed inky dark at its centre, to the tawny daylily with its brilliant orange petals, and the Ruby Spider that started golden near its stamen and shaded into a fierce, vivid red at the tips. In full bloom, Dad's garden looked like a shattered rainbow fallen to the earth.

When he lost his battle with cancer, we saw him off with flowers. Anything else was unthinkable. But it wasn't the same—clipped and stored in vases, on stands, and in a spray across his casket—it just wasn't his garden. But it was the best we could do. There were pastel carnations, roses in scarlet and white, and, of course, lilies.

After the service, I encouraged friends and family to take the flowers. There were so many, and they deserved to be enjoyed for as long as they lasted. When everyone else had gone, I gathered a little bouquet for myself from what was left. All the flowering lilies were gone, so I took a stem with two buds still firmly closed.

The bouquet went into a vase and was, sadly, mostly forgotten. I took Dad's death badly. I'd honestly thought he'd pull through and beat the disease that had been dragging him down for thirteen months. I was lost in a terrible place and couldn't find a way out.

Several weeks went by. The carnations turned brown, curling in on themselves like dead spiders. The roses shriveled, and petals blackened and fell off their stems. The Baby's Breath went dry and crunchy, eventually flaking away. I ignored it all. I couldn't get up the energy to throw them out.

And then, after another sleepless night, I sat down in the kitchen, looked up, and felt like I'd been punched in the chest.

The lilies had bloomed.

It had been weeks since they'd been cut. All the other flowers had long since rotted away, but there they were — creamy white petals dusted with golden pollen, perfuming the air with the faintest hint of sweetness.

And it was like he was there again, with his hand on my shoulder. I could almost hear him saying that everything was going to be all right. It would hurt, and the hurt would never really go away, but it would get better. It would be okay.

And things did get better — not quickly, and not all at once, but eventually. I clutched at that moment and held it close through the dark times. I believe it meant that my father had a message for me, and he'd said it the only way he could — with flowers.

— A.L. Tompkins —

15

Death Cannot Separate Us

Death ends a life, not a relationship.
~Jack Lemmon

Before my husband Bill died, we often talked about whether there was an afterlife. We hoped that there was something beyond this world, and that somehow communication could take place once death occurred. We had plenty of time to talk about these things because my husband's battle with prostate cancer lasted for ten and a half years.

Shortly after his forty-sixth birthday, he was given the news that he had cancer. Neither of us had worried about his prostate biopsy after a positive rectal exam. I didn't know much at all about the prostate, if truth be told. I didn't even know how to pronounce it correctly. What little I did know (or thought I knew) about prostate cancer was that it was something that old men got, and they didn't die from the disease. Boy, was I wrong about that.

I had no idea when the phone rang that day that we were about to embark on a losing battle that would last for more than a decade. One minute, I was a thirty-two-year-old, stay-at-home, home-schooling mother of three young sons. The next, I was a prostate-cancer researcher, advocate and primary support system for a man with cancer.

The first year was a flurry of activity, with hormonal therapy, prostate surgery and its recovery, followed by seven and a half weeks of pelvic radiation. Despite everything that we had thrown at his cancer, we were told it was incurable one year after his diagnosis. They said he had two to four years. Over the next nine and a half years, he fought with all that he had to beat the odds so he could stay with his family and watch his sons become men. Ten days after our youngest son's eighteenth birthday, Bill died.

Five years after his death, I was faced with another trauma that could have easily ended in tragedy. I received a call one morning that our oldest son had been shot just outside Fort Campbell, Kentucky. Living on the coast of Maine, it took me almost twelve hours to get to his bedside. On my flight to him, I prayed a lot, as well as asked my late husband to be with him and keep him safe.

To my shock, when I arrived at my son's bedside in the trauma unit at Vanderbilt University Medical Center in Nashville, Tennessee, he was hooked up to a respirator. He had been shot three times in the back, and his skull had been fractured from a hard blow near the temple. Eventually, his sedation was lifted, and he slowly became conscious. When they knew he would be able to breathe on his own, they pulled the breathing tube from his throat. As soon as it was removed, his first words were "Daddy, Daddy."

Though my son has no recollection of seeing his father during his unconscious state, I cannot help but wonder if my husband heard my plea and somehow acted on it. After a three-week hospital stay and a long recovery over the next year, my son was able to return to a full and active life. I will always believe that my husband was with our son during those crucial hours following his shooting and somehow intervened.

Then, several years later, I had a severe case of the flu that put me in bed for a week. It left me in a very weakened state for nearly a month. My two elderly dogs had died a few months before my sickness, so it was the first time in my life that I didn't have the comfort of a dog beside me when I was ill. At the time, I was living on an island off the coast of Maine where I had provided end-of-life care for my parents who had recently died seven weeks apart. I didn't know many people there, so I felt alone and isolated during my sickness.

More than a week into it, I reached out to my deceased husband in a moment of complete and utter desperation. I looked toward the heavens, lifted my hands to the sky, and said, "Okay, Bill, send me a puppy. You have to send me a puppy." Though I wasn't sure if he heard me or not, I had a sense that a puppy would soon come my way.

The next morning, I opened my e-mail to find a message from a breeder whom I had contacted after my last dog died. I had asked her about upcoming litters. When she had not replied, I assumed she was no longer in business. The breeder's e-mail began with an apology because she had just seen the e-mail that I had sent six months before. As luck would have it, her dog had just had a litter of ten black Labrador Retrievers. Some of the pups were born on March thirty-first, and some had been born on April first.

I had wanted a male, but only one of the puppies was born on the first, the tenth anniversary of my husband's death. I didn't ask which one. Over the next four weeks, I enjoyed viewing pictures of the puppies on social media until the day arrived that I could visit them. I played with them for forty-five minutes before I asked that important question. I had a distinct bond with one of the pups and held my breath hoping that he was the one born on the first. He had been the first to come to me, and when all the others had gone to sleep, he just sat there staring at me. As luck would have it, or perhaps it was divine intervention, the one I felt connected to was indeed the one born on April first.

The breeder had put different colored collars on the pups when they were born. Little did she know that the light blue collar she had put on my pup was the same color used for prostate cancer awareness.

This puppy has been my constant companion and brought me so much joy. I no longer feel alone because he is always by my side. He has been such a wonderful gift, and a continuing link to my husband. Our love was so strong that even death cannot separate us, and I will continue to look for those special signals and signs from Bill.

— Wendy Newell Dyer —

16

Horse from Heaven

The wind of heaven is that which blows between
a horse's ears.
~Arabian Proverb

Growing up, my whole world revolved around the one hour a week that I was able to sit in a saddle and ride a horse. My mom would make me take a bath as soon as we got home because she said I smelled like a horse. She made it sound like something undesirable. As I waited for the tub to fill, I would press my jeans to my face and breathe in the scents of saddle leather mixed with the earthy odor of a horse. I couldn't imagine even the most expensive perfume smelling any better than my pants did after a ride.

When I wasn't riding I was dreaming about riding, talking about riding, reading about riding, and counting the days until I could ride again. At the top of every Christmas list was the same request — a horse. I wished on birthday candles, falling stars, pennies in fountains, and the first robin of spring. In winter, my mom and dad would shovel the snow into one big pile, and I would crudely fashion it into a horse and ride it for hours.

"Do you think Whitey will come back this year?" Mom would ask at the beginning of each winter.

"I guess, but I wish I had a real horse that wouldn't leave when it got warm," I would say.

My mother's response was always the same. "I'm sorry, we just can't afford a horse."

"You would never have to get me another present again," I'd promise.

"I wish I could buy you one, but it's a luxury we don't have the money for. Be thankful you can take lessons. Those are expensive enough," Mom said.

My passion for horses continued into adulthood. Unfortunately, riding was put aside as I contended with student loans and living expenses, and then a mortgage with my new husband. Just when I had a handle on things and began to consider riding again, my mother was diagnosed with Alzheimer's. Every visit left me drained, empty, and disheartened.

After a five-year battle, my mom passed. I didn't know what to do with my extra time now that I wasn't taking care of Mom. I wandered around the house aimlessly, with no focus.

"Why don't you get that horse you always wanted?" my husband suggested.

"Oh, no, I couldn't do that," I said.

"Why not? It's always been your passion," he said.

The thought of achieving my lifelong dream invigorated me again. I did some research and decided to adopt an American mustang. My application was approved, and after hours of poring over every picture and description of horses online that needed homes, I finally decided upon the one I wanted. He cost $125 to adopt. I planned on signing the adoption contract and paying my fee the next week.

A day later, a large envelope came in the mail from my sister. Inside was a note that read, "Here are a few things of yours I found in Mom's drawers while cleaning them out." Included were various items such as pictures I had drawn, my baptismal certificate, and a kindergarten report card. I came across a plain white envelope with my name on it in my mother's distinct handwriting. Inside was a $100 bill, several $2 notes she had saved when they came out, and a handful of Susan B. Anthony dollar coins. The hair started to stand up on my neck as electricity ran down my spine. I didn't have to add them up to know the total came to $125. My tears dampened the envelope.

I used that money to adopt my horse, whom I named "Wydee"

after my winter snow pony. The difference was that this one didn't leave in the spring. My mom finally got to buy me a horse, from heaven.

— Amy Rovtar Payne —

17

Closing Caption

We loved with a love that was more than love.
~Edgar Allan Poe

We sat at the kitchen table, huddled around my ancient laptop, watching snapshots of Rickey's life as they transferred over from the digital camera and appeared on the screen. The process was painstakingly slow. I waited impatiently, my nephew David by my side, just as he had been since his uncle Rickey—my husband of sixteen years—had passed away forty-eight hours earlier.

I glanced at the download status bar at the bottom of the screen: 2% remaining.

"We're almost done, kiddo," I said, yawning loudly. Though we were both exhausted in every manner imaginable, neither of us would get any rest until we had finished compiling and editing the tribute video for Rickey's visitation the following day.

David gave two thumbs-up, sighed and stretched. I removed my glasses, wiping them clean with my shirt. I rubbed my bloodshot eyes and tried to recall what day it was. I'd been so busy getting everything in order for Rickey's funeral. When was the last time I'd slept? Or eaten? Or even showered?

The laptop dinged, snapping me back to the task at hand. I opened the movie-making program and began importing over 200 photos. David watched over my shoulder, and we noticed that several of the thumbnail images had come across with a banner beneath them that said simply "digital camera" while the rest remained captionless.

With the download now complete, David and I had to sort through hundreds of images from Rickey's life, string them together like pieces of a puzzle, and set them to music. We scoured the image gallery in search of the perfect picture to use for the closing. When we reached the final page, there it was: a portrait of Rickey in his ball cap and jacket, smiling with his glass of sweet tea. The photo was taken a couple years prior at Cracker Barrel, one of Rickey's favorite restaurants, when our then five-year-old great-niece Trystan had swiped the camera and taken a handful of random pictures. As I opened my mouth to tell David we'd found the picture, he stood up suddenly and started gesturing excitedly, pointing toward that very photograph.

"Yep, that's the one we're gonna use for the finale," I said, sharing his enthusiasm, happy that he seemed to be thinking along the same lines.

"No, Aunt Mandi, look!" he said with such urgency that it almost frightened me. He reached up, his hand trembling, and pointed directly beneath the image of Rickey and his sweet tea. My mouth dropped open; I couldn't believe my eyes. I squeezed my eyes shut quickly a few times, and then opened them. Once again, I was sure I was dreaming. There, in big bold letters beneath the image, was a caption that read: "I love you."

"Oh, David, tell me you see it, too!" I said excitedly, even though he had been the one to point it out initially. I double-clicked the thumbnail so we could see the actual picture, praying silently the words weren't some computer glitch that would vanish into thin air. When the photo expanded to full size, both of us stared in awe and amazement at the bright white words "I love you" that were emblazoned across the picture.

David hugged me so tightly that I thought I might faint as tears spilled down both our cheeks. Then he smiled slightly and shook his head.

"Uncle Rickey loved you so much; he wanted to make sure you never forget. He still loves you even now. He always will," David said.

I tried to speak, but for the first time in my thirty-six years, I had no words that could express everything in my heart — the joy, sorrow, thankfulness, excitement, awe and pure exhilaration that filled me as I realized that just because our life together had come to an end didn't mean that our love ever would.

I grabbed my cell phone from my back pocket and quickly snapped a shot of the screen filled with my special message, just in case anyone wanted proof or thought I was hallucinating in my moment of mourning. I posted the picture on social media, eager to share our love story with everyone.

***

Just over two years later, I was going through an especially difficult time emotionally and missing Rickey more than I ever thought possible. I thought of my "I love you" moment and selfishly longed for another. I was at such a low point, so lost in my grief and heartache that I could barely function from one day to the next.

One of the few things that kept me going was my parents' upcoming fortieth wedding anniversary. My sister Rachel and I had decided to make a slideshow celebrating Mom and Dad. We included a variety of images, from black-and-white childhood photos of our parents to group pictures that expanded as our family grew. Rachel and I couldn't decide, however, whether to include any photos with Rickey. He had been a part of our family for close to two decades, and everyone grieved for him a great deal. We didn't want to bring down the mood of what should have been an occasion to celebrate. After much debate, we went ahead and added pictures of Rickey, feeling that not doing so would be like trying to erase a huge part of our family album.

Rachel and I gathered at my kitchen table much like David and I had done, transferring files into the movie-making program. As my favorite picture of Rickey and me filled the screen, this time it was I who pointed excitedly at the screen.

"Rachel, do you see it?" I whispered, again unable to trust my own eyes. She nodded rapidly, and then pointed at the bottom of the image where "I will always love you" was written in white type. I wept tears of joy as I snapped another photo of a message from my sweet Rickey.

I thought back over the life we had built, the love and laughter we had shared, and I finally understood how unbelievably blessed I had been.

— Mandi Smith —

18

Veggie Soup

For me, cooking is an extension of love.
~Hedda Sterne

When I was young, one of my favorite ways to spend a weekend day was cooking with my grandmother. We'd pick out a recipe, make a trip to the grocery store, and put on a musical to watch while we made a delicious meal together.

My grandmother was happiest when she could cook for her friends and family and have everyone gathered at her house for a good, hearty meal. Her vegetable soup was one of her favorites. Anytime her children, grandchildren, or neighbors were sick or recovering from surgery, she would make a big batch for them.

About a year after we lost my grandmother, I decided it was time to make her famous vegetable soup. I found the recipe that I had written down years ago but I felt her loss. I couldn't remember a time when I made one of her recipes at home that I didn't need to call her at least once for help.

I retrieved the beef soup bones from the freezer, various vegetables I had purchased that morning, and my enormous stockpot. My grandmother never made small batches; there were always plenty of people to feed, and any leftovers could be frozen in the deep freezer. I turned on the TV and heard the joyous vocals and tap dancing of Fred Astaire and Ginger Rogers resound through the kitchen. At that point, I just stared at all of the ingredients for a while before having a minor meltdown.

"Hey, hey, you've got this. You've made this enough times with your grandmother. It's going to turn out amazing," my husband reassured me as he walked into the kitchen to comfort me.

"I don't know. What if the amounts are off, and it turns out horrible?" I countered. My grandmother never measured anything; she just added ingredients as needed, so it was hard to write down accurate recipes.

"You are an incredible cook, just like your grandmother. You have the base ingredients to start with, so start small. You can always add as you go. That's a big pot to fill, but I am sure you will get it just right." He gave me a big hug.

As my breathing slowed, and I finally began to calm down, something shifted in the freezer and made a loud, clunking noise. We both turned our heads, startled in the moment.

"Well, that's something to add to the list: clean out the freezer." I rolled my eyes, and then smiled at my husband.

I walked over to the freezer and opened the door. A sealed bag of food came flying out and slid across the floor. I picked up the package, and as I was reaching to place it back on the shelf in the freezer, I read the writing on the package. I began laughing and crying at the same time, as I closed the freezer door and turned to show the frozen-food bundle to my husband.

"It's vegetable soup," I said in disbelief. "I totally forgot I had any left. This is from the last time my grandmother and I made soup together, shortly before she passed away." My husband looked up from the plastic bag of frozen soup with a twinkle in his eye.

"You see, everyone is reassuring you today. I don't think there is any possible way you can fail at making this veggie soup."

I defrosted the frozen soup, and tasted it here and there to compare as I put ingredients together that day. Once it was a perfect match, I put the remainder of that soup I had made with my grandmother into the soup I made that day. Every time I make a batch of veggie soup, I freeze one package and save it for the next time I cook. That loving batch of soup from my grandmother is a part of every batch of veggie soup I make, reminding me that her love for and ability to cook also resides within me. She is here in spirit to guide me through all my cooking endeavors.

—Gwen Cooper—

19

The Earrings

The dragonfly brings dream to reality and is the
messenger of wisdom and enlightenment
from other realms.
~Author Unknown

S itting cross-legged on her bedroom floor, I was sifting through
the contents of my deceased son's jewelry box with my widowed daughter-in-law. "Oh, here," she said as she handed me
a small, pastel-colored paper bag. "Jake bought this for you
earlier this year and said it had significant meaning. I'm not sure why
he didn't give this to you before he died." Puzzled, I took the little
package and slowly peeked inside. What I saw took my breath away.

It was early December when she gave me that package. I had been
living in a fog for five months at that point, as my twenty-nine-year-old
son, Jacob, had died very unexpectedly that June.

I had repeatedly asked for a sign from God that my son was
okay. About six weeks after his death, I had been sitting in a nature
area atop a hill when I had brazenly challenged God. "God, if Jake is
happily with you, I will see a bird when I look up." I raised my eyes
and slowly scanned all around me. Nothing. Not a blue jay, cardinal,
wren, or crow. There wasn't even a fly or bee anywhere. My entire
body sagged in disappointment.

But something told me to tilt my whole head upward. I did…
and gasped. I was not graced by the presence of any bird, but rather
surrounded by dragonflies flitting over my head. These dragonflies

were huge — as big as small birds. And not one, nor two, but an entire swarm danced and darted over my head. That was the only time in my entire life that I have seen dragonflies that size, and so many clustered together.

I was astonished and bewildered. Where had they come from? I was not near a pond, lake, or water reservoir of any kind. And I had been looking out at the view and had not seen anything coming this way. But now, they hovered just above my head, performing delightful acrobatics.

I was fairly certain no one would believe what I was seeing. I had to pinch myself to make sure I wasn't hallucinating! Since I could not take my eyes off this vision, I blindly snapped a couple of photos. And then, for just a brief second, I turned my sight downward. When I looked up again, they were gone! Every single one had disappeared in the blink of an eye. I stood up and repeatedly turned in a circle. There was not a single dragonfly, let alone a cloud of them, anywhere. As instantaneously as they had appeared, they vanished.

Trying to make sense of it, I went home and researched what I had witnessed. In my quest, I discovered that dragonflies signify spiritual transformation. In Japanese culture, they are also a sign of resurrection. My request for a solitary sign was multiplied exponentially with the swarm that appeared. But that was not all. This sign was especially meaningful as my son was enamored with Japanese art and symbolism.

Dragonflies had never meant anything to me prior to that experience, so my son would have had no reason to buy me a dragonfly gift. That's why I was so stunned when I opened the little bag my daughter-in-law handed me five months after my son's death and found a pair of dragonfly earrings. Suddenly, my experience of the dragonfly visit took on a whole new meaning, and dragonflies became extremely significant.

When the Michigan weather warmed again the following spring, I began noticing dragonflies in the oddest of places. One would fly around me on my porch. One would appear as I walked, or while I waited at the ice-cream stand. One even aligned with my driver's window as I pulled into a park my son was fond of. When I would walk with his children, they would often land on the hats they were wearing. Needless to say, each time it was like Jacob was tapping me on the shoulder and saying, "Hi, Mom! I love you, I'm still with you, and I'm doing great!" To this day, every time I see a dragonfly, I feel comforted. I feel embraced. And I feel reassured.

— Rose Robertson —

20

By the Light of His Torch

She did not stand alone, but what stood behind her,
the most potent moral force in her life,
was the love of her father.
--Harper Lee, Go Set a Watchman

While my father held several different jobs in his life, I truly believe that, in his heart, he was a writer. As a child, I remember watching him as he worked tirelessly on his novel, night after night, for years. Unfortunately, his passion for writing outlived his time on Earth. Sixteen years ago, he wrote his last words.

Not long after the funeral, I sifted through his effects, finding an old manuscript he had written: a romantic account of my mother. I was delighted to read his charming, affectionate words. Those words conjured images of a classic, romantic movie of bygone days, with my father and mother in the lead roles. Fearing that I might lose this treasured manuscript, I gave it to relatives for safekeeping.

Four years ago, I decided to become a writer. At the time, I thought I was just looking for a professional change of pace. Eventually, I realized that I was actually searching for a true sense of purpose in the second half of my life.

As I wrote, I often thought of Mom and Dad. Not surprisingly, memories of how I felt when I first read that old manuscript started to flood my thoughts. Feeling deeply sentimental, I asked my relatives for the manuscript. They spent days looking for it — with no success. They surmised that it might have fallen victim to several home-remodeling projects and had been lost in the shuffle when workers reorganized their belongings.

Although I was crestfallen, I continued writing, always thinking of my father and mother. Consequently, many of my new stories centered on my parents, continuing to re-fuel other long-forgotten memories of them. It wasn't long before I yearned for that manuscript again. I decided that I had to find it myself. I wasn't going to give up on it that easily.

Soon thereafter, I searched through my relatives' garage, where the missing manuscript had last been seen. After hours of rummaging through storage cabinets, I found many discoveries, including several binders that held my father's writing. Unfortunately, the manuscript was nowhere to be found.

Still, I was glad to find my father's other works in the binders, and I took them home with me. When I arrived home, I enthusiastically reviewed the contents of these binders. Proudly, I rediscovered Dad's breathtaking eloquence. Some pages showed vocabulary terms he had jotted down — an old-fashioned, handwritten thesaurus to help him craft his essays. On another page, he had begun a handwritten address book. At the top of the page, he had written my name in his beautiful cursive penmanship. Delicately, I ran my fingers across those three letters — Mai — almost feeling his presence next to me as I did. Seeing my name on that page, I wasn't expecting to be as emotionally affected as I was. I suppose when we miss our loved ones, even the simplest things that would have gone virtually unnoticed before can be precious after they are gone.

Eventually, I started to consolidate the contents of the binders, and I found reams of blank notebook paper in them. By the time I was finished I had a ten-inch stack of blank notebook paper. I wasn't sure what I was going to do with it.

That stack of notebook paper was still confronting me the next day. I had no place to store it, so I thought about just throwing it in the recycling. But then it occurred to me. I did occasionally use paper when I wrote my screenplays, essays, and stories. What better way to collect my thoughts than to use the very same paper that my father, the aspiring novelist, used when he was still alive? Suddenly, I saw this old notebook paper in a completely new light. I had searched for one buried treasure — my father's manuscript — and found another one in its place.

Since its discovery, I have used my father's notebook paper every day, being truly inspired by it, and by him. It almost feels like he is sitting by my side, writing with me. As a result, I have created over a dozen new short stories as well as the outlines for two new screenplays. It is as if Dad and his words are living on, speaking to me through his paper — at least, this is my worldly explanation for the fact that story ideas are flowing from me like a river.

Some people may say that it's just a simple coincidence, but I prefer to think that with this gift of my father's paper, he is passing the torch to me, to light my way through the darkness, as I pick up where he left off. Perhaps this is more than just a stack of old paper — it is how I am going to find my true purpose in life.

Dad ran out of time before he could live out his dream, so I'm doing my best to live out a dream for both of us. Then I can finally say, "I'm a writer, just like my father."

— Kristen Mai Pham

21

Flowers from Gary

Love is something eternal; the aspect may change,
but not the essence.
~Vincent van Gogh

My husband and I were relocating to a new town due to my work. Everything would be new to us since we had never been there before.

I went ahead to begin my new job and find us a place to live. My husband, Gary, stayed behind to pack up our possessions. He would join me in a month.

Two weeks later, two police officers arrived at my work. They told me my husband had passed away earlier that day. They had located me from some paperwork at the previous house. It was a blood clot to the lung, which killed him suddenly. I was devastated.

A few weeks later, I received a piece of mail claiming I had won a free bouquet of flowers at a local florist. I figured it was junk mail and set it aside since no one knew me, and I had not entered any contests.

A few days later, on the day my husband had been due to join me, I found the gift certificate again. Feeling low, I thought maybe some flowers would cheer me up.

When I arrived at the florist, they assured me that the gift certificate was indeed legitimate, and I had won the contest. She asked me what kind of flowers I wanted. Teary-eyed, I explained how I had lost my husband Gary not long ago, and I wanted something to cheer me up. The florist said, "Just a minute. I have something perfect for you."

A few minutes later, she came back with a beautiful arrangement of potted plants. She said I didn't need flowers that would die in a few days; I needed plants that would continue to live as I would. I was crying by now and thanked her very much. Then I asked if there was a way to see who had submitted my name in the contest.

"You don't know?" she said. "They were from Gary."

Ten years later, the plants are still thriving.

—Linda Eiffert—

Finding Faith

22

Still Helping

I cannot forget my mother. She is my bridge.
~Renita J. Weems

I t was a relief to sink into the couch next to my husband at the end of a long and busy November day — at least until I glanced down and noticed my bare hand. The gold wedding band that never left my finger was missing. "No!" I gasped.

Life had been full of losses recently. First, there was a stubborn knee injury that had significantly impacted my mobility. Next, there was the departure of our closest family friends to a city a thousand miles away. But by far the most painful blow was my mother's death earlier that spring.

My mother was only sixty-six years old when she lost her third battle with breast cancer, and her death had left a gaping hole. She'd been the center of our close-knit family, nourishing us with her legendary cooking, her faith, her sense of humour, and her wisdom. I was forty-two when she passed, a grown woman with five children of my own. And yet, up until her final months, I'd still call her when I needed parenting help, cooking advice, or encouragement. Now she was gone.

A wedding band was a tiny loss in comparison, and yet it was one loss too many. I blinked back tears.

"It'll turn up," my husband said, putting his arm around my shoulder.

I didn't share his confidence. I'd spent the entire day Christmas shopping, visiting countless stores in three shopping malls in two separate towns. My ring could have come off anywhere. Nevertheless, I made a list and started calling as soon as the stores were open the next morning. No one had turned in a gold wedding band, but every customer-service clerk and store manager I spoke with promised to notify me if one did show up. While I waited, I searched our minivan and our house from top to bottom.

Several days passed, and there was still no sign of the missing ring. "We'll get you another one," my husband promised. But I didn't want another one. I wanted the gold band that my husband had put on my finger when we'd exchanged our wedding vows. I wanted the gold band I'd worn for the past twenty-three years.

I was still hopeful that my ring would somehow find its way home, but when it hadn't reappeared after two weeks, I stopped at a nearby jewelry store and chose a simple silver band. I spent as little as I could. This wasn't a replacement — it was simply filling in for the ring that really belonged on my finger.

Months went by, and I did my best to make peace with the losses in my life. There were times I was sure I felt my mother's presence, reassuring me that she wasn't really gone — even if I couldn't see her or hear her voice. But the ache remained.

Suddenly, it was March thirteenth, the first anniversary of her death. I woke up feeling out of sorts, and I found myself snapping at my husband and children over breakfast. Recognizing that I needed space alone to process my grief, I drove the half-hour to my mother's grave. It was overcast, and I had the small, hilltop cemetery to myself. There was no bench nearby, and the earth was too damp to sit on, so I simply stood above my mother's headstone. I tried speaking with her in my mind, but the gesture felt empty. My mother wasn't in the ground under my feet. What we'd buried there was just an empty shell; her spirit was somewhere else — somewhere bright and beautiful, but unreachable to me.

I stayed at my mother's graveside for several more minutes, allowing the tears to fall. When the wind had dried my face again, I turned and began walking carefully back toward my vehicle.

As I descended the small hill, I felt a measure of peace settle over me. My mother lived on, of that I was sure. I would see her face-to-face one day, and when I did, she'd be young and radiant again. Until that day came, I'd just have to rest in that faith.

I was a different person when I returned home later that morning. I apologized to my husband for my irritability over breakfast — and then asked why he was grinning.

"Hold out your hand," he said. "No, your left hand."

I stared in disbelief as he slipped a familiar gold band onto my ring finger.

At the very moment I'd been visiting my mother's grave, our two youngest had made an unexpected discovery in the pile of composting leaves on the far side of our driveway. Four months after it had gone missing, my wedding ring had reappeared — on the very anniversary of my mother's passing.

"Thank you, Mom," I whispered.

— Rachel Dunstan Muller —

23

The Piano

All that I have seen teaches me to trust God
for all I have not seen.
~Author Unknown

My father was forty-five years old when I was born. Although he had always enjoyed perfect health, he worried that he would not live long enough to see his children grow up and have families of their own. It gnawed at him. And it didn't help that his father had died at age seventy-seven.

Throughout my childhood, I was told to make the most of the time I had with my father, and I did. When he turned eighty, I was so relieved.

Just before his eighty-second birthday in 1998, my father announced he had to have surgery. There was a narrowing in his carotid artery, and he was at risk of having a stroke. We were told the surgery went well, but when I saw my father in the recovery room afterward, he looked stressed.

"Pop, what's wrong?" I asked.

"The nurse said my blood pressure is high, and she told me to relax. How can I relax? She scared me half to death," he said.

"Did the doctor say anything to you about it?"

"I haven't seen the doctor, just the nurse."

Dr. Engel was at the nurse's station. I went over to him and said, "Excuse me, doctor. Why is my father's blood pressure high?"

"It's just slightly higher than normal," he said. "Your father is going to be fine."

"He doesn't think so. When he woke from the surgery, the nurse told him his blood pressure was high. He's scared. Will you please tell him he's going to be okay? It'll mean more coming from you." Dr. Engel went to my father and assured him that the surgery went well. When he heard he could go home in the morning, he relaxed and slept peacefully for several hours.

At 4:35 a.m., my father had a stroke. He was stabilized and transferred by ambulance from St. Agnes to the stroke center at the White Plains Hospital. It was the longest two-mile ride of our lives. Lying in the hospital bed, my father looked like he was at death's door. Just eight hours earlier, he had been sitting up, telling jokes, and looking forward to going home. Now he was weak, could barely talk, and his face looked sallow. The surgery that was supposed to prevent a stroke had caused one. I felt betrayed by Dr. Engel — and by God. It wasn't God's fault, of course, but nobody could tell me that then.

When I left my father's room, Father Castellani was sitting in the waiting room with my mother. She had called and asked him to come to the hospital to pray with her. When they went to the chapel, my mother asked if I wanted to join them. I didn't, but I went anyway.

We sat for a long time in the tiny chapel. I couldn't stop thinking about my father, who was one floor above us. While Father Castellani and my mother prayed, I sat and stared at my hands. Silent. Nervous. Lost in thought. Suddenly, a man's voice jarred me from my brooding. "Your father is going to be fine," he said. It was almost a whisper, but there was no mistaking that it was a man's voice or that I had heard it.

Dr. Engel had said those exact words to me in the recovery room. I looked up, expecting to see him standing in the aisle, but no one was there. Father Castellani was the only man in the room. He was still seated next to my mother, praying. I was about to interrupt them to ask if they had heard what I heard, but the voice stopped me. "Let them be. I am here because of their prayers. Your father will be all right."

Neither my mother nor Father Castellani looked up to see who was speaking to me. They couldn't hear him. Why was I the only one who could hear the voice? And where was it coming from? It was frightening, but at least the message was comforting. And, strangely enough, I wanted to hear more.

Ready to listen, I closed my eyes and concentrated on the gentle voice. "Your father's health will improve. He will be sent home next week. But the incision will open, and he'll go back into the hospital for five days. He'll have physical therapy and then exercise at home. He'll regain his speech and mobility. But his hand will take a year to heal."

My father did get better. He was released from the hospital but rushed back that night when the incision popped open. There was blood everywhere. Five days later, he came home to stay. Physical therapy helped him regain much of his strength, and his speech returned to normal. But he hated physical therapy, and it hadn't improved his left hand at all. So he did his own form of exercise at home instead. He walked every day until his limp was gone. And he played the beloved upright piano his father had given him when he was eight years old. He couldn't play nearly as well as he used to — his left hand dragged on the keyboard, and it sometimes fell lifeless onto the keys — but he kept playing.

I watched my father as he learned to play the piano all over again. It broke my heart to see him struggling with it. He had always been an exceptional musician. One day, he got so upset that he slammed the fallboard shut, got up, and walked away. As he walked down the hallway to his bedroom, he mumbled, "I'll never play the piano again."

I bowed my head and prayed silently. "God, please help my father. The piano is his life. If he stops playing it now, I'm afraid it will kill him."

After his walk the next day, he went to the piano, looked at it, and walked away. But the following day, he came back and began playing the scales with his left hand. He played slowly, but with determination. Soon, he grew tired and stopped. Each day, he played longer than the day before. As the days progressed, he played the scales faster and louder. The strength in his left hand was coming back. By summer, he was playing all the old songs he once played with his band. There were plenty of mistakes, but it sounded great to me. By fall, his hands were moving up and down the keyboard like lightning. The house was alive with music.

I will always be grateful for that extraordinary day in the chapel, and for my father's full recovery. In fact, he lived long enough to see not only his children, but his grandchildren grow up. He even got to hold his first great-granddaughter in his arms. He played the piano every day and lived to be ninety-five years old.

—I.M. Lush—

24

The Difference a Day Makes

*Between the earth and sky above, nothing can
match a grandmother's love.*
~Author Unknown

I sat on the edge of the bed in my hotel room staring at the little hourglass flashing on the digital pregnancy test. It felt like the longest three minutes of my entire life. Then it happened so quickly I had to do a double take to make sure my eyes weren't deceiving me: PREGNANT.

The word was clear, but I was having trouble seeing through my tears. Could it really have happened that quickly?

Just two months earlier, my husband and I had decided to try for our first child. Despite the heartache we had gone through during the past year, it seemed like the right time to start a family.

After taking two more tests — both displaying the same result — I ran to pick up my cell phone, desperate to share the good news with someone... anyone. Naturally, I wanted to call my husband, but I was out of town on a business trip, and this was the kind of news that could only be shared in person.

I punched in my best friend's number, but my fingers stopped short of pushing the Send button. It simply wouldn't be right to tell her — or anyone for that matter — before my husband. I sighed and set down the phone. I would be home in forty-eight hours, but I knew they would feel like an eternity.

As I lay down on the plush hotel comforter, I placed one hand over my non-existent bump. Despite being only three weeks pregnant, I could sense the little life inside me. That is when it hit me. There was one person I could tell, and I knew beyond a shadow of a doubt that she would keep the secret.

"Guess what, Grandma?" I called out. "I'm pregnant! Can you believe it?"

Despite having passed away eleven months earlier, I could sense my grandmother in the room with me. She and I had always been close — we even shared our middle names — and that feeling didn't go away after her death. I closed my eyes, picturing her in the armchair by the window.

"I know you are. I am so happy for you!" I imagined her saying. "You are going to be a great mother."

"I wish you could be here to meet the baby," I said softly.

Six weeks later, on the anniversary of her death, we were ready to tell my parents about the pregnancy. The day was sure to bring my mom a decent amount of heartache, and I wanted nothing more than to turn that pain into joy.

Reaching across the dinner table that evening, I handed her a box that was addressed: To Our Family's Newest Matriarch. Inside was a heart-shaped locket with the word GRANDMOTHER scrawled in beautiful cursive across the front. We both cried, but I am certain my grandmother did nothing but smile from her view in heaven that night, happy to pass the torch to her own daughter.

My due date, October 19, had been thickly circled on the calendar since my first doctor's visit. By June, we found out we would be welcoming a little boy into our family. By the start of my third trimester, I had absolutely everything prepared. The nursery was decorated; there wasn't a truck, train, or bear onesie that I hadn't purchased; and I had gone to all of the parenting classes. It seemed as though I was made for pregnancy since the whole thing was going off without a hitch — until it didn't.

On a particularly warm October morning, I walked into my doctor's office expecting nothing less than a perfect report, just as I had received during every other prenatal visit. I was supposed to have my checkup the previous day, but a last-minute conflict at work forced me to push back my appointment.

"Do you know what preeclampsia is?" my doctor asked.

I had heard the term before in reference to high-risk pregnancies, but I never dreamed it would happen to me, so I simply shook my head.

"It is a very severe pregnancy complication," she replied. "You need to get to the hospital right away to deliver your baby."

Going into labor under emergency circumstances was so far off my birth plan that I should have panicked, but I didn't. Instead, I felt calm, with a peace that surpassed all understanding. Sure, some might say it was because I was in denial over the magnitude of the situation, but I truly believe I had God by my side, keeping me calm when my world was starting to spin out of control.

Within thirty minutes, I was at the hospital, hooked up to monitors and tubes, and an IV dripping magnesium into my veins. My risk of seizure was high, so there would be no getting out of bed and nothing to drink, not even ice chips. Through the various bouts of pain and medication, the rest of my time in labor was nothing but a fuzzy blur.

Then, from out of the pain, came a sensation that was undeniably strong. I knew without a doubt this was it — I needed to push. With my mom and husband by my side, it took only five minutes for my son to be born. The pushing was excruciating, but the reward was so worth it. I had my little man on my chest, his shrill cry calming my nervous heart. It was all going to be okay.

After a few hours of recovery, I was starting to step back into the world of the living again. The bleariness from the medications was wearing off, and I could properly take in the miracle that had just unfolded.

The doctor informed me just how serious my complications had been, letting me know they would need to extend my hospital stay for observation. Had it not been for the one-day delay in my checkup, they likely would not have discovered the issue in time. A single day could have meant the difference between life and death for my son and me.

I glanced over at the whiteboard on the wall where the nurse had written my son's birthdate: October 7, 2015.

The hairs on my arm stood straight up as a knowing smile spread across my face. It was just too perfect to be a coincidence. I looked down at the sweet little boy sleeping on my chest.

"Happy birthday, Elijah," I whispered into his ear. "And happy birthday to you too, Grandma."

— K.C. Runkel —

A Woodpecker with Purpose

Reason is our soul's left hand, Faith her right.
~John Donne

My two dogs and I were taking a Sunday afternoon walk along our favorite trail beside the St. Croix River. The brisk November day left the marina there deserted, with the big yachts moored on land and covered for the winter. As we headed up the trail from the beach to the marina parking lot, I stopped dead in my tracks. There before me, directly in my line of sight, was the largest woodpecker I'd ever seen. The largest one native to Minnesota — a pileated woodpecker — was clinging to the side of a post. Measuring almost twenty inches high, this black bird had bold white stripes, a bright red cap and an impressively long beak that he used to excavate food from within the wooden post. Clearly, this bird was the inspiration for the cartoon character Woody Woodpecker!

The dogs and I had walked this trail along the St. Croix River many times, and I had never seen a pileated woodpecker there. In the twenty-five years I'd lived in the area, I'd seen pileated woodpeckers only a few times. And even then, I'd only gotten a fleeting glance of one high up in a tree or heard them drumming deep in the hardwood forest in the state park, their characteristic bass rhythmic sound resonating throughout the forest. I heard pileated woodpeckers more often than I saw them, so I knew they were around. But these large birds are known to be elusive, even to the intrepid birdwatchers who search for them.

Surprisingly, this woodpecker perched right at my eye level as I walked up the trail with my two fifty-pound dogs. Fortunately, we were nearing the end of our walk, so the dogs were tired and willing to wait quietly on their leashes as I whipped out my camera and started taking pictures. I was in awe that this amazing and usually shy bird had not flown away as we approached. Clearly aware of our presence, keeping one eye on us, the woodpecker continued to poke his beak into the nooks and crannies of the post as I snapped over forty photos. After a few magical moments, he flew off into the nearby woods.

Not long after I returned home, I read a posting written by my friend Jessie. I was stunned to learn that her fiancé Carl had been tragically killed in an accident in North Dakota where he'd been working. During the wee morning hours of November eighth — the day before my woodpecker sighting — a semi-truck had broadsided Carl's vehicle, and he was killed instantly. He was only thirty-five years old. My heart ached for my friend, knowing in that split second that the life Jessie and Carl had been planning together was gone. Carl was a child of the North Woods of Minnesota, where Jessie and Carl had both grown up. He was a musician and animal lover with a tender heart for all creatures. Jessie was consumed with grief.

As I continued reading what Jessie had written online, the hair on the back of my neck stood up, and I got goosebumps. Jessie wrote: "The day that Carl died, we all gathered at his mom's house. The day is a blur, the grief incomprehensible. But a couple of good things happened that day that stick in my memory. One was the pileated woodpecker that showed up outside the dining-room window, where we were all sitting. The woodpecker sat there for a long time and stared in at all of us. I laughed and said, 'Leave it to Carl to show up as a woodpecker!' Some people get a sign from the beyond in the form of eagles or hawks or some other noble creature. Our lovable, joking woodsman, Carl, showed up as a funny-looking bird! Carl, the logger, a bird of the woods. It was a moment of laughter because it was 'so Carl.' I'm quite certain that he laughed along with us."

Jessie told me that several friends and family had seen pileated woodpeckers that weekend. The mystery of the friendly woodpecker was solved! Although I hadn't yet learned of Carl's passing when I saw the woodpecker, I had seen it the day after Carl had passed away. When I shared my woodpecker photos with Jessie, she wasn't surprised to hear that Carl had appeared as a pileated woodpecker to yet another person in her life. Carl, whose spirit was set free in the wee morning hours on the North Dakota prairie, appeared in the form of a cartoonish bird to let us know that he had ascended, and to leave us with a smile and a sense of wonder.

I sent Jessie a woodpecker totem that I found in a local shop. It's a small silver disc, about the size of a quarter, with a pileated woodpecker on the face. Jessie now lives in Uganda, where she works with widows and orphans to help them with their grief, and teaches them empowering self-sustaining life skills. There are no pileated woodpeckers in Uganda but Jessie carries the totem in her pocket, and Carl lives on in her heart.

How can a person's spirit convince such an elusive creature to show itself so boldly to people? I don't know, but if anyone could, it would be Carl. I don't know *how* it happened, but I know that it *did*. How else can we explain all the out-of-the-ordinary pileated woodpecker sightings the weekend of Carl's passing?

—Jenny Pavlovic—

26

Believe in Miracles

Love is the great miracle cure.

~Louise Hay

I know he has arrived before I ever see him. Heads turn in his direction, and if he stops for just a minute, he draws a crowd. He walks through the halls with a swagger that is saved for the truly confident.

His name is Augie. He is a six-year-old Goldendoodle with a strawberry-blond coat that is made for petting, and his manners are impeccable. He is a trained therapy dog who visits patients in the hospital where I work as a dialysis nurse in Fredericksburg, Virginia. I have seen Augie come through the hospital, stopping for anyone who wants to pet him, and I have seen him go into patients' rooms. But I had never witnessed Augie providing the therapy that he was trained to give until I saw him with Mr. M.

Mr. M had been in ICU for many weeks and endured many medical complications. His wife rarely left his side. Family and former colleagues visited, and I quickly learned that, in his younger years, Mr. M had been a force to be reckoned with — if you were intent on breaking the law, that is. Prior to his retirement, Mr. M had worked as a canine police officer and developed strong bonds with his four-legged partners. It was a natural transition when, upon retiring from the police force, he became a trainer for the next generation of fearless police dogs. Sadly, Mr. M had been attending a training program for police dogs when he fell ill.

Although he was awake, and his beautiful green eyes were open, there was little indication that he was aware of his surroundings. Mrs. M was undeterred by the lack of response and kept talking to him while she exercised his arms, hoping he would make some effort to move them himself. I watched Mrs. M work with her husband's hands, opening and closing them. She told him gently that he needed to move his hands so he would not lose the use of them, but he did not seem to be able to do it. He moved his eyes to look at her when she spoke to him, but he didn't, or couldn't, move his head toward her voice. His bright green eyes seemed to shout, *I'm in here! I'm trying!*

Cue Augie. When the handler brought him to the door, it was as though Augie knew he had to make this visit. He sat at the doorway, his eyes fixed on Mr. M until he was invited in. Then he walked over to the bed and plopped down his big head, gently nudging Mr. M's hand. I took Mr. M's hand and placed it on Augie's head as I introduced them. The miracle started unfolding as the connection was made. As Mr. M felt the soft, curly fur under his hand, I could see him straining to move. And then, with fierce determination, he moved his hand ever so slightly. He moved his head, too, to try to look at Augie. It was incredible!

There was no doubt in that moment that Mr. M was not only aware of what was happening, but he was making a huge effort to participate in it. Augie's handler and I looked at each other and spoke the same word: "Powerful!" With tears in my eyes, I looked over at Mrs. M. She didn't look astonished; instead, she looked like she knew all along that this miracle would occur. In that moment, I knew two things: Mr. M was going to recover, and I had been forever changed. To see miracles, I only need to believe in the possibility that they will happen.

— Jacqueline Gray Carrico —

27

Sonja's Message

*Faith is to believe what you do not see; the reward of
this faith is to see what you believe.*
~Saint Augustine

I was checking e-mail when a photograph of Sonja popped up on the computer screen. Did I accidentally hit the wrong key? I did have this image in my photo files. I paused a minute and stared at the image of my best friend, who'd died the prior year. Her shoulder-length brown hair was styled nicely, and her wire-rimmed glasses made her look smart. She wore a suit jacket, an open-heart necklace, and a wide grin.

"Hello, Sonja," I said aloud. "I was devastated when I heard about your accident. Does heaven have a special place for writers?" The room was quiet. I spotted a book on my desk that had recently come in the mail. "Guess what? Chicken Soup for the Soul reprinted my story in a new book."

I shook my head. Was I going crazy? My husband might think so if he heard me talking to myself.

During the next few days, the same photo of Sonja kept appearing on my screen. At first, I said, "Hi, Sonja," but when it happened again and again, I felt uncomfortable. I'd quickly click on another screen.

Sonja and I had met over a decade ago in my writing group. Forming a group wasn't my idea. Pam, a friend of mine who was legally blind, convinced me that feedback would improve our writing. We had tried a literary group, but some members scoffed at Pam's religious articles and lacked the patience to accommodate her disability. We needed kinder folks.

I'd tacked a notice on the library's bulletin board: "Christian writing group starting. Meetings once a week. If interested, please call." Along the bottom I'd written my number on fringed strips. Would anyone want to share stories? I figured we'd be lucky to fill the chairs around my dining-room table, but the phone continued to ring, and four women joined us, including Sonja Herbert.

Sonja stood out from the rest. She was older, spoke with a German accent, and always dressed up for meetings. The stories she wrote were about experiences she'd had while growing up in post-WWII Germany. I thought I'd moved a lot as a military wife, but she'd spent her entire childhood in a traveling carnival.

Perhaps Sonja and I bonded because we were both far from home. She'd married an American G.I. and come to the U.S. with him years ago. My husband had recently retired from the Navy and taken a job in Oregon, so I was thousands of miles away from my family in New York.

Both of us had also taken spiritual journeys. Sonja's memoir dealt with her search for God as a young adult. While attending English classes in Germany, she'd met missionaries and become a member of the Church of Jesus Christ of Latter-day Saints. I was raised Catholic, but my brother's death when I was young later made me question what I was taught. I asked, "Is the Bible true? Are Jesus and heaven real?" I wanted to believe, but how could I be sure?

At our meetings, I avoided being the person who said the opening prayer, and I remained silent while the others talked about churches they attended. One day, Sonja looked me straight in the eye and asked, "Which church do you go to, Mary?"

I squirmed in my chair. "None of them," I admitted. "My husband and I moved often in the Navy. I tried a few, but it was hard to keep starting over."

Sonja raised her chin and smiled as if she saw right through my excuse. She'd found me out! I wasn't a Christian writer. I'd started this writing group solely for my blind friend's benefit.

The more I got to know Sonja, the more I admired her. She'd

excelled in college despite a sporadic education during her formative years. She'd had the courage to leave a bad marriage and she had taught on an Indian reservation to support her six children. Although English wasn't her native language, Sonja was the best writer I knew. Her determination to be published was contagious. We encouraged each other to aim high, and to submit work to Chicken Soup for the Soul and other publishers.

A few years later, Sonja and I hugged goodbye. She moved to Utah with her second husband, and then they lived in Germany for a while. I followed her blog, "German Writer," and when she returned to the States, we exchanged manuscripts by e-mail. I was so happy when Sonja found a publisher for her memoir.

We drifted apart when we both took jobs. I worked as a substitute teacher, and she became a translator. "We need to start writing again," Sonja said, but our lives were hectic. There never seemed to be enough time.

On a rainy morning in 2015, I received an e-mail from Sonja's blog. Her daughter wrote a note: "German Writer has passed away." My heart skipped a beat. A car had struck Sonja as she crossed the street on her way to work. I walked around in a daze. Questions I'd wrestled with in the past returned: Do we go to heaven after this life, or is death the end?

The following year, Chicken Soup for the Soul sent me a copy of *Chicken Soup for the Soul: For Mom, with Love*. It was a compilation of stories that had been published in earlier volumes, including one of my own. I imagined Sonja would've been as proud as I was to have one of her old stories in this book. That's when her photo started to pop up unprompted on my computer.

I e-mailed Ken, Sonja's husband. "Has anything like this happened to you?"

"Not exactly," Ken wrote. "Sometimes, I get little 'nudges' from Sonja in the form of thoughts that, like the picture you talk about, just suddenly pop into my head. I can feel she's near, and I do talk with her. She loved you as a friend, so I'm not surprised."

Shortly afterward, I was reading *Chicken Soup for the Soul: For Mom, with Love*. As I turned the page, my eye caught the name beneath the next title: Sonja Herbert! Goosebumps broke out on my arms. Was this why Sonja's picture kept coming up on my computer? Had Sonja's spirit been "nudging" me to look for her story? I remembered this one about her mother-in-law helping her after her divorce. Now both our stories were together forever in one book.

Elated, I e-mailed Ken and told him the good news. I wrote a comment on German Writer's blog announcing that Chicken Soup for the Soul had reprinted Sonja's story and added: "Even after her death, Sonja continues to affect the world with her writing."

I hung Sonja's picture near my desk. One day, I looked up at her big grin and laughed out loud. If I truly believed she'd communicated with me, then I must believe in an afterlife!

What if that were the whole point? Sonja knew I had been struggling with my faith, so she'd found a way to let me know her spirit lived on. Every time her picture popped up, it was as if she were saying, "Believe, Mary! Believe!"

— Mary Elizabeth Laufer —

28

Heaven Cent

To live in hearts we leave behind is not to die.
~Thomas Campbell

I hung my jeans in the closet at the top of the stairs as I half-listened to the television droning in the living room below. I bent to scoop up several pennies that lay on the closet floor. *They must have fallen out of my pants pockets,* I thought absentmindedly as I closed the door.

Normally, I would have done my chores to the sound of the radio or one of the CDs from my collection. That day, though, I didn't have the heart to listen to songs, upbeat or otherwise. The man who had nurtured my appreciation of music — my dad — had passed away only the day before.

Our shared love of music had started early when Dad taught me my first tune on the piano. If I closed my eyes now, I could still see him transcribing an old folk song into an arrangement easy enough for me to play as I eagerly waited by his side.

Through the years, music was the one thing that bonded us. It seemed that, though we were devoted to one another, we didn't always agree on much else. But when it came to music, we were both on board. We enjoyed the same artists, shared facts and fascinations about them, and often sat together, listening and commenting on instrumentation and arrangements. When I sat down to play the piano, Dad would invariably comment at the end of my performance. "I really enjoyed that," he'd say, even though my level of skill was nowhere close to his.

During the two years of Dad's health decline, I cared for him in his home with the help of some wonderful aides. As I puttered in the kitchen, I often heard him in his bedroom down the hall singing along with the radio or tapping out a beat on the table next to his bed. When he had enough energy, he would come to the keyboard and entertain us with his favorite selection of jazz standards, swing tunes and oldies. It seemed that there, he was ageless. Those were bright moments in a dark time.

How long, I wondered now as I climbed back up the stairs, *will it take before the world seems bright again? How long before I enjoy a song again?* I opened the closet door and hung a few T-shirts on hangers. I thought I had gotten all the pennies off the floor earlier, yet there lay several more. I grabbed them and put them in my pocket before returning to the first floor, the television still droning out the sounds of some old movie. As I reached for the remote to change the channel, I noticed another pair of jeans to be put away. I certainly didn't feel like going up those stairs again, but I grabbed the pants and made my way back to the second floor. I opened the door. Was I losing my mind, or was that closet growing pennies? This time, I scooped up a handful of coins.

My friend Elizabeth would have called these "pennies from heaven." Having lost her dad only a few months earlier, she told me how, each time she went to visit his gravesite, she never failed to find a few pennies there. "It's a message from my dad," she explained. "He's telling me he's still watching over me."

Well, I knew about pennies from heaven, too, but in a different context. I knew it as the title of one of my favorite songs from Dad's repertoire. While I would have liked a sign, too, a bunch of coins strewn in a public place or even in my closet hardly qualified as a message from beyond as far as I was concerned. I closed the closet door once more, determined not to climb the stairs again that evening.

Now, where did I put that remote control? I wondered as the sound of the television began to irritate me more and more. I had just laid hands on it when a song began to play. I recognized it instantly. It was "Pennies from Heaven."

Now there was no denying it: Dad was sending me a message. For me, there could be no surer sign. After all, music was always the way Dad and I connected best. I smiled as I jangled the coins in my pocket. *Thanks, Dad, for the music. For the pennies. For the sign. Thanks, Dad, for everything.*

—Monica A. Andermann—

29

The Mystery of a Miracle

Miracles occur naturally as expressions of love.
The real miracle is the love that inspires them. In this
sense, everything that comes from love is a miracle.
~Marianne Williamson

My parents were getting older but they were always on the go, and I became frustrated when I couldn't reach them. So, I purchased a cell phone for them and provided a quick tutorial on its use. It was a flip phone, so it was pretty easy to use and had only basic functionality. I didn't even attempt to teach them how to retrieve voicemail as that was too complicated for them.

Unfortunately, my father's hearing was impaired, and he had a hard time with the volume limitations of the earpiece. Therefore, the phone was always carried by my mother, which wasn't a big deal since they didn't go anywhere without each other. My mom became pretty proficient with the phone, and she called family and friends on a regular basis from her new toy.

Five years later, my mother died after a short illness. My father kept up appearances for the children and grandchildren, but nothing really brought him solace.

About two years later, I was adjusting the battery on my father's cell phone and I discovered several unplayed voicemails. One was from my mother! I put the phone on speaker so my father could hear it. "Hi, John. Where are you? It's me... Angie!" My father looked at me in disbelief and called out, "That can't be!" I explained to him that the date stamp on the message was from more than two years ago. We played it over and over. I hadn't seen my father's face light up like that in years! I forwarded the recording to my siblings, who were also shocked, but thankful for my mother's message from heaven.

There were a number of things that just didn't make sense. As I mentioned, while my mother was alive, my father didn't carry the phone because of his poor hearing. The voicemail function wasn't used because they didn't know how to use it, nor were they even aware of the password required for retrieval. My parents had this phone for years, so my mother definitely knew my father wouldn't be accessing any messages. So, why would she have recorded this one, specifically to him, on the cell phone? I can't explain it.

As technology advanced, I got a newer phone for my father that had improved volume. He also learned how to retrieve voicemail, especially so he could replay the priceless, saved message from my mother. While very little brought comfort to my dad after my mom's passing, the sound of her voice, and hearing her say his name, were blessings to him. I know she got him through some of his most difficult days with her eight simple, recorded words. He died two years after we found this message from heaven, and now I'm sure my mother knows exactly where he is — with her, for eternity.

— Susan Sellani-Hosage —

All Cats Go to Heaven

What greater gift than the love of a cat.
~Charles Dickens

Losing a loved one is always hard, but being in my twenties and having to say goodbye to my best friend of eighteen years was unfathomable. She had always been there. She was there when I moved from my toddler bed to my day bed. She was there for my sixth-grade graduation, high-school graduation, college graduation, and wedding day. She was there throughout my awkward teenage years when I had no other friends. She was there for every breakup and heartache, volunteering her services as the world's cuddliest Kleenex. She was there after every major surgery.

She was a part of me.

And a part of me was actually convinced that she was invincible. She had, after all, survived the Neighborhood Cat-Poisoning Massacre of 2005, as well as the Great Tree Rescue of 2007, when my dad had to stand on top of a ladder on top of a bucket on top of a tractor just to get her down. She had won every fight she entered in 2009, no matter if her challenger was the German Shepherd next door or the alligator in the pond. She was fearless.

I tried to choke back my fear as I approached her for the last time. Her face lit up when she saw me. She tried to meow but no sound came out, so she silently laid her head in my lap instead. I stroked her matted fur, coated from the mud of the rain puddle she had walked through earlier in her delirium. "It's okay now. Mommy's here," I whispered as

I petted her body, now so small and frail beneath my hands.

I kissed her stubborn forehead and whispered that it was okay to let go. I would still love her and be with her again. I prayed that she would not suffer and would go peacefully in her sleep, and she did. I was grateful for that, and that I got the chance to say goodbye.

During the drive home from the vet, I had a crisis of faith. I have always believed wholeheartedly in a heaven and an afterlife for human souls. But I was suddenly panic-stricken. Where did animals go? Their souls go to heaven too, right? I needed to know, and I needed proof.

I prayed desperately, *Dear Lord, please, if my cat is safe with you, just give me a sign that my Sugar is okay. That song I used to sing to her all the time — "Suga Suga" by Baby Bash — just let me hear it once, and I'll know....*

As soon as I had the thought, I dismissed it. How stupid could I be? I was expecting to hear a fifteen-year-old song on the radio — a song that everyone else had forgotten. To make matters worse, if I even had a chance at all of hearing it, it would have to be on a Flashback Friday when some of the radio stations play oldies. But it was Sunday. I gave up on the idea as quickly as I had it. I didn't want to set myself up for disappointment and more heartache.

After getting home and crying in my lunch, I logged onto Facebook to browse through some photos of her. Suddenly, I came across a post that one of my friends had sent me. It was a funny video compilation with various songs playing in the background for comedic effect. In that two-minute video, a certain song started playing at 0:36 seconds. That's right: "Suga, Suga." I was elated. But still, being the cynical human that I was, I chalked it up to mere coincidence.

Then, that same week, Walmart released a new commercial — one that featured the song "Suga, Suga." That commercial played every time I turned on my TV. Why would Walmart choose a fifteen-year-old song to promote their products? I'll never know, but I wish I could shake the marketer's hand and thank him or her for renewing my faith — and for reassuring me that all cats do, indeed, go to heaven.

— Kaitlin Hodnett —

31

The Garden's Embrace

Where flowers bloom so does hope.
~Lady Bird Johnson

My mom knew I loved flowers, especially gardens lush with roses. Since I am blind, I can touch their soft petals and breathe in their sweet scents. Chirps, tweets, and twitters from all the resident birds are music to my ears. These scents and sounds create a vivid picture in my mind. Gardens give me the atmosphere to meditate in my own private cathedral.

A couple of years after our wedding, my husband Don and I were able to buy our first home, a new construction. Don planted our lawn with help from friends. They put in sod, but we still needed colorful accents so we were pleased when family and friends bought us housewarming gifts of bushes or trees. My mother brought us a rosebush. She and I had always loved that poem that starts with "Roses are red…."

"Aren't roses very hard to grow?" I asked, though, because Don and I didn't know what we were doing.

"Oh, you'll figure it out," she said. But year after year, that rosebush refused to bloom. Don moved it around our property, chasing the sun to find the perfect light. We watered and fertilized. We talked to it. Nothing happened.

Twenty-five years later, Don burst into the sun porch. I heard the surprise in his voice. "You'll never believe it!" he said. "Mom's rosebush has a flower on it." From the beginning, we had always called it "Mom's rosebush," not "ours."

The next time she visited, Mom walked out the door to see the single bloom for herself. Now, she walked more slowly and used a cane. She stood before the buds and stared. "I hope this doesn't mean that I'm going to die," she said. I swallowed hard. She was ninety years old, but the thought of her not being with me hurt too much.

The following spring, my mom died and I took it very hard. The sweater that she used to wear as we sat in our garden was still hanging in our closet, and I found myself pressing my face into it to breathe in the floral fragrance that she had worn for years.

The summer after her death, Don stood in the doorway and called me into the garden. "Come outside. I want to show you something." He guided me to our old friend, Mom's rosebush. When he described the blooms, I gasped in disbelief. I touched hundreds of glorious red flowers. I had been struggling to find some comfort in faith. Was this Mom's sign telling me she was happy? This time, my tears flowed freely, as I thought back to the verse I had learned from her when I was a child, "Roses are red."

— Carol Chiodo Fleischman —

Signs from Above

32

Chicken Soup for the Soul

The Force Be with You

*Death is a natural part of life. Rejoice for those around
you who transform into the Force.*
~Yoda, Revenge of the Sith

I'd experienced loss piled upon loss: my mother's death from cancer in 2010, followed seventeen months later by the death of my husband. Then, in January 2013, the doctors who had been treating my grandson's cancer for more than two years informed us there was nothing more they could do.

For as long as his health allowed, Jacob lived each day with a zest for life that inspired everyone around him. During his many hospital stays, he'd save the cupcakes he made with volunteers and the little prizes they gave him to share with his siblings. Even during the short period of time he was cancer-free during the previous two-and-a-half years, he'd thought about others, collecting toys to take to the hospital for other children going through treatment. How could we bear to lose such a generous little boy? Our hearts ached, even as we attempted to give him a sense of normalcy.

Jacob spent many afternoons at my house, drawing pictures of *Star Wars* characters. He loved anything related to *Star Wars*. He'd pass the time in the hospital and at his many doctors' appointments by playing *Star Wars* games on his Game Boy.

His obsession with all things *Star Wars* prompted me to take him to The Core comic-book store in Cedar Falls, Iowa for their free comic-book giveaway in May. I'd chosen this particular store because they were also offering a prize of a free autographed photo of Jeremy Bulloch, who'd played Boba Fett in the original *Star Wars* trilogy.

The small store was so crowded that we had to wait in line outside. When we reached the head of the line, I noticed the man at the entrance staring at Jacob's bald head.

"We have a big *Star Wars* fan here," I said, introducing Jacob.

"Did you know that Jeremy Bulloch, the actor who played Boba Fett, will be here in June?" the man asked. I informed him that not only were we aware of it, but we were hoping to win one of the tickets for a signed photograph.

Once inside, the many displays of *Star Wars* merchandise drew Jacob's rapt attention. He gravitated toward an enclosed glass case. Leaning his forehead against it, he peered inside intently. The entire case was filled with *Star Wars* figures. Normally reticent, I was surprised when he began pointing at the figures and rattling off the characters' names.

"I hear we have a *Star Wars* fan in our store," Mike, the owner of the store, said as he approached us. Jacob nodded shyly.

Then Mike knelt in front of Jacob, meeting his eyes before looking up at me with a questioning gaze. He must have seen the answer to his unspoken question in mine.

"Did you know Jeremy Bulloch is going to be here next month?" Mike asked.

"Yeah," Jacob said. His eyes lit up with excitement.

"We're hoping to win the autographed picture," I informed Mike. He looked from me to Jacob as if carefully considering his next words.

"I want to personally invite you to meet with Mr. Bullock before the public does and then have dinner with him later."

Wait, what? I didn't know whose eyes were wider — Jacob's or mine.

"Mom, too, of course," Mike hastened to add.

"Grandma," I corrected automatically. "But what about his dad? He loves *Star Wars,* too."

"Grandma and Dad," he agreed. "We'll work out the details later." He handed me his card, and I fumbled for one of mine in my purse.

The whole encounter was surreal. I hadn't requested special treatment for Jacob. Yet he'd just nabbed a private meeting with an actor from his favorite movie. When I asked Mike later what had prompted him to invite Jacob to the supper and a private meeting with Mr. Bulloch, he said it was the man at the front door — a cancer survivor who'd recognized a fellow warrior.

I'll never forget the look in Jacob's eyes as the dignified English actor spent an hour catering to the whims of a small child. Jeremy Bulloch's intriguing British accent seemed to relax our little boy, who never spoke a word outside of his repeated "yeah."

A team of Mandalorian Mercs — a *Star Wars* costume club that heard about the terminally ill *Star Wars* fan — brought him a helmet they'd designed. Presenting it to him, they dubbed him an honorary member of their organization. As my son-in-law Ben and I watched from the sidelines, television and newspaper reporters' cameras flashed. For one amazing day, Jacob was the star whose smile lit up a room.

Just a few days later, Jacob was too ill and weak to enjoy much of anything. He spent the last fifty days of his life on the couch, his mother sleeping on the floor next to him. He died in mid-August.

A month later, a friend invited me to accompany her on a birthday trip with six other women to see Michael Bublé in concert. Before he began singing, Michael Bublé announced a special guest in the audience, and cameras panned to a boy sitting near the front. I gasped with recognition at the meaning behind the small, bald head, and tears slid down my cheeks, fresh grief over my recent loss.

I was subdued as we drove home the next day, silently grieving Jacob. Halfway home, we stopped for gas and a bathroom break. As we piled back into the van, Chris, who'd been in the same seat on the way to and from Nebraska, called out, "Hey, look what I just found! This wasn't here before. Does Frankie still play video games?"

The other women laughed. The son in question was in college.

"What is it?" Evelyn, the driver and owner of the vehicle asked, turning a little in her seat and craning her neck to see.

"It's a Game Boy game," Chris replied as she handed it to the woman in front of her. I felt a distinct prickle at the back of my neck.

"Did your son own a Game Boy?" I managed to ask past the

lump forming in my throat. Evelyn shook her head. Even as the game reached my hand, I knew. I turned it over, and Evelyn glanced at the *Star Wars* game in my palm.

"That's not mine. I cleaned this van several times before this trip. I don't know where that came from."

I did. I clutched it tightly all the way home, where my three youngest daughters waited for me. When I told them what had happened, seventeen-year-old Emily snatched it from my hand and popped it into her sister's game system.

"Cool. There's a game saved on here," she commented, pushing a button to begin playing it. "And a back story just popped up," she continued, reading silently, before lifting widened eyes to meet my expectant ones.

The words on the screen? "The Force is stronger than death."

—Mary Potter Kenyon—

33

Seven Simple Notes

Music gives a soul to the universe, wings to the mind,
flight to the imagination, and life to everything.
~Plato

It wasn't that I had anything against harmonicas. Of course, they never produced the dulcet tones of a French horn or the haunting melody of a violin; still, they were considerably more portable, infinitely cheaper, and immeasurably easier to play. But as my husband and I were strolling along the picture-perfect oceanfront of Carmel, California, I might have preferred listening to Handel's "Water Music" or even The Beach Boys' "Surf City" rather than a syncopated rendition of "The Boll Weevil Song" on his Hohner Golden Melody.

"Larry, I know you're practicing regional folk songs to complement your Southern States social studies unit, but we're on spring vacation. Couldn't we listen to the sounds of the surf and calls of the seabirds — just for a while?"

He wrapped up the final notes of the "Just a-lookin' for a home" chorus and slipped the harmonica into the pocket of his tennis shirt. "Sure, babycakes," he said with a wink. "That way, I can hold your hand for the rest of the walk."

Did I mention that, occasional harmonica-playing notwithstanding, I was fully aware that God had blessed me with the perfect husband?

Larry had always been in love with life. In addition to being a top-notch fifth-grade teacher, he was a natural athlete, switching effortlessly from basketball to running to tennis to weight training. A devoted volunteer at our local Humane Society, he spent much of his summer teaching at-risk, inner-city kids how to interact with animals and treat them with kindness and compassion. His stress-reliever was music: belting out his favorite tunes while accompanying himself on classical guitar. While away from home, he substituted the handy-dandy, pocket-sized harmonica for his Gibson. And, maybe best of all of his talents, there was the way he could always, no matter the circumstances, make me laugh.

That week along the California coast was a trip we had dreamt about for years. Miraculously, it far surpassed our expectations. The weather was idyllic, the hotels delightful, the sights enchanting. On the flight home, Larry took my hand, sighed with contentment, and said, "That was the vacation of a lifetime." At the time, I couldn't have imagined how true that statement would turn out to be.

***

It started out to be an ordinary May morning — sipping coffee and discussing our plans for the day. And then, in one life-altering moment, Larry was on the floor at my feet, leaving me alone forever.

***

"I know this is not the way you would have wanted it," my longtime friend Celeste said to me many months later. "You'd rather go back to California with Larry. I know you were planning to return for your next anniversary. But please consider traveling back with Lori and me. There might be some painful memories, but I think there will be some good memories, too."

I knew she had my best interests at heart. I knew she thought I needed to get out of my cocoon of grief and face the past in order to move on to the future. "But back to all those places we first saw together?" I said. "I just don't know if I'd be able to handle it."

Celeste looked me straight in the eye. "You know Larry would want you to do this, don't you?"

No fair, Celeste, I thought. But I knew she was right.

***

The only bad part of flying to California is changing planes at O'Hare International. The cacophony of undecipherable loudspeaker messages, rumble of rolling suitcases, and raised voices of passengers on cell phones trying to be heard over the chattering crowds assail the senses. All this while trying to hang on to a carry-on, purse, boarding pass and ID card, and take a final sip of lukewarm coffee at the last wastebasket before security. Not to mention those interminable, snaking lines leading up to the harried TSA agents' desks.

But there we were — Celeste, Celeste's friend Lori, and me — on our way to the California coast. We had already cleared the initial agent's amazingly polite interrogation and were on our way to remove shoes, belts, etc., and approach the metal detector. Of course, I was excited about the trip, but I was simultaneously remembering the previous one, as well.

"The last time Larry and I went," I told Celeste as she pushed her tray of belongings along the conveyor belt, "the metal detector buzzed at him, and the TSA guy wouldn't let him through without a search." I smiled at the memory. "Then Larry remembered that he had stuffed his harmonica into the back pocket of his jeans."

Celeste, knowing Larry's penchant for ever-present music, began to smile, too — and then...

Over the din of the crowd, I heard it: seven simple notes — played on a harmonica. Of course, I assumed it had to be — it must have been — an internal soundtrack, my mind somehow bringing the past into the present. What else could it have been?

I looked at Celeste — and her expression told me that she had heard it, too. I didn't know what to say.

Celeste turned to her friend Lori, in line right behind her. "Did you hear that music?" she asked.

"Yeah," Lori said, matter-of-factly. "It was that tall guy over there playing the harmonica… Oh, I guess he's gone." Seven simple notes….

***

Now, if I'd written the script for that incident, a scenario in which Larry shows me that he approves of the trip — that, in some form, he'd be right there beside me — my guess is that I would have included an overture of delicate harps, resonating violins and triumphant trumpets. But not Larry. As always, he'd want to have the last laugh, and to make me smile right along with him. A harmonica… and seven simple notes.

— Joyce Styron Madsen —

34

Mom's Gladioli

*Flowers are those little, colorful beacons of the sun
from which we get sunshine when dark,
somber skies blanket our thoughts.*
~Dodinsky

My mom still lived in the same high-rise apartment building in Brooklyn, New York where I was born and raised. Although my mom lived in the heart of the city, she loved to garden. We lovingly referred to her as a "Windowsill Gardener." If she had a seed, she would plant it. Peach, avocado, and mango pits took root into miniature trees. Sweet potatoes made for a beautiful, leafy plant. Herbs were lined up on her kitchen window and used in her fabulous meals. Violets, marigolds, and begonias also adorned the windowsills. But her favorite flower, the gladiolus, couldn't grow in her apartment.

Mom loved visiting me in my suburban New Jersey home after I got married. For her, it was a little reprieve from the city hustle. I was outside with my one-year-old daughter when my husband Harold drove up to the house with my mom one weekend. Mom busted out of the van, calling across the lawn, "Wait until you see what I got you!" As I walked over to the van, Harold opened the door to reveal the back seat loaded with plants and flowers. Mom was beaming. "So, when can we start planting these?" Violets, coleuses, rosebushes and other plants and flowers filled the whole back seat and floor. "Here," my mom said, as she handed me two bags full of gladiolus bulbs. "My favorite!

They will look pretty planted up against your house."

After lunch, my mom and I got to work digging in the rich soil. It took us about an hour to plant everything. We were dirty and sweaty as we stood proudly surveying our work. The yard looked beautiful with all the flowers and plants. "I saved the best for last," Mom said as she held out the bags of gladiolus bulbs. We got right back to work. We dug holes alongside the front of my house and tenderly dropped each bulb into the ground. By the time we were done, we had planted twenty-four bulbs. Once the gladioli bloomed, they would be a shocking bright red — my mom's favorite color.

Over the course of spring and then into summer, Mom would call for flower updates. "How are the gladioli?" was always the first question she'd ask. "Call me when they're about to sprout," she instructed. When she visited, she would always putter around in the garden, tending all the flowers, but she took extra time with the gladioli.

Mom hadn't come for a visit for about three weeks when I noticed that some of the gladioli had buds. I called to tell her they would probably bloom soon, and she came the next weekend. "Not quite in full bloom yet," Mom said, as she examined each delicate bud. The next morning, bright and early, she was walking around the garden. She gestured for me to come out. By the smile on her face, I had a feeling the gladioli had bloomed. Sure enough, there they were, opened up in all their red glory, pointing toward the sun. My mom was beyond excited.

During the next few years, it became our tradition to work in the garden together. Every spring, mom would bring more flowers. Every mid-July, she would pamper her prized gladioli when they bloomed.

In July 1988, my mom visited for the last time. Two weeks later, I got the call that she had passed away from heart failure.

During the next few years, it was a comfort to see the gladioli blooming in my garden — a reminder of my mom and our tradition of gardening together. As my family grew, we moved to a larger house. I dug up every gladiolus bulb and planted them along the entrance of our new home. Come spring, I waited with bated breath for the gladioli to sprout. They never grew. I was devastated. The gladioli had made me feel close to my mom; they were my connection to her.

In years to come, I was never able to grow my mom's gladiolus bulbs or even newly purchased bulbs. No matter what I did, I couldn't grow them. Eventually, I gave up. One day, while shopping, something compelled me to turn and look at a decorative watering can. Leaning against the can was a small bag of gladiolus bulbs. There were only three of them, and they were yellow gladioli, not the brilliant red my mom loved. I tossed them in my cart anyway. When I got home, I planted the bulbs, although I knew it was a lost cause.

That summer, I was missing my mom more than ever. The twenty-eighth anniversary of her passing was approaching, and my heart was getting heavier with each day. I didn't have much desire to do anything, and I was neglecting my garden. One late afternoon, I forced myself to weed my overgrown flowerbed. To my surprise, one single gladiolus stalk with three tiny buds peeked through the tall grass. That triggered a rare smile from me.

The next day, I left to visit my daughter for a three-day weekend. "Make sure you keep an eye on my gladiolus," I told my husband. "Call me if it's about to bloom!" I instructed, sounding like my mom.

I arrived home late Sunday evening, exhausted, and went straight to bed. The next day was the anniversary of my mom's death. I was moping about when I remembered the gladiolus. I went outside and couldn't believe what I saw. Not only did three beautiful gladiolus buds bloom, but they were a bright red, my mom's favorite color, even though the package had indicated they would be yellow! My spirit lifted instantly, and my heart felt lighter. What an amazing gift my mom had given me. She sent me her favorite flower when I needed her the most.

— Dorann Weber —

35

A Cottontail Message

I am convinced that these heavenly beings exist and
that they provide unseen aid on our behalf.
~Billy Graham

Zack was the youngest of my three older brothers. As children, we were inseparable. As adults, we followed our individual paths, but always reconnected eventually. The bond we shared wavered from time to time — as it does with siblings who may not agree on everything — but it never disappeared altogether. If anything, when we resolved our issues, we became even closer.

Growing up in a strict Catholic environment, Zack and I often speculated in whispers about death and the afterlife. Were all the stories true? Was there really a heaven? We even pinky swore that whoever passed first would let the other know with a sign.

Those conversations, long forgotten, were revived when my brother's lung-cancer diagnosis impacted our lives. After every hopeful option known to modern medicine was exhausted, we received the heartbreaking prognosis. He had only a few months left.

He chose to die at home. Two weeks before we lost him, he and his wife asked me to stay with them to help out. I went willingly.

"Remember our promise when we were kids?" he asked me weakly one day. "The one about sending a sign?"

I hated the defeated turn his conversations had taken — the ones that always began with "When I'm gone" or "Before I die…" I wanted to scream at him, to insist that he remain optimistic and not give up — that miracles happen. Instead, I nodded. I knew he needed closure, so I let him speak.

"Yes," I choked.

"I'll do it," he replied as his lids drooped. "If I can…"

His words trailed off, and his eyes closed as exhaustion overcame him.

Within moments, he was asleep. I rose from my chair beside the hospital bed we'd installed in his living room and tiptoed into the small kitchen. It was almost three o'clock. I opened the refrigerator, took out a bowl of chopped vegetables, and made my way out back and toward the cedar hedges.

The little, wild rabbit was already there, waiting like he did every day, with his wary stare and his twitching nose. I set down the bowl and backed away. He hopped over and started nibbling.

My brother had named him "Van Gogh" due to his missing half ear — a result of some past altercation with an unknown predator. Only Zack could hand-feed him. Though we had all tried since my brother was confined permanently to his bed, Van Gogh would not approach anyone else. He would finish his treat and scamper back to wherever he came from. My brother asked about him every day, and we assured him that we were taking care of him and would continue to do so.

That night, Zack sank into a coma. The next morning, he awoke for only a moment, and then passed away. I was with him, holding his hand.

As his wife, Lise, and daughter, Jessie, wept softly across from me, I leaned closer to his now-still body and whispered in his ear.

"Don't be afraid. Be at peace, and remember to let me know you're okay," I pleaded, kissing his forehead one last time and releasing my fingers from his limp ones. "Goodbye for now."

A half-hour later, the doctor arrived. Removing his stethoscope, he somberly and officially acknowledged what we all knew. The finality of the declaration caused the many gathered family members to break into fresh sobs.

Shortly afterward, the funeral-parlor attendants came. They gently and respectfully transferred him onto a gurney and took him away. We would not see him again. His express wish was that he be cremated immediately. A memorial service would be arranged at a later date.

I watched numbly as he was wheeled past me. Dry-eyed, I forced stoic control for the benefit of his daughter, who clung to me helplessly. I held her close and waited. The sign would come. I knew it would. He had promised.

I don't know what I expected: A rainbow? A clap of thunder? Doves? All I knew was that Zack said that he'd let me know he was fine — that this wasn't the end of his once vibrant spirit. I waited, but nothing happened. He was simply lifted into the hearse and driven away.

Over the next few days, I waited for my brother to reach out to me. He didn't. I arrived the day before his memorial service to help my sister-in-law with last-minute preparations. I felt sure Zack would contact me somehow with a spiritual message — perhaps at the ceremony, the church, or his gravesite.

At three o'clock, I asked Lise if Van Gogh's bowl was ready.

"He never came back after Zack died," she informed me sadly. "No one's seen him since."

"There were a lot of people here that day. Maybe they just scared him away for a little while," I soothed.

"Maybe," she replied. "I hope so."

I stepped outside to look, but the rabbit was nowhere to be found.

The next day, we buried Zack's urn containing his ashes. Throughout the graveside prayers, I anticipated that much-awaited communication, but was again disappointed. No profound miracle took place, no incident that could connect me to him on a spiritual level.

For months, I continued to hope. In my heart, I felt he was safe, but I still yearned for his heavenly validation.

That following summer, my husband and I decided to visit Zack's grave, and then stop to see Lise who lived about a half-mile from the cemetery. We stopped at a vegetable stand to buy some fresh produce and then drove on our way. The cemetery road led directly to my brother's freshly mounted headstone. We stopped, and I opened the passenger car door. Before I could step out, a movement beside Zack's cross caught my eye. I gasped when I spotted a cottontail rabbit — one with a half ear missing — Van Gogh!

I stared in shock as he hopped toward me, stopping only about three feet away. Motioning to my husband to stay quiet, I slowly reached into a bag in the back seat to pull out the celery I'd just purchased. Breaking off a leafy stalk, I held it toward Van Gogh. He approached, snatched it from my shaking hand, and ran back into a thicket directly to the side of us.

Tears poured from my eyes. The odds of that rabbit finding his way to where Zack was buried were astronomical. I had received my sign. When I looked at my husband, his eyes were as wide as mine.

I told Lise what occurred. For weeks afterward, she continued to leave a bowl of food at my brother's grave. It was never emptied, and we never saw Van Gogh again. He'd delivered his message. His work was done. I now know my brother lives on and is at peace. And, finally, so am I.

— Marya Morin —

36

Heavenly Star Balloons

For my part, I know nothing with any certainty, but
the sight of the stars makes me dream.
~Vincent van Gogh

Every day after school, our granddaughter Casey would walk the bike path behind her middle school to our backyard gate. As she ate a snack, we would often sit at the kitchen table or on the patio and watch all the students, joggers, and bikers go by "our corner of the world." Between our property and the bike path is a water canal, bridge, and twelve trees along the bank. We installed an almost-invisible wire horse fence so we could still enjoy the view.

We decorated that corner of the lawn with an antique wheelbarrow that was filled with multi-colored flowers in the summer; two old wagon wheels with ornamental grasses; and several pink honeysuckle vines and red barberry bushes. It is a colorful and pleasant area. When Casey's hamster, Herbie, died, she asked, "Grandma, can I bury him in our corner of the world? It is the perfect spot because I will see his grave every day and never forget him."

"Yes, of course. We will give Herbie a little funeral," I replied.

We bought a special wooden box with a lock on it and a garden paver with purple flowers stamped on the top as a marker for his grave. After we buried Herbie beside the wheelbarrow, she prayed, "God, here is Herbie, my first pet. I will miss him very much, but I know he will be happy with you in heaven. Amen."

Casey was an honor student who loved school, especially reading and writing. Her favorite pastimes were going to the school library and the bookstore where we spent many hours together. Occasionally, she would ask me to read a book after she did so we could talk about it. Sometimes, we traded books. But writing was where her artistic talent shone. In the first paragraph of a story or essay, she often captured the reader with a dramatic or whimsical statement. When her amusing poem about outdoor education week was published in the middle-school newspaper, she was embarrassed and proud at the same time.

Although she was highly successful at school, Casey struggled daily with poor health. She had been born with severe eczema that would cause her to scratch frequently, and asthma that challenged her breathing. By eating a healthy diet and faithfully using eczema soaps, ointments, and prescriptions, she tried to eliminate the itching, but nothing worked. As she grew into a teenager, the eczema and asthma worsened. Her arms and legs became riddled with scars, scabs, and open wounds from the intense itching and scratching. It was often painful for her to go up and down the stairs in middle school and high school because the raw skin would become more irritated as it rubbed against her clothing as she walked. In order to heal properly, she would have to stay home for several days at a time.

Missing school was depressing for her because it was hard to keep friends if she wasn't at school. Making matters worse, she couldn't wear tank tops, T-shirts, shorts, and capris like the other girls. She was a beautiful girl, but wore long sleeves and jeans in public because she was embarrassed and afraid of being bullied. As her condition rapidly and gravely disintegrated at the age of seventeen, going to doctors and taking serious medications that didn't work became her life.

Then, without warning, I received an early-morning phone call from my daughter saying that Casey had died. With heavy, grieving hearts, my husband and I went to help her. Jamie was inconsolable over the death of her only child. We brought her home with us and made the funeral arrangements for our granddaughter.

A week after the service, Jamie was sitting on our patio deep in grief and crying when she heard rustling in the trees behind our house. Coming in the back door, she informed us, "There must be an animal like a raccoon moving around in the trees. It is kind of scary because I have been watching and waiting, but so far nothing has come down."

Just before lunch, I went out to the back yard to fill the birdbath with water. As I stood there, I heard a commotion in the trees. Looking up high in the branches of the old cottonwood trees and the thorny Russian olive tree, I didn't see anything.

Late in the afternoon, my husband shouted to us, "Come and see what was trying to get through the trees to our corner of the world. You will not believe this."

Running to the window, we saw an unbelievable sight. Pressed against the wire horse fence was a white star balloon above Herbie's grave. Even though it was a sturdy foil balloon, it was miraculous that it hadn't been punctured from all the rough tree limbs. As we wondered how it got through without a scratch, it slowly dawned on us that it must be from Casey, reassuring her mother that she was okay and in heaven.

That perfect, white star balloon stayed there for a few weeks comforting our entire family. We took pictures to prove it had happened, and we even saved the balloon after all the air leaked out of it. Of course, we didn't know at the time, but that was only the first star-balloon visit.

Several months later, Casey's Uncle Jerry walked into what was her favorite coffee shop, and a gold star balloon slowly drifted over in front of him and stayed there. With a big smile, he told us, "I was totally caught off guard, but I definitely felt that Casey's fun spirit was letting me know she was there."

The following summer, Casey's Uncle Jim was sitting on his fourth-story balcony when a blue star balloon flew up to his level and lodged in the tree in front of him. Since only birds and squirrels had ever come up that high, he was delighted to ask, "What are the odds of this happening? It must be another star balloon from Casey."

Casey's birthday was in April, close to Easter Sunday. It had always been a festive time for the family to get together and celebrate both occasions. Sad and deeply missing her again this year, we colored Easter eggs and dyed two in her favorite color of purple. After our holiday dinner, we walked family members out to their cars. As we hugged goodbye, they looked up and gasped. Quickly lifting their cell phones, they took pictures of the heavenly purple star balloon floating above us. Our angel was here again!

— Brenda Cathcart-Kloke —

37

Fran on Facebook

When you are sorrowful, look again in your heart, and
you shall see that in truth you are weeping for that
which has been your delight.
~Kahlil Gibran

She was all white — white uniform, white cap, white stockings and immaculately clean white shoes. She was an experienced, no-nonsense nurse with no tolerance for mistakes. Everything was serious.

I, on the other hand, was a wet-behind-the-ears, eager-to-please puppy of a nurse, uncertain and afraid, but wanting to do great things. I was scared to death of Mrs. Stentz the first time I met her. We worked together for a few tense months and then parted ways.

Twenty-five years later, I was sitting in our hospice office when Fran Stentz re-entered my life. Immediately, I realized that my shoes were scuffed and looked for a way to duck under the desk. But Fran had changed, and so had I. The years had mellowed her, while they had forced me to grow up.

Fran and I became friends. I'm sure that it was the calling of hospice that bound us together. Fran was a very quiet person, who spoke best with her eyes and her soft touch. She had retained her focus and attention to detail, but a quiet, passionate compassion drove her. She elevated our team and made us want to be the best we could be.

Sharing patients with Fran taught me to see people and their families in new ways, to care intensely about the events in their lives and move to help. She didn't just provide competent care, but she sometimes raked the leaves or weeded a garden for her patients. She cared for them, and for some reason she loved me, too. To be loved by Fran was a beautiful gift.

Fran retired reluctantly from nursing, and still she cared for me. I would receive a text message telling me to stop in if I were in her neighborhood for lunch. The table would be set, with soup simmering and salads in place. In her quiet way, Fran asked simple questions and continued to make me think beyond myself. If I lingered over lunch, her eyes would go to her watch, and without her saying a word, I would remember that my lunch break only lasted a half-hour. We continued catching up over dinners, telephone calls and even a vacation together. She was supportive when I left hospice and began working on the palliative-care team.

In a strange turnabout, Fran became ill, and I became her palliative-care nurse. It was torture for me, and she recognized that. With her soft hand on my hand, her warm brown eyes looking into mine, she told me quietly that she wanted me there but was worried about me. "Is this too hard?" Although I wanted to cry out that I could not do this, I knew I would regret it forever if I did not, so I joined Fran as she walked her final journey. She knew when the time had come for her to call upon hospice, and she guided me.

I went to visit Fran after her admission to the hospice program. It was a poignant, sweet relief to sit in her living room as a friend. I thought we would have time together as she completed her journey. I wanted to ask her things I had always wondered about: What was she thinking and feeling? What was most important to her? She had always been my teacher. There were more lessons I was ready to learn.

We sat in her living room one afternoon and chatted as we had for years. When it was time for me to go, she reached out her hand, pulled me down into a hug and whispered, "You have been the light in my life." They were the last words I would hear Fran say. She took a turn and was admitted to the Compassionate Care Center the next week. I visited her there on a Saturday afternoon. Her daughter took a break while I was there, and though I sat quietly with my hand on

Fran's arm, she did not speak again. As I rose to leave, I whispered, "I love you, Fran." Her eyes opened, and I was blessed with one final Fran smile.

I waited all the next day, not wanting to intrude on the family time. I could envision what it would be like in her room. I knew they would be waiting, alternating between feelings of peace and grief. Finally, evening came, and I decided to simply send a text message to Fran's daughter. I received a reply soon after. Fran had taken her last breath at the moment her daughter received my text.

My heart was broken. Tears streamed down my face as I told my husband that Fran was gone, and then I escaped to the solitude of my car and began to drive aimlessly. I talked to her as I drove. Over and over, I asked, "Where are you? Where are you right now? I want to know where you are." Finally, I was spent. I pulled off into a park before going home and pulled out my phone, knowing that I needed to let some of our mutual friends know that Fran had passed. As I sat with phone in hand, I went to Facebook and scrolled absently. A saying popped up:

> Family isn't always blood.
> It's the people in your life who want you in theirs;
> the ones who accept you for who you are.
> The ones who would do anything to see you smile
> and who love you no matter what.
> Share if you agree!

It seemed so clear and perfect in that moment. I shared and tagged Fran. In a matter of seconds, someone liked my post and, to my astonishment, it was Fran! To this day, I have no explanation. I asked Fran's daughter at the funeral if she had perhaps had her mother's phone in her hand and hit "Like." She simply stared at me and shook her head.

The funeral was beautiful—perfect for Fran. I smiled as the vocalist began to sing "I Come to the Garden Alone." This had been my father's favorite song. I closed my eyes and had a clear vision of

Fran. She was standing between my father and my stepfather with her arms around both of them, watching me as she smiled her gentle Fran smile. To this day, I think she watches me still.

— Sara Conkle —

38

The Sign

Trees are the earth's endless effort to speak
to the listening heaven.
~Rabindranath Tagore

M y cousin Tim and I stood together at the plot where his ashes would be buried. "I have a question to ask you, Mare," he said. "I need someone to do my eulogy, and I trust you most. Would you be willing to say a few words at my funeral?"

"Wow, that's a lot to take in. Let's hope you are around for many years. Who knows, you might speak at mine first."

"I don't think it will be years. I pray for one more year." He was unemotional.

I gulped and said, "I would be honoured to do a tribute for you. How will I know if you liked it or not?"

"Don't worry, I will send you a sign," he said confidently.

That was the last conversation we had about his request. We both knew that the day would come sooner than we wanted. He had AIDS, and it was 1992. Tim was dying of the virus, not living with it like so many today.

We grew up together. We were next-door neighbours, and our mothers were sisters. We lived along the side of a busy road in Northern Ontario. It wasn't even a village, just a few houses beside the King's Highway.

Tim was the first newborn I ever laid eyes on. His red face peered at me as I stood on my tiptoes looking into the bassinet at the midwife's house in the next town. I stared at his little hands, and I knew from that moment on he was different. He was special.

I was the first person with whom he shared his secret about being homosexual. My response was a little insensitive. "Oh, my God, Tim, I knew you were gay before I knew what gay meant." He just wanted to hang out with the girls, not play hockey or baseball with the boys. We played "house" by the hour, and he was my little buddy.

The years of puberty were hard on his self-esteem. He was bullied and teased, even by those who loved him most. We were all confused.

After college, he moved to the city and then to Miami's South Beach. Then, in the mid-1980s, he got sick. He moved home to try to get answers.

He told me years later that he came to my house to tell me the day he learned he had acquired immunodeficiency syndrome, but I wasn't home. I didn't learn that he was seriously ill until 1991.

One day, I was up north visiting my father when the phone rang. To my shock, it was Tim, and I'll never forget what he said. "I need to spend some time with you soon, Mare. I have the big 'A.'" Stunned, I promised to call ahead the next time I was going to be in town.

We connected a number of times over the next two years. Then one Friday in August, on the spur of the moment, I cancelled all my appointments and was able to get a cottage for the week near Tim's parents. Tim and I watched the Summer Olympics on television and talked nonstop for the week. That was the visit when he asked me to do his eulogy.

The next spring, I was in the middle of a transfer from one city to another for work when my aunt called the office. She put Tim on the phone, and he told me he didn't have much longer. I told him I would be there as soon as I could. I drove twelve hours to see him for five minutes. He was a skeleton, and I nearly gasped when I saw him. We laughed and cried and said goodbye.

He passed two days later on a beautiful June evening in 1993.

The memorial service was the following Saturday. I was prepared and focused. I gave my eulogy and then played "I Will Always Love You" by Whitney Houston. A graveside service took place immediately after the service at the same spot he and I had stood the summer before. As his sisters laid red roses on his grave, an unexpected wind picked up. The pine trees over our heads swayed and swooshed loudly for a brief moment and then stopped. I looked skyward, and when I looked down the female clergy looked me right in the eye and said, "I think someone is trying to tell us something."

And there it was. Goosebumps covered my arms, and I smiled. As promised, he sent me the sign of approval, and I heard it without question.

— Mary Lennox —

39

Don't Tell Baba

More and more, when I single out the person who
inspired me most, I go back to my grandfather.
~James Earl Jones

I remember the Sunday afternoon gatherings of the relatives at my grandparents' home in a New York City suburb. With three adult daughters, one adult son, their spouses, and grandchildren of all ages, it was invariably a full and loud house.

We were first, second and third generations of Slovaks. Grandma, in Slovak, was called Baba, and Grandpa was Dedo. I called him Dedecko, a form of endearment.

Of all her grandchildren, Baba loved my cousin Millie the most. Since Millie and I were both ten, I remember wondering why Millie always got to sit on Baba's lap, but I was never invited to do so.

When Dedecko was not mingling with the adults, he'd be playing games with my twelve-year-old brother, Dee. Then one day I noticed Dedecko watching me. He must have seen my wistful expression as I gazed longingly at the display of affection between Baba and Millie because he suddenly called me over to play with the "big kids." I was elated. From then on, whenever Dedecko and Dee played together, I was included. Soon, even Millie would slip off Baba's lap to join us.

With adults, Dedecko was the rough and intimidating patriarch of the family. His presence alone could evoke fear in all the grown-ups, but with us children he would be as gentle as a teddy bear. Even though he loved all his many grandchildren, he related best to Dee, Millie and me. He knew how to think like us and make us laugh. When we had his attention, I completely forgot about wanting to sit on Baba's lap.

About once a month during these visits, Dedecko would send a signal to the three of us. No one would notice how we'd disappear with him. Mischievously, with his finger at his lips indicating "Shush," he'd meander down the hall and we'd follow. He'd stop by the linen closet and take one final dramatic glance around to make sure no one was watching. We knew what he was about to do, and we were always excited. He'd quietly open the closet door, reach in, and pull out three single dollar bills from between the sheets. He'd hand one to Millie, one to Dee and one to me. Then he'd always say, "Don't tell Baba."

A dollar was a big deal to kids our age, and it made us feel special.

This went on for several years. Every few weeks, we three kids made our trip down the hallway to the linen closet, stood outside and waited for Dedecko to "surprise" us. We kissed him, thanked him and giggled as he said, "Don't tell Baba." We never did. I don't know to this day if Baba knew about his private stash.

When we got older and started earning our own money, the dollar bills no longer meant as much, but that gesture showed that he loved us. That meant more than money. This pleasant tradition continued throughout our teenage years.

Eventually, Baba died peacefully in her sleep. Dedecko was heart-broken and lost. He sold everything, including the house, and moved to Florida. He soon returned, however, missing his loved ones as we missed him. He moved into the apartment with my mother and me. The three of us grew even closer. I spent every afternoon after school chatting and laughing with Dedecko. He was the father figure I never had. When I wanted to move out of New York, I was concerned about leaving him. I felt as if I were deserting him, but he told me, "Go, Evka. Go. Make your own life. I will always be with you."

I never saw my grandfather again.

I moved to the West Coast, but I kept wondering if I had done the right thing. Mother was at work all day, and Dedecko would be home alone. Had I abandoned my dear grandfather?

When he passed away, I felt guilty that I had not been there for him at the end.

I missed my roots and my family. It took a while to make new friends. Many a lonely night, I considered returning to where I had grown up and giving up the dreams I had envisioned for myself in a new and exciting town.

Eventually, I bought my first house. I had taken nothing with me but my clothes and my cat when I moved. Slowly, I purchased furnishings and supplies to make my house a home.

One day, as I was arranging my belongings in my new house, I found myself thinking of my childhood. As I reached into my closet and pulled out a pair of sheets to change my bed, I remembered my grandfather and his secret stash of dollar bills. Dedecko had been gone several years by then. And then something shocking happened. There, between the sheets that I had purchased a month earlier, three one-dollar bills appeared!

It hit me like a ton of bricks. I felt like my Dedecko was still with me, assisting my transition from girlhood to adulthood. I knew then that I could make it on my own.

I sent one dollar to my brother Dee and another to my cousin Millie, who were still living in New York. I wrote a note to each, saying: "Look what I found in my linen closet between the sheets."

A few days later, I received two messages on my answering machine — one from Dee and one from Millie. Each one said simply, "Don't tell Baba."

I'm sure they were both smiling when they left those messages. I certainly smiled when I heard them.

— Eva Carter —

40

Just Dropping In

I miss thee, my mother! Thy image is still the deepest
impressed on my heart.
~Eliza Cook

How foolish I felt! I was holding up to the ceiling a letter for my mom to read! Mother had been dead for a year, and I missed sharing precious teaching moments with her.

My student Judy, a timid speaker, had won a trophy in a Speech and Debate Contest, eligible for the National Finals in Boca Raton, Florida. After graduation, Judy had written a long, loving letter of thanks for my hours of coaching.

I used to mail these "brag notes" only to my mother, who enjoyed rejoicing over triumphs for my students, especially the less gifted. "My spiritual grandchildren," she called them. She had once traveled to our huge New Jersey high school from her home in Pittston, Pennsylvania, to watch my winning Mock Trial team, and she enjoyed chatting with my students.

But tonight, she was gone. I was propped up in bed, reading my mail, and said aloud, "Mom, how I wish you were here to read Judy's letter. Can you see it from heaven?" And I held up the letter to the ceiling.

At that moment, I heard a funny, crinkly sound, like a mosquito walking on cellophane, and then a "plop" on my pillow. It was a photo of Mom, taken right before she died. The day I snapped it, she had playfully posed among the branches of our pink mimosa tree.

Weeks ago, I had Scotch-taped this picture to my bedroom wall, high above my headboard, and forgotten it. The tape had now dried up on the wooden wall and had slowly released the precious photo.

I saw my mother's face smiling at me from my pillow. She seemed to be saying, "Oh, yes, I can see it! How lovely!"

— Sister Josephine Palmeri, MPF —

A Message from Dad

Blessed are those who mourn,
for they shall be comforted.
~Matthew 5:4

My beloved father passed away in October 2017 after a very long illness. From the day I was born, we had a special bond and a wonderful relationship. He required a lot of care in his last years, and I was blessed to be able to keep him at home with me and care for him. His wish was to be buried in New York with my mother, so I flew there with his body from our home in South Carolina.

Understandably, it was a very difficult trip that I had to make by myself. I had severe back problems and required a wheelchair to get around the airport. After my plane landed in New York, I was asked to wait until the other passengers had deplaned before my wheelchair would arrive. After I thought they were all off the plane, I turned around and saw that a young man was still in the row behind me, getting his belongings together. I had turned on my phone when we landed, and it was resting on the seat beside me. It started ringing and playing *The Marines' Hymn*, which is my ringtone.

Before I could pick it up or even look at it, the young man said, "Oh, I know that song. Semper fi, ma'am."

I replied, "Semper fi, young man." He told me he was in the Marines for ten years and had served two tours in Iraq and Afghanistan. I thanked him for his service, and he had a questioning look on his face about my connection to the Hymn. I told him my father had died, and I was bringing him back to New York for the funeral. I said he was a World War II Marine who had served in the 1st Marine Division in Okinawa and Saipan.

The young man said, "Oh, my goodness, my grandfather was in the 1st Marine Division in Okinawa." At that moment, I knew that my dad was trying to reach me through this young man. I started to cry, and he said, "May I give you a hug?"

I said "yes," and as he hugged me, he whispered in my ear, "Don't worry. Everything is going to be okay." Those were the last words my dad had said to me before he slipped from consciousness for the last time. I thanked the young man, and he went on his way. Then I looked down at my phone to see who had called. There was no call. I searched and found nothing—no missed call, no connected call. I turned the phone off and on again, and still there was no record of a call. The last call had been registered the night before. I was puzzled, but it became more and more apparent to me that I had received a message from my dad. He knew what a difficult time I had ahead of me, and as he had always done in life, he tried his best to comfort me.

My friend picked me up at the airport, and as soon as I got in the car, I handed her my phone and asked her to look for the last call. She found the call from the night before and nothing else. There was no call that morning, and yet the phone had clearly rung and played the Hymn an hour before!

—Jeanne Cassetta—

42

Earned Faith

'Tis impossible to be sure of any thing
but Death and Taxes.
~Christopher Bullock (1716)

It was February 2, 2018 — a Thursday. I walked down the handicap ramp of the church I served in the Hudson Valley area of New York, and I spotted a piece of folded white paper on a patch of bare ground. I sighed; I was in a rush. My arms were full of cooking supplies for a free lunch program that I was holding on Saturday at the First Baptist Church of Monticello. I needed to deliver these items before going to work. The paper could wait until my return that evening for our prayer service. I attempted to dismiss it as I loaded the items in the car, but I couldn't.

White against brown, perfectly folded on a patch of earth the snowplow had cleared two days earlier, it appeared as if it had been carefully placed in the very center of the only non-white spot of the dirt parking lot. I was about to slip into the driver's seat when I sighed again. I felt like the paper was drawing me to it, and I rationalized the feeling with several explanations. One, it was litter, and I wanted to keep the church parking lot neat. Two, I might have dropped something. Three, it could have blown there or, lastly, someone had been parked near there after I left the day before. The church is in the middle of nowhere with no businesses around and very few houses. It was possibly a Realtor's, as the building was up for sale. It definitely had not been there the prior morning. I would have noticed it, and it wasn't something the plow had uncovered for it was too clean, too neat. Whatever it was or however it got there, I knew I had to pick it up.

As I reached down, I found the paper to be surprisingly free of any ice. As I read the contents, I got goosebumps all over. It was a W-2 form, from an East Liverpool, Ohio company I never heard of — from the year 2003! Why was a fifteen-year-old W-2 form from Ohio lying in a parking lot in New York State? But it was the person's name on the form that shocked me. It was the name of a dear friend who had passed away more than a year before.

There was no earthly reason for this dry, pristine white paper to be on this piece of frozen ground. Al had never visited this church in the three years I was pastor. He was busy in his own church and then too ill that last year. His widow, Annette, had only come here once about six months earlier — and what possible reason would she have had for carrying such an item? It could not have been lying there for any length of time as I or someone else would have seen it.

I needed to pray about my next move. I could not visit Annette that day or the next several days as my schedule was packed. Occasionally, she came to the Friday night Bible study, but I knew I would see her on Monday when I volunteered at the 1st Way Life Center that she ran. At least by then I might have an answer to this mystery.

It snowed again that night, and the bare ground was once again covered in white.

I brought the paper with me on Friday. Even though Annette showed up for the Bible study, I could not speak to her alone afterward as I had to drive one of the ladies home. On Saturday, I left the slip of paper on my desk rather than risk getting it dirty while preparing and serving the free lunch.

Busy cooking, I almost didn't hear the light tap on the kitchen door. I looked around for one of the church members, but they were busy in another room. So I wiped my hands and opened the door to find Annette standing there smiling.

"Annette!" I cried as I hugged her and pulled her into the warmth of the kitchen. "What are you doing here?"

"I woke up this morning, and I believe God told me to come and help you today." She shrugged out of her coat and put it near mine, reaching for an apron. "I wasn't planning on coming as I usually spend Saturday with my granddaughters, but I felt God nudging me to come here. The girls never get up early on the weekend anyway."

"Well, I have something to tell you."

"Wait, please," Annette interrupted. "I feel I have to ask you to pray for someone who has been heavy on my heart."

"Sure, who?" I replied.

"Dr. Douglas."

"Dr. Dougy?" I asked. He was the OB-GYN who rejoiced when announcing my last pregnancy and mourned with me when I lost it. It was in his office almost twenty years earlier that I met Annette, who was his receptionist. "Didn't he pass away a couple of years ago?"

"Yes."

"Annette," I said gently, "you know I don't pray for the dead. Do you want me to pray for his family?"

"No, I have to explain." She interrupted me again, clearly feeling something powerful. "I keep wondering if he made it to heaven. He was such a part of Al and my family's life for a while there. He was engaged to one of my daughters, and during that time Al and I actually moved to Ohio to help Dr. Douglas open a clinic there. We moved back to New York after the engagement ended. When he died unexpectedly so young, I always wondered if he had time to get right with God."

"I don't know what is going on, but I have to tell you something." I told her what I had found. But for some reason, I said I found it Friday instead of Thursday. She listened, and when I told her the name of the company on the W-2, she nodded.

"That was the name of the clinic."

"Well, I don't understand how that paper got in the Woodbourne parking lot," I replied, feeling slightly frustrated. "Could God be trying to tell us something?"

"Well, since it was Friday you found it…"

"Did I say Friday?" I shook my head. "I'm sorry, it was on Thursday I found it. We had snow Thursday night, and I never would have seen it on Friday."

"Thursday?" she cried. "Thursday? Well, that was Dr. Douglas's birthday!"

"Well, since it was Al's W-2, maybe they finally ran into each other in heaven and decided to let us know," I replied, laughing with joy. "How great is that?"

—Camille A. Regholec—

Heavenly Reassurance

The Interview

God has not taken them from us. He has hidden them
in his heart, that they may be closer to ours.
~Author Unknown

His name was Mark, and he was my first real boyfriend. He was a tall, blond hunk of a guy, with electric blue eyes. He was a senior and on the football team. He would walk me to class and grin at me as he dropped me off at the door. That sideways smile always made my heart flutter. When class was over, he would be there, casually leaning against the wall, books resting on his hip, and take my hand to walk me to the next class or to the lunchroom to sit and talk. He taught me to drive his car, me shifting gears as he pushed the clutch, sitting on the center console with his arm draped across my shoulders.

It was everything a first love should be.

Sadly, as many high-school sweethearts do, we drifted apart after graduation. He joined the Navy, and I moved with my mother to the West Coast to start a new life. We stayed in touch sporadically, but as the years passed, we lost touch with one another. Now and then, something would bring him to mind, and I would wonder how he was, and if he ever remembered me as fondly as I thought of him.

News filtered back to me that he was battling multiple sclerosis. A mutual friend saw him in our hometown and called to tell me that not only was he fighting MS, but he had been diagnosed with leukemia as well. He was struggling to get around with two canes, but apparently his famous grin was still as bright and happy as it had always been.

I thought a lot about the young man I had known and the dreams we shared. When my workday was done, I looked up his phone number to call him and catch up. I am not a person prone to "stage fright" or shyness. For some strange reason, though, I could not dial the number. I sat there staring at the phone, seemingly at a loss for words. Finally, I decided I would wait a bit.

A week or so later, a girlfriend of mine from home sent me a message on social media that Mark had died. I was filled with such sadness that I'd not called to talk to him; it had been so unlike me to hesitate. It haunted me for weeks afterward, a chance I should have taken to connect with someone I had loved so much.

I have been lucky to make my childhood dream job a career. Being on air as a radio personality has been a great joy for me. As an avid book reader, I often do interviews with authors so that I can share my love of reading with my listeners.

One morning, I was scheduled to interview a famous psychic medium to promote her new book. As a rule, interviewers do not request personal readings — as a gesture of respect. We talked at length about some of her experiences in assisting the FBI and police on cases, and how her gifts affected her everyday life.

As the interview drew to a close, she suddenly stopped in mid-sentence. She asked if it would be all right for her to tell me the message she was receiving.

To be honest, I have always been a bit of a skeptic, but here we were live on-air, and I was curious.

She was quiet for a moment. Then she said, "It's Mike, no, Mark. Mark is here, and he wants you to know something very important."

I think I was holding my breath at this point, and she continued, "He wants you to know there was a reason you couldn't call him that night. He wants you to know that he stopped you and doesn't want you to feel sad anymore."

She explained that he had been in a deep coma that night, hovering between worlds. He had been drawn to me, sitting there. He had put a hand on my shoulder and whispered to me, "Wait," believing that if I got no answer and left a message, his not returning it would hurt me. He wanted me to know that he remembered everything in the same way I did, with a smile and with love. Our time had been important to him, too.

By now, the tears were streaming down my face. *How could she possibly know?* She asked me if this had relevance to me somehow, and I managed to confirm it. She told me he was no longer in pain, and that he would always be an angel watching over me.

Finally, as the time of our interview concluded, she hesitated and laughed a bit.

"He wants to know," she said, "can you still drive a stick shift?"

With that, she disconnected, and there I was, live on-air, and a complete mess.

That night, I called his mother, who was still living in our hometown. She shared with me about his son and the love he had for him. She told me of the coma that he had been in for several days and the night he passed, surrounded by those who loved him.

Some say these messages are just wishful thinking. Some say there are no such things as angels.

I can't help feeling that I have been touched by one, and I will never be the same.

— Cj Cole —

44

Life Is for the Living

Mother, the ribbons of your love are woven
around my heart.
~Author Unknown

The first hitch in our travel plans occurred when our luggage did not arrive in Atlanta. My normally calm husband, Ken, shouted at innocent airport personnel. We finally filled out forms and were told we'd be contacted when the luggage arrived. We were scheduled to fly on to Johannesburg, South Africa, the next morning for a long-planned three-week visit with dear friends, and this was no way to begin.

We returned to the hotel after dinner and were dismayed to find no message or luggage. "What are we going to do?" I asked my husband. "We've spent months planning this trip. How in the world can we cancel now?"

Ken put his arm around my shoulders. "We'll be on that plane tomorrow morning. What you're wearing now will work out fine for the next three weeks." Then he laughed.

I used the toiletries the airline had supplied and went to bed imagining two different scenarios: wearing the same clothes for three weeks straight, or going on a big shopping spree upon arrival.

I'd finally drifted off to sleep when the phone woke me. "Mom, it's Kirk. Uncle Paul called a few minutes ago." He hesitated before saying, "Grandma died tonight."

I clenched the phone. My eighty-seven-year-old mother had been in a nursing home for well over a year, body and mind deteriorating rapidly. Dying was a blessed release. I understood that, but why now?

"Did Uncle Paul say what the plans are?" I felt Ken's hand on my shoulder, rubbing gently but sending a clear message of comfort.

"No, nothing's been set. Didn't you talk to him and your other two brothers about this before you left?"

"I did, Kirk. I told them that if we were still in South Africa when it happened, we'd probably not return for the funeral. I said my goodbye last fall when I visited Grandma. At least then, she was aware and knew me, but I realized it was our final visit. But now — I'm just not sure what to do." My hand kept smoothing the comforter on the bed until I broke the silence. "The doctors said three months ago she had only days left."

My son did his best to give me a guilt-free way out. "If there's a funeral right away, I'll go for you. You and Dad should continue with your trip."

"I'll call in the morning with our decision. You phone your sister and tell her." I choked on the final words.

Ken put his arms around me. "We'll do whatever you want."

Suddenly, the man who proclaimed we'd go on with or without our luggage had changed completely. His concern for me took precedence over everything else.

The big question was: What did I want? I wanted to go on this long-planned trip. I wanted to honor my mother at a service for her. I wanted to talk to her. I could barely swallow around the lump in my throat.

I lay down and reviewed a conversation I'd had with Paul only days earlier. I suggested that, if the worst happened, they have a burial immediately and then a memorial service later when we could all be there. My brother hadn't readily agreed, but he didn't veto my idea either. It sounded reasonable to me then, but it suddenly seemed selfish.

But was it? We'd spent a lot of money on airfare, our friends had reservations at places we'd travel to, and they'd arranged visits and activities with others. They'd worked hard on plans. Even so, I wrestled with my conscience in the darkness. Ken's even breathing let me know he was asleep. I lay there for what seemed like hours.

Suddenly, I heard my mother's voice. "Go. Life is for the living." Did I imagine it, or was it real? As if in answer, she repeated it. "Go. Life is for the living." I could not see her in the darkened hotel room, but I felt a warm presence close to the bed. Had she come on the wings of an angel?

The voice and message were clear and strong. This was the mother I'd known for so long, not the very ill woman I'd visited in the nursing home months earlier. I reached out from the side of the bed, but felt nothing. I had only the memory of the few words she'd spoken.

My heart beat faster. I shivered and moved closer to my sleeping husband. I spent the remainder of the night thinking about the vibrant person my mother had been up until the past year. I had no doubt that it was my mother speaking to me and advising me as she had always done when I needed her most.

The sun hadn't made an appearance yet when Ken rolled over and put his arms around me. "What have you decided?"

Before I could answer, the phone rang again. Our luggage had arrived.

I related my nighttime message from Mom, wondering if Ken would think I'd gone around the bend. He never questioned what I told him and agreed with my decision to go on with our trip. Quietly and quickly, we got ready for our overseas flight after he retrieved our luggage.

Before leaving for the airport, I called my brother to tell him my decision. "Do what you have to do," he said. He hadn't censured me, but I knew my mother approved, and that was all I needed.

I called both our children to tell them what we'd decided. Each said they'd hoped that is what we'd do. Karen laughed when I told her about the message. "That sounds just like Grandma," she said.

I boarded the plane with a heavy heart, but I had Ken's love and support plus a wonderful message from Mom to sustain me. Her words gave me the strength I needed during the visit with our friends and their family, all of whom were so kind to me. Whenever I felt sad, I remembered my mother's sage advice: Life is for the living.

Later that spring, I prepared a photo board of Mom's long and full life for her memorial service. Our guests studied the pictures, many commenting on how full of life she'd always been. They listened as I read a tribute I'd written, many nodding their heads at one thing or another. She lived her life to the fullest, and so would I, thanks to her advice.

— Nancy Julien Kopp —

45

Be Positive

*Granddaughters use grandfathers as their entourage in
both real life and their imaginary fairytales.*
~Author Unknown

I was parked under one of the big trees in the parking lot, and I couldn't stop crying. My shift started in ten minutes, and I knew that I needed to pull myself together before then. It was a perfect Southern California day, but my heart was hurting too much to enjoy it. For some reason, I couldn't stop thinking about my grandpa.

Earlier that morning, I had had a doctor's appointment. My husband waited in the lobby for me while they took blood samples before leading us back to a small office with a picture of Yoda on the wall that said, "Fine, it will be." My heart jumped a little, and I wiped my palms down the thighs of my slacks when our specialist, Dr. Young, entered the room. After some brief greetings, Dr. Young dove straight into why I was, at the age of twenty-five, sitting in the infertility office.

In very technical terms that took me a series of questions to understand, Dr. Young explained that something had gone very wrong with my reproductive system at some point.

"Probably while you were still in the womb yourself," he said. He explained that the year my husband and I had spent "trying" for a baby had been futile, given that my body was not capable of creating life. Dr. Young informed us that there were medical avenues that could potentially provide us the gift of parenthood, but chances were slim — about 20 percent. That was when I started crying.

As I sat in the parking lot attempting to pull myself together, I had a strong yearning for one of my grandpa's skinny-armed, too-tight hugs. He'd been gone for three years, and I felt that I particularly needed him today.

Sitting in my car, I spoke to him. My relationship with God was "under construction" at the time, so I spoke to who I was comfortable with in hopes that Grandpa could maybe put in a good word for me, or at least pass along some comfort to get me through the day.

"Please help me. I just want a baby. I want to be a mom. What do I do, Grandpa?"

Just speaking to him made me feel calmer. My tears slowed to a stop, and I finally noticed the beauty of the day. I felt like I could, in fact, get through this, because I was no longer alone.

Just as I was collecting my things to get out of the car, my phone buzzed to life. A new e-mail flashed across the screen. I clicked it open and saw that it was my blood test results from my appointment that morning. One link read Blood Type, and I was surprised that in all the time I'd been on this earth, I had never found out my blood type. Out of curiosity, I clicked it first. It loaded for a moment before my result appeared in large, bold letters: B POSITIVE.

It took me a second before I realized that I was holding my breath. There it was, my little bit of wisdom from my grandfather wrapped in a bit of his customary comedy. Grandpa had sent me a very literal message; all I needed to do was be positive that everything would work out. I laughed. "Okay, Grandpa, okay."

That morning was three years ago. Now I spend my days chasing twin toddlers around the house. And I am constantly reminded of our new family motto: "Be positive." My daughters and I talk to Grandpa often, and I'll never be able to logically explain why my garage smells like pipe tobacco from time to time seeing as no one in my home smokes. But in my heart I know it's him checking in, happily looking down on the two beautiful, little girls he gave me the courage to work so hard for and reminding me that a little positivity can go a very long way.

— Audrey Zelenski —

46

More Than a Dream

*While we are sleeping, angels have conversations
with our souls.*
~Author Unknown

Mama was dying in an Austin nursing home. For several days, she floated in and out of a coma, and when she was awake, her dementia obscured reality. Then one day, it was as though she awoke from a nightmare. She looked at my sister and me and asked fearfully, "Where have I been? I don't remember the last few days or weeks or months."

We explained that she had advanced dementia. Strangely, she wasn't in the throes of dementia at that moment. She was as clear-headed as she was in her younger days. My sister and I were astonished and wondered how this was possible. For the next day and a half, we had our mother back — the mother we knew before dementia consumed her brain. It was a gift we couldn't explain, one we were thankful for as her life waned. Then just as abruptly, the dementia took hold again.

That night, I couldn't leave her. I slept in a chair at her side, holding her hand. Suddenly, she blurted out, "No! I am not going anywhere with you. I'm not ready!"

I bolted up in my chair. "Who are you talking to, Mama?"

"Shush, I'm not talking to you." She waved me off with her hand.

"Who are you talking to?" I asked again.

She gestured a circle around the bed. "Those people," she said. I saw no one. My mother and I were alone in her nursing-home room.

She soon fell asleep, as did I.

Later in the night, I woke again, this time hearing a young girl's voice coming from my mother. She was looking straight ahead, with a sweet, childish smile crossing her lips and a child-like sparkle in her eyes.

"May I see my father now?" she asked in the high-pitched voice of a young child. I watched, mesmerized. She got some kind of response, one I couldn't hear. "When may I see him?" she pressed further. Mama must not have liked the second response either because a look of sadness filled her eyes as she said, "Okay."

I wondered who she had been talking to. Was someone from the other side telling her that it was her time to cross over? Was she trying to drive a bargain that she would cooperate if she could see her beloved father who died before I was born? I never had the chance to find out. She fell into a coma, never returning to consciousness.

I'd been there for days, before and after her miraculous return to lucidity. The nurses said she was hanging on because she knew I was still there and didn't want to leave me. They had seen it many times before and encouraged me to go home and allow her to die. I was torn. How could I leave her in her final days, hours and moments? The nurses assured me that she would pass soon after I went home. Reluctantly, I left. My sister was with her, and I knew Mama would not die alone, but it still grieved me that I wasn't there when she passed a day after I left.

A few days after her funeral, I sat on my couch feeling miserable and wishing that I could hear from her one last time. I decided that I would ask her to contact me. I spoke out loud to Mama, telling her that I regretted we didn't get one last goodbye and imploring her to send me a sign that she had arrived safely on the other side.

"Please," I told her, "don't send a rainbow or a butterfly because that won't catch my attention. Send a sign that will knock me on the head, something that will scream at me that it's you."

I went about my day, largely forgetting my plea. It was like buying a lottery ticket. Sure, I buy them occasionally, but I never actually think

I'll win. When I asked Mama for a sign, that's all it was — a wish. I didn't think anything would come of it.

That night, I dreamed that I was sitting at a desk, writing. Something called me away. When I returned, I found a note below my own handwriting on the page, written in my mother's distinctive hand. I was dreaming, but I clearly felt my heart miss a beat.

"Honey, I heard you. I arrived safely, and I'm fine. I love you, Mama."

As comforted as I was by her words, it was what I read below her writing that caused me to bolt upright in bed, gasping for breath and awakening my husband.

"What is it?" he asked, a little alarmed.

I told him about calling out to Mama earlier in the day and asking her to contact me. When I told him about Mama's note, his eyes widened. Then I relayed what I had read afterward. It was a note written by my father. I had not seen my father's handwriting since he died thirty years before, but I knew it was his. My tears fell as I told my husband what the note said:

Jeffree,
Your mother is with me now, and we are watching over you.
Love, Daddy

My husband asked why my father's note shocked me so much.

"At first," I told him, "I thought that maybe because I wanted so badly to hear from Mama that I'd imagined she contacted me in the dream. But when I saw Daddy's note, in handwriting that I knew was his, I realized it was all quite real. They really did contact me. And they did it in a way that I could not mistake for something else."

It was no accident that they chose to write to me in a dream. Writing has always been a big part of my life. That was the knock on the head that I needed to be convinced it was them. They knew that was the perfect way to get through to me.

The dream occurred thirteen years ago, but it might as well have been last night. It's as vivid as ever. I know that I received something extraordinary — a message from beyond, as well as the certainty that my parents are watching over me, and I will see them again one day.

— Jeffree Wyn Itrich —

47

Halfway Home

Life is eternal and love is immortal;
And death is only a horizon,
And a horizon is nothing save
the limit of our sight.
~Rossiter W. Raymond

The worst thing I could imagine had happened. Maureen, my beautiful, headstrong twenty-three-year-old sister, was dead. Mo had lived her life at 200 miles per hour, taking too many chances, most in the name of love for her family and friends. She was known for driving out late at night to rescue people who had run out of gas or to pick up folks who needed rides. So perhaps it was no great surprise that she met her fate in a car, at four in the morning, as her beloved Datsun crumpled against a utility pole on an Atlanta street.

While my parents and sister lived in Atlanta, most of our extended family was living in New York and my husband Steve and I were in Philadelphia. I can't recall now the blur of what happened next: our trip south to deal with insurance, the funeral home, and the casket. We made endless calls to loved ones, sharing the horrible news.

The one person we deliberately didn't tell was Grandma Berrigan. Grandma had dementia. What would be the point of saddening her? She would forget and would have to be told again and again when she asked. We felt there was no harm in keeping the truth from her.

Several months after Mo's death, my mom flew up to New York. Mom approached Grandma's house, her heart sinking. She anticipated the familiar litany of questions. Grandma always asked about the grand-daughters in birth order. What would she say when it came to Maureen? And so it began that day. She asked for me, but then skipped Mo and asked about my younger sister, Carolyn.

There was a pause. Grandma continued, "And the little one… who died."

Mom sat in shocked silence. No one had told her about Maureen's death. She was positive of that.

Calmly, Grandma went on. "Maureen. Yes. She comes to me, you know. Sometimes at night, sometimes when I'm sitting in my chair. She talks to me. Maureen didn't want to go out that night, you know. She wanted to stay home with you. Her friends called after you were asleep."

My Lord, thought Mom. She remembered finding Mo's scrawled note on the kitchen table in the early dawn, after the police knocked on the door. *That's right. But how could she…?*

"Dear, Maureen needs you to stop crying. She is fine. She's very happy, except that she's worried about all of you. Your tears are holding her back from where she needs to go next."

The incredible visit continued. Grandma was more alert than she had been in years, not repeating a single question. When at last they parted, she took Mom's hands in both of hers and squeezed. "Maureen loves you so much. Please know that."

Grandma lived quite a few more years. She and Mom never had another lucid conversation. Grandma never mentioned Maureen again to anyone. But the miracle of that afternoon stayed with us. My sister had reached out to us through my grandmother. Maybe Mo felt we wouldn't have believed it if she spoke to us directly.

A priest friend, when we told him the story, had a thought that made sense to us. He said that perhaps people with dementia live with one foot on earth and one foot in heaven. Grandma was halfway home, and she was like a bridge to the other world.

It has been thirty-six years now. Maureen was joined by my grandma and my parents. The rest of the family is reassured that we will all meet again.

—Elise Seyfried—

48

Hudson Phones Home

Be thou the rainbow in the storms of life.
The evening beam that smiles the clouds away,
and tints tomorrow with prophetic ray.
~Lord Byron

O n July 26, 2017, I lost my twenty-year-old son Hudson to suicide. He was an extraordinary example of what a person should be and spent his time here making the world a better place in every way. He studied engineering in college, spoke to school officials about why they needed solar energy, traveled the world studying humanitarianism and sustainability, and made everyone who met him a new best friend.

The week following our tremendous loss, I sat in the living room retelling stories of our boy with my two daughters, Dakota and Delaney. We were startled when Hudson's cell phone rang suddenly from across the room. It was sitting on the kitchen table on top of his Bible. We all jumped up from the couch and ran to the phone. On the screen, it said, "Caller unknown." We all looked at each other and knew it was Hudson. He had extensively studied circuit boards in college and actually had a job putting circuit boards together, so we felt as if manipulating electricity and phones would be easy for him from the other side.

At that very moment, the bright sun from behind the house beamed through the sliding-glass doors and caught our attention, as did the rain clouds through the front door. I looked at the girls and said, "Go out back. He's going to send us a rainbow." As the girls ran out the back door, I ran out the front and looked up at the sky, waiting for a message from him. As I searched the sky, I heard a scream from behind the house. "Mom, come quick!"

I pushed open the front door and ran as fast as I could to the back of the house, overlooking the lake. It was then that I saw the biggest, brightest rainbow I've ever seen in my life. As we jumped up and down in pure excitement, the rainbow transitioned into a double rainbow that dipped down into the calm waters of the lake. It was like nothing I had ever seen before. It looked so close, as if we could touch it. We cheered and screamed his name at a job well done.

The girls laughed and said, "Mom, I've never seen you this happy my whole life." And I was, knowing that my boy was reaching out to us from the other side. As I quickly grabbed my cell phone from my pocket to take a picture, I heard a voice in my head that said, "Mom, live in the moment." Ironically, I had said that exact thing to Hudson many times.

I replied, "But I have to take a picture or no one will believe this." As I disobeyed his request and went to snap the photo, the entire scene went blank, and the rainbow disappeared. I laughed so hard because I knew he was behind it. Shortly thereafter, another pastel rainbow appeared and stayed around quite a while, even for my picture.

Ever since that day, I can say, "Hudson, show me a sign that you're here. Send me a rainbow." And, without fail, one will show up. It may be a reflection, a sticker, a song, a word or an actual rainbow in the sky, but he will always send a rainbow.

As I type this out, I'm in the jury duty waiting room, and I suggest that we start jury karaoke. The woman in front of me says, "I have a song in my heart." I ask her what that is. She says, "Somewhere over the Rainbow." And there's my sign, right on cue. That's just the kind of son Hudson is… always sending a sign when I need it.

— Chris Lowe —

49

A Gift from My Mother

When a baby is born a flower begins to bloom in her
continuously, this flower is the love of her mother.
~Debasish Mridha, MD

I t was the day after my mother's death. I had spent the past twenty-
four hours in a whirlwind of emotions and tasks. The reality of
her passing hit me over and over again.

We were staying at a modest motel in nearby Banning, in
a neighborhood by the highway and the train tracks that was filled
with rundown pickup trucks and junkyard dogs. I went out for my
morning walk anyway, warily.

Then, I spotted a dog. He didn't have that lean hungry look that
stray dogs usually have. And he wasn't a mutt. What was a Basset
Hound, with those weepy eyes and hanging jowls, doing in Banning?
And why didn't he have a collar?

He was just sitting in the road as if he were waiting for me. As I
got closer, he started hobbling toward me, with a limp on his left side.
My mother had also had a limp from a severe car accident years ago.
I never thought of my mom as crippled. That was just the way she
walked. This dog wore his limp the same way — not apologetic or in
pain, but just as a natural part of his gait.

The sorrow of my mother's passage immediately lifted as the dog
and I walked together. He seemed to belong to me, trotting along like
we had been walking together every morning.

In the periphery, I could see a few crusty yard dogs coming our way. Dogs like this are often not treated very well, which accounts for their unruly behavior. They were suspicious of us. Strangers rarely came wandering up these roads, not without a pickup truck, a gun, or both.

The five dogs circled us. They were acting hostile and I was starting to worry.

"My dog" sat down right in the middle of those aggressive dogs. I tried to call him away, but he sat there calmly, as if he was a mediator in a family squabble. I was nervous for him.

Suddenly, a nearby barn door opened, and a man called off the dog pack. He gave me a look as if I didn't belong in his neighborhood, so I turned around and began heading back toward my motel.

As the Basset Hound and I approached the train tracks, I tried to shoo him away, hoping he'd take a side street and find his way home. But he stayed by my side.

A train screamed in the distance. I didn't have a leash and I was afraid the dog would take off across the tracks and get hit. Luckily, he was smart. He stood still while the train passed in front of us. And then, with the caboose receding in the distance, he trotted forward by my side as we continued back to my motel.

Up ahead, the main intersection of Banning was waiting to test us again. As we proceeded, would this dog stay by my side and out of traffic? Could he tell red lights from green ones? Again, he minded the traffic perfectly.

After we turned, I noticed him sniffing the trashcans, at which point I kept walking, hoping he'd find his way home or get attached to someone else. I walked about a half-block, and when I turned around to check on him, he had vanished.

To this day, I wonder if this fellow was a gift from my mother, telling me she was okay. The similar limp, the appearance of a purebred dog in the middle of this dangerous neighborhood, and his ability to protect me as those stray dogs circled — it all seemed very much out of the ordinary. And then there was the way he vanished when the danger was over.

I don't question it. I just know my spirits were lifted immediately, and I was able to cope with the ensuing grief of the day — all because of that sweet, brave dog who had my mother's limp.

— Mary B. McGrath —

50

Checking In

A father is neither an anchor to hold us back nor a sail
to take us there, but a guiding light
whose love shows us the way.
~Author Unknown

It was the wee hours of the morning when I got the news that I expected. We had been holding a vigil at my father's bedside in the hospice unit for two weeks, but when it finally became clear that we were not helping him we all went home. Dad didn't want us to spend the night there trying to sleep on uncomfortable chairs or pacing in the hallway, and he didn't want us to be there when he passed. He was such a protective father and grandfather.

That morning, as I drove to the funeral home to finalize arrangements, I pulled into a gas station. My mind was reeling, filled with the emotional events of the last few days. My cell phone rang and it was my good friend Suzie, who said, "I found a penny today. Most of the time, I think of my mom, but today I knew it was from your dad. Did he pass?"

"Yes," I sobbed.

When our conversation ended, I thought about what Suzie told me. I was feeling overwhelmed with guilt because I hadn't been at my father's bedside at the end. It was incredibly hard to honor his wishes and leave him there to pass on his own terms. I yearned for a sign, something to let me know he was okay and with God.

At that same moment, from out of nowhere, a woman approached my car. Tapping the driver's side window, she asked, "Excuse me, but could I have a penny?"

A penny? I thought. That was a strange request. *Why a penny?* "Sure," I answered. *What was the harm in giving her a penny?* As I grabbed my purse, all the change flew everywhere. I managed to scoop up the only penny among the coins and handed it to her.

"Thank you!" she gushed.

I assumed she owed it to the cashier inside the convenience store, but she simply got in her car and drove away. I watched, stunned. Involuntarily, I shivered, and then a warm feeling filled my heart. Immediately, I knew it was Dad giving me a sign so I could be at peace.

In the first few months after he died, I found pennies everywhere. There was one on the floor near his casket, one in the church at the funeral, and one sparkling in the grass at the cemetery. Often, I'd find pennies on the pavement when I opened my car door, especially if I was parked at one of his favorite places. But the most predictable penny sightings were at my grandsons' sporting events. Dad loved those boys deeply and enjoyed cheering them on in every sport they played.

The pennies themselves are significant in that every one is always a shiny new 2014 penny found heads-up. That was the year he died. I'm positive that this is Dad's way of guaranteeing I won't miss his signal.

Just when I think the penny sightings have stopped, a new one turns up in an unexpected place. I pick it up, smile, and say, "Thanks, Dad."

Recently, I faced a difficult health decision. I weighed my choices and went to church to pray. During the Mass, I had my eyes glued to the floor to hide my tears. When it was time to leave the pew to receive Communion, I lifted my eyes to the priest. When I looked down at the floor again, in the exact spot I had been staring at for an hour, a shiny penny gleamed. My heart felt lighter. I picked up the little gift. "Thanks, Dad."

Arriving at the doctor's office the next day, I felt a little better about the decisions I'd made regarding the treatment. Nonetheless, I had butterflies in my stomach. I waited forty long minutes to be called back to an exam room. As the nurse said my name, I spotted a shiny penny at my feet. In the nick of time, Dad was showing me that he agreed.

— Terry Hans —

51

Growing Wings

No matter how hard death tries, it can't separate
people from love. It can't take away our memories
either. In the end, life is stronger than death.
~Author Unknown

I had kissed my mother goodbye in her palliative-care bed a few weeks before she passed. Then I had hopped on the plane that took me home, all the way across the country. I flew back for her funeral, which to date remains the most peculiar day of my life. I woke up in the morning with the full weight of finality bearing down on me. I shared tears with my family and, oddly enough, even a few fond laughs. By evening, I felt washed out, like the sky after a storm.

I didn't know it then, but my mother had told my dad that she would send a sign from the other side if she could. After the service, we gathered around her grave in the shade of a centuries-old sugar maple. As the priest arrived, the shuffling and whispers quieted.

In the peaceful silence, a large butterfly fluttered in our midst. Some say it was white. I remember it with powdery bronze wings bordered in yellow lace and blue dots: a mourning cloak. What I remember most is the tangible awe that united us as the butterfly circled the assembly before rising out of sight into the deep blue sky.

After a few more days spent with my father, brother and sister, ordinary life resumed. Back home, I planted an apple tree in my mother's memory, but it died after its first winter. I missed Mom immensely. I had been missing her on a daily basis for years since we lived so far apart, but now I kept forgetting that I couldn't just pick up the phone and talk to her.

The books on how to cope with grief did not help. Everybody said that time heals, and I knew it was true, but the healing didn't begin for me until I found a book of testimonials about contact with the afterlife. I cannot say that I was fully convinced, but the thought that my mother's spirit or awareness might still exist comforted me and made her death easier to accept.

Over the years, my mother has made multiple appearances in my dreams, usually in situations that make no sense whatsoever. Still, it is always nice to catch a glimpse of her. Once in a blue moon, I have a dream that leaves a more lasting impression.

A few months after she died, I dreamed I was walking from my house to the end of our long driveway to meet my neighbour. She is a small, dark woman, her face lined with age and worries. As I approached, a golden light enveloped her, and she was not my neighbour anymore but my mother, beautiful and smiling. I walked into her arms, and she hugged me for a long time. I felt bathed in love so pure, warm and wonderful.

Happiness became easier after that.

The next time I dreamed of my mother, I was standing on the porch of my childhood home, watching her silhouette walk down the road. She wore cargo pants, hiking boots and a huge backpack, things I have never seen her wear in life. She brought presents for the two granddaughters she never got to know very much, and she was coming to say goodbye. She gave me another hug brimming with love, and then went on her way. Where she was going, she didn't say.

I wondered if there are different stages to the afterlife. Is the proverbial light at the end of the tunnel a rite of passage that one willingly walks into when ready to cut ties with earthly life? She was fifty-two years old when she learned she was dying. She had made her peace with the fact, but she certainly had not been ready.

It has been twelve years since she died. I still miss her.

After the dream when she backpacked to wherever she went, I thought this would be the end of those cherished dreams. However, close to the anniversary of her passing this year, she came back — a tourist with two large suitcases and a broad smile. I was overjoyed, and that joy accompanied me for days afterward.

I don't recall that she ever spoke to me in those otherworldly encounters. As much as I would like to hear her voice again, I know that words cannot begin to describe that powerful feeling of love that she gives me in these dreams.

After I cut down the dead apple tree, a new shoot pushed out of the ground in its place. It must have come from a stowaway seed, for it did not look like its McIntosh predecessor. This spring, it flowered for the first time: a profusion of fuchsia blooms that blew in the breeze like butterfly wings.

Caterpillar to butterfly, seed to tree. Death is certainly an end, but I like to think that it is not *the* end. Longing has replaced my grief. And whatever happens after death, memories and dreams have kept my mother very much alive in my mind and heart.

— Caroline Lavoie —

52

Dream Baby

A mother's love for her child is like nothing else
in the world. It knows no law, no pity.
It dares all things and crushes down
remorselessly all that stands in its path.
~Agatha Christie

I stared at the black, empty screen. My heart was pounding in my chest. There was nothing there, but how couldn't there be? I waited to hear the sound that would put my fears to rest; yet there was only silence.

"Honey, I'm sorry. What happened can't really be explained but…" said the tech.

My husband's trembling voice cut her off immediately, "Where is it? Why can't we see it?"

I knew the baby was there. It was gone though, and I was told what happened was called "a blighted ovum." Sometimes the baby begins to develop and suddenly stops… dissolving away into blood clots in the sac. At least that's the only thing I remember them telling me.

My husband held me as the tears poured out, reality finally hitting me. "I don't understand. Is it my fault?" I asked no one in particular. My husband tried to comfort me, but I knew he was using all his strength not to begin weeping, too.

I was taken to give some blood after the news. Sitting in the waiting room with mothers and their babies felt like torture. I had wanted so badly to see my baby.

I wanted to be angry with God, but as I looked up at the ceiling to talk to him, no words came. It felt as if he was staring at me with the same sadness he knew I felt. "I'm not angry with you, God. I'm not angry," were the only things I could say. It was true. No matter how I wanted to feel about the situation, something in my heart felt comforted still.

My husband and I shared many sleepless nights and long talks for months after the miscarriage. Grieving was a long hard road, and many people didn't seem to understand the struggle. I hated hearing people say, "Maybe it was for the best?" How could it be best for me to lose my baby? I think only people who have lost a baby can understand just how painful it is.

A year later, I had a dream. It was one of the most vivid dreams I have ever had.

I was running out of the back door of my house, following a laughing toddler with long black hair. As I reached her with my arms outstretched to lift her, I woke up.

I remember the hair on my arms sticking straight up after that dream. I went about my day normally and took out my Bible for some devotional time. I opened to a random page and the first words I saw echoed in my mind: "'Sing, O childless woman, you who have never given birth! Break into loud and joyful song, O Jerusalem, you who have never been in labor. For the desolate woman now has more children than the woman who lives with her husband,' says the LORD." My heart skipped a beat because for some reason I knew this verse was speaking to me.

The very next day I took a pregnancy test, and it was positive.

Today I have a beautiful toddler with long black hair down to her waist. My husband and I were beyond happiness when we saw her in the first ultrasound and heard the beating of her heart. Even in our happiness now, however, we don't forget our angel baby that lives in heaven. That baby will forever have a special place in my heart.

—Rachel Bliss—

Chapter
6

Answered Prayers

The Best Wedding Gift

A sister is God's way of proving
He doesn't want us to walk alone.
~Author Unknown

It was about to happen. I was getting married! My sister Laurie and I had been rehearsing for this day since we were little kids. Imagining ourselves to be June brides just like Mom, we paraded down Maple Street garbed in old lace curtains and clutching bouquets of hydrangeas plucked from the bush in our front yard. Of one thing we were certain: We would be the maid of honor in each other's wedding. But God had other plans.

Laurie was sixteen and I was eighteen the night I sat at her bedside holding her hand, and we had our last conversation this side of eternity. "I'm not afraid to die," she told me, "but I am sad I never got married and I'll never be your maid of honor." In a matter of hours, cancer claimed her life.

And now—thirty-two years, three months, and twelve days later—I was getting married. I was fifty years old, for crying out loud! Who could have imagined it would take me so long to snag the man of my dreams? Sometimes, truth is stranger than fiction.

My fiancé Augie and I had a private "wedding dress reveal" in the church sanctuary before our guests began to arrive so the two of us could pray together. When it was my turn, I prayed, "Lord, I have an unusual request to make—and it's okay if you say 'no'—but I was wondering if it would be possible for my sister Laurie to watch our wedding this afternoon." Feeling foolish, as if I were asking the impossible, I continued, "Could you at least let her know I'm getting married? I know she'd be happy. And please tell her our good friend Erica is my maid of honor, although I wish it were her...."

Later that day, things were winding down. The buffet tables were nearly empty, the cake had been cut, I had thrown my bouquet, and we were about to leave on our honeymoon when my Aunt Evelyn pulled me aside.

"Did you see Laurie during the wedding?" she asked in whispered tones. My response was a look of confusion. Of course, I remembered my earlier prayer, but I had shared that with no one but Augie. Disappointed, she said, "Aw, shucks. I was hoping you saw her, too."

"What did you see?" I asked, my interest piqued.

"While you and Augie were saying your vows," she answered, "I glanced at your maid of honor and couldn't believe my eyes. It was as if Erica's face had become the face of Laurie. And she was positively radiant. She smiled. She paid close attention. And then when the preacher declared you 'husband and wife,' she was gone. Please tell me you saw her."

Tears welled up in my eyes. "I can't say that I saw her, but I do believe you." And I told her about my pre-wedding prayer.

Now that's what I call a wedding gift!

—Janet L. Revino—

54

Promised Child

The value of consistent prayer is not that He will hear
us, but that we will hear Him.
~William McGill

"Welcome, Baby Sarah!" was written across the sheet cake in bright pink cursive lettering. And it broke my heart. I stood at the buffet table, fingering a napkin as I blinked back the tears and attempted to compose myself.

Don't get me wrong. I was happy for my friend Janet and her soon-to-be-born baby, but I'd been struggling for more than a year to get pregnant again with no success. I'd just been to my doctor, and the conversation was bleak.

"You need to start infertility treatments again," she began. "Listen, fertility drops dramatically even in fertile women your age... and no one would ever consider you a fertile woman. You need to get on it or give up. You simply don't have time to waste."

She was right. No one would consider me a fertile woman. I'd had twelve surgeries to address my endometriosis and polycystic ovary syndrome and two years of infertility treatments before giving up and then, miraculously, conceiving my son. I should have been happy. After all, I had a baby. So many women in my infertility support group could not say that. Maybe I shouldn't be so greedy.

But I felt my daughter. I felt her. Her soul seemed to dance around me during the day, and visions of her lived in my dreams at night. I wanted — no, I needed — this child of my dreams to manifest in the flesh and join my family.

However, the cost of infertility treatments was prohibitive. We were able to afford them with my son because I was still working, and we were double-covered by insurance. But when my son fell from our second story, fractured his skull and nearly died, I quit my job to stay home and help him deal with the residual effects of his fall. We'd been through so much to save and protect this first child. Couldn't we just conceive his brother or sister to help him progress and fill out our family? Now, however, there was no secondary insurance coverage. And after paying the enormous co-pays for my son's hospitalization and surgery, there wasn't anything left for the luxury of infertility treatments.

"Didn't Cindy do a good job on the cake?" I felt Janet's baby bump brush up against me before she'd even finished her sentence. I took a slow breath to steady myself and not pull away from my friend. "Are you okay?" she asked kindly.

That was one of the reasons why I loved Janet. In the midst of her joy and celebration, here she stood, reaching out to me, knowing how painful this day would be for me. I closed my eyes to ward off the tears and nodded my head.

"Everything looks so nice, Janet," I began. "How are you feeling? It's getting close." I'd been avoiding Janet in the last few weeks. It was hard for me to see her growing belly and her happy glow while each month of her pregnancy that passed just made me less likely to conceive.

But I stood and talked to my friend. I took a tour of the nursery in a bittersweet dance of joy for her and pain for me before we headed back toward the cake.

"Everyone, a toast!" Janet's husband stood behind the cake with his glass of sparkling cider raised to the sky as he reached his arm around his wife. Guests moved in closer as glasses were filled and raised to the couple. "Here's to my beautiful wife and my soon-to-be daughter. To the blessings of family and the indescribable joy of our little one. Thank you all for joining us in our happiness and helping us to celebrate the wonder of new life."

With shaking hands, I raised my glass and sipped a toast to my friend's blessings. Then I slipped away from the table to find a quiet space to regroup.

Why? I lifted a silent prayer. *Why can't I have a baby? I'd be a good mother. I'd honor the gift you would give me. My son needs a sister. I need this daughter. The rest of the world has babies at the drop of a hat. Why can't I have one? I know this child. I already love this child. Please, God. Please!*

And, suddenly, an answer came.

Stop! While the loving voice in my head didn't "say" the words I heard, the message was, nevertheless, clear as day and as concrete as the ground I was standing on. *It's done. Your baby is coming. By Sarah's first birthday, you will have a baby.*

Suddenly, the deepest peace I'd ever known filled my body and instantly settled me down, ending my painful longing. I knew the voice was correct. I was sure to my very bones that my prayer would be answered.

Two days later, Janet had her baby.

***

The room was decorated with pink balloons and crepe paper. Presents were piled high on the far side of the dining-room table. Up close, a white sheet cake sat in the spot of honor. Pink frosting spelled out, "Happy Birthday, Sarah!"

Janet laughed as she answered the door, and Sarah tried to toddle out. "Let me catch her!" she said as she grabbed the wiggling child's arm and pulled her back into the house. She took my gift and set it on the table as my son chased after her daughter and joined the chaos of giggling children.

"How are you?" asked Janet as we walked over to the easy chairs and other moms.

"I'm good," I said, lowering myself to the easy chair as the first tear fell. Yet, within seconds, that first timid cry began to grow and strengthen in volume. "Oh, honey," Janet soothed. "It's okay. It's really okay." But this time my friend was not addressing me. No, instead, her comforting words were directed to the tiny bundle in my arms.

Instantly, the other moms joined in with soft coos and words of solace. And as they soothed, I smiled. Then, having settled in, I discreetly lifted my shirt and kissed the top of her head as I lay my newborn baby, Mary, to my breast and nursed this sweet child of heaven's promise — born just in time for Baby Sarah's first birthday.

— Susan Traugh —

55

Full Circle

The tie which links mother and child is of such pure
and immaculate strength as to be never violated.
~Washington Irving

My mother had died when I was four years old. I can't explain why — maybe because I was too young to know better — but I never really missed her. I had an amazing support system of strong women to nurture and take care of me — until the time came to plan my wedding.

I had watched friends go through the process of planning a wedding, and it always included their mothers. Their mothers tore out pictures from magazines, helped create guest lists, chose china patterns, and sometimes — okay, a lot of times — put in more than their two cents' worth. While some of my friends wanted their mothers to go away, I wanted mine more than ever.

As I entered the wedding salon that day, I wasn't aware of how much I longed for my mother. I was ecstatic to be starting this journey. I had pictures of wedding dresses I liked, and I had plenty of dreams for the day. As I slipped on the first dress, the saleswoman, who was hearing-impaired, marveled at how lovely I looked.

Innocently, she said, "Your mother will love this one." I let it go. Then I tried on dress number two and got comment number two. "Wow, wait 'til your mom sees this one."

Now, I was getting uneasy. "Please stop. My mom passed away and won't be coming to see me," I pleaded. Unfortunately, the saleswoman had turned away so she couldn't read my lips. She continued talking about my mother through a dozen dresses until I couldn't take it anymore.

I blurted it out: "Please stop saying that."

There, I said it; I expressed my hurt.

I had never really expressed sadness to anyone about losing my mother, but now I did. I pulled my big sister aside; she was like a surrogate mother to me. I didn't have to say much. The fact that I was standing in this perfect bridal salon wearing a designer wedding dress and crying pretty much said it all.

My sister did her best to comfort me, telling me that Mommy was with me, looking down from heaven, and all of the other clichés one says to someone crying over a lost one. But I wanted and needed more than that. And when we arrived back at my sister's house, I got more than I could have hoped for.

For the longest time, my sister and I had quarreled about the location of my mother's wedding ring. My sister had worn it on her wedding day, and I had hoped for the same honor. But it was missing.

My sister swore she had passed the ring on to me, but I knew she had not. I knew that if I had something so valuable, I would have put it in a very secure place.

The loss of the ring was another blow to my already fragile state. I begged my sister to search for it, and she did, to no avail.

Until that day. After the bridal salon, I had returned to my sister's house to help watch her two little girls while she did some unpacking. A new piece of furniture had just been delivered in which my sister was going to display her collection of teacups and teapots.

Carefully, she unwrapped teapot after teapot until we heard a *clink*.

As she removed the lid from the teapot, she gasped and froze. Her tear-filled eyes said it all. Inside, nestled among other pieces of jewelry, was my mother's wedding ring. Beautifully worn, nicked in a few spots, missing a stone or two, but… absolutely perfect in every way that mattered.

My mother was with me. This day was symbolic in so many ways. I was all grown up, getting married, and yet experiencing the feelings of that little four-year-old girl who didn't understand those feelings back then. I missed my mom and longed for her to be with me. And now, I knew for sure that she was.

— Deirdre Twible-Kenny —

56

Not Until She Graduates

Prayer is not asking. Prayer is putting oneself in the
hands of God, at His disposition, and listening to His
voice in the depth of our hearts.
~Mother Teresa

As a physician, I'm trained to think logically. But every now and then, something will happen that defies all reason — a bona fide miracle. Take the case of Patricia Baxter.

Patricia, a middle-aged librarian, took delight in mothering her spirited daughter, Julie. At her yearly physical, Patricia was more interested in discussing Julie's winning soccer goal than her creaky knee and heartburn.

One year, however, Patricia mentioned weeks of unexplained exhaustion, nosebleeds, and sinus infections. My stomach tightened as potential causes — all bad — came to mind. After a thorough exam, I sent off blood tests, which confirmed my worst suspicion: acute leukemia. The leukemia cells — called blasts — had crowded out all her healthy bone-marrow cells. Hence the anemia, bleeding, and infections.

Patricia completed six cycles of chemotherapy. Baldness, nausea, exhaustion, and blood transfusions became her new normal. Despite how wretched she felt, Patricia insisted on leading Julie's Girl Scout and youth groups. "I don't know how much longer I'll have with Julie, so I don't want to miss a thing. With God's strength, I can do it, even with leukemia."

It was a blessing that Julie had not degenerated into a

"you've-ruined-my-life-and-I-hate-you, Mom" time bomb like so many fifteen-year-old girls. In fact, the cancer brought them closer. Patricia's greatest worry wasn't dying; it was leaving Julie to fend for herself during her formative years.

One day, after a rough cycle of chemo, Patricia gripped my hand and said, "Please pray this chemotherapy works." With tears in her eyes, she added, "I don't need to grow old—I just want to see Julie graduate from high school. Is that too much to ask?"

As a mother myself, I understood. What if it were my daughter? I squeezed her hand and promised, "I will pray for you every single day, and I'll get my staff and prayer group to pray, too."

Her face relaxed. "Thank you. All we can do is pray. The rest is in God's hands."

Pray, I did. Every day. Multiple times a day, along with my nurse and prayer group.

We all rejoiced when blood tests revealed the blasts had disappeared. For a few glorious months, Patricia remained in remission. Then the unthinkable happened: The leukemia returned.

"We'll resume chemotherapy. It worked before, so it will likely work again," the hematologist reassured us.

Except it didn't.

"We'll try a stronger drug," he insisted. But it also failed. Patricia then joined an experimental drug trial, but had to drop out when she developed a blistering rash all over her body. A bone-marrow transplant was out because no one in the family was a match.

Patricia was out of luck.

As leukemia advanced through her bone marrow, she required platelet transfusions on a near-daily basis. While not a cure, the transfusions kept her from bleeding to death. Unfortunately, with time, her immune system developed antibodies that chewed up and destroyed the platelets within hours of being transfused. This put Patricia at risk for severe internal bleeding.

Despite her bleak prognosis, Patricia's faith remained unwavering. Her one persistent prayer? "Please, God, let me see Julie graduate from high school."

But God appeared to be in no hurry to answer our prayers. Life threatening infections landed Patricia in the hospital frequently. Then disaster struck. Patricia suddenly hemorrhaged into her lungs and brain, and within hours, she was comatose and ventilator-dependent. Things spiraled down and became so hopeless that the hematologist informed us, "She won't survive the night. I've written a DNR order, as there's no point in prolonging the inevitable."

I pored over Patricia's chart looking for something—anything—I could do to improve her condition. No luck. I offered up one last heartfelt prayer: "Please, God, grant Patricia a miracle. Let her see Julie graduate."

I exited the room, suspecting I'd never see Patricia again this side of heaven. My eyes pooled, as I'd grown close to Patricia and her family.

Miraculously, Patricia survived the night, and over the next few days, her platelet count slowly began to increase. Even the blasts disappeared!

What was going on?

Within days, her breathing improved enough to come off the ventilator, but she remained in a coma. Would she ever wake up? If so, would she end up brain-damaged?

Several days later, Patricia woke up, and she was singing praise music! She could move all four extremities, walk, talk, and swallow water. How had she sustained such a massive brain hemorrhage and come out unscathed? And why had the blasts disappeared?

It made no sense until Patricia shared her near-death experience with me. "While I was in a coma, Jesus appeared to me in a translucent robe and said He would heal me long enough to see my daughter graduate from high school. He said I would live three more years, so I should make them count. 'Give your daughter life lessons and memories to last a lifetime,' Jesus told me. Then He disappeared, but I felt such a peace and joy. I knew He'd answered my prayer."

God had granted her a miracle, and I had witnessed it.

As promised, for three years, Patricia remained in remission. She cheered at Julie's soccer games, helped her select a prom dress, and adjusted her graduation cap and gown. Patricia recorded a collection of tapes with life lessons for Julie's graduation gift. "Something to remember me by when I'm gone."

Patricia wept as she dropped Julie off at college, marveling she had lived to see this milestone.

Unfortunately, after Julie's first year of college, Patricia's leukemia returned with a vengeance. Despite aggressive chemotherapy and a bone-marrow transplant donated by a stranger whose marrow matched hers, Patricia died from an overwhelming infection.

Everyone was devastated. Why would God heal her for only four years? Why not permanently? I'm convinced we will never understand this side of heaven.

I worried how Julie would handle her mother's death. Would she lose her faith and become jaded? I prayed not.

Since Julie attended an out-of-state college, I lost contact with her until a few years later. She now worked as an oncology nurse at a local hospital and still marveled at how God had granted her mother an additional four years. Julie showed me a photo of the family riding mules to the bottom of the Grand Canyon the summer after Julie graduated from high school. They had made precious memories.

"We both knew she was here on borrowed time. Those extra years with Mom meant everything to me — they were a gift from God. Besides, I haven't really lost her, right?"

I must have looked puzzled, so Julie went on to explain. "Mom's in heaven, and someday I'll join her. It's just a matter of time until I'm with her again."

I hugged Julie goodbye and then offered up a prayer of thanks that Julie had weathered her mother's death with a maturity and optimism far beyond her years.

— Sally Willard Burbank —

57

A Promise Fulfilled

The bond between friends cannot be broken by chance;
no interval of time or space can destroy it. Not even
death itself can part true friends.
~St. John Cassian

It's amazing how clearly I can remember the moment Nancy and I first met and became best friends more than sixty-five years ago. There we were, two young girls on opposite sides of the street, walking home after the first day of school in the warm September sunshine. She was the new girl in the neighborhood, but I was too shy to introduce myself. When I snuck a quick peek, she caught me and waved. I smiled back with a timid, "Hi."

Our houses were less than two blocks apart in the mostly Italian-Catholic neighborhood of Southeast Portland, Oregon. We were both nine years old and in the fourth grade.

For the remainder of grade school and throughout high school, we were as close as any two best friends could be, sharing our most intimate secrets with each other and spending as much time together as possible. It seemed as though we could read each other's thoughts, probably because we thought so much alike. We loved telling people we were twins. We weren't lying, just fantasizing about what we wished were true.

As we grew into adulthood, our unique bond grew with us. We double-dated, stood up for each other at our weddings, and were together for the births of our children. We promised each other that we would never grow apart, and nobody would ever come between us.

Regrettably, as our kids grew older and became active in sports and other activities, we stopped spending as much time with each other. But I always felt her closeness. Even when we didn't talk for years at a time, we were together in spirit.

When the phone rang on a hot August afternoon in 2001, it wasn't Nancy, and it wasn't good news. "Oh, Connie," her mom stammered between agonizing sobs, "I have sad news! Nancy has terminal pancreatic cancer. I knew you'd want to know."

Of course, I wanted to know — I *needed* to know. My thoughts raced back through the years. I was going to lose my best friend — the girl who had been my other half for the majority of my life.

When I called Nancy, she could tell by the tone of my voice that I knew. "Mom called you, didn't she?"

"Yes. When can I see you?" I pleaded impatiently.

Nancy responded with her usual calm, understanding nature. "Anytime. I'm always here."

"I'll be there tomorrow morning! Do you need anything — anything at all?"

"Just you," she responded.

She knew it was important for me to be with her; we had been there for each other through the happiest and saddest of times.

I showed up at her door the following morning with a huge bouquet of freshly picked sweet peas from my flower garden. The beautiful blooms and familiar fragrance were reminiscent of our carefree childhood summers in the fifties.

Throughout the following couple of weeks, we spent countless hours together. Nothing had changed between us in all the years. We were still those two school-aged best friends. We laughed and cried. We hugged and talked candidly about her impending death.

Her final promise was that she would do everything possible to reach out and let me know that she was still there for me. We believed in our hearts that not even death could separate us.

Nancy passed away surrounded by her loved ones exactly fifty years from the day we met. Of course, I was there holding her sweet, frail hand until the very end.

Her funeral was held at the Catholic church in the old neighborhood. Although I was not Catholic, I'd visited the church on numerous occasions, including Nancy's wedding and my grandmother's funeral. But this was the saddest visit by far.

Several days before her death, I'd written a touching poem for my best friend. After I read it to her, we cried and comforted each other with a long, loving hug.

Nancy's family asked me to read the poem at her funeral. And though I'd spoken quite eloquently at funerals before, my voice trembled as I recited the sweet memories of our youth.

Although the church was full, I felt profoundly alone as I made my way back to join my mother and daughter on the wooden pew. "Nancy," I whispered through my tears, "I really need a hug from you!"

And, just as she'd promised, Nancy confirmed that she was there for me in the most miraculous way.

Immediately following the concluding rites, the kind, elderly priest made his way from the casket in the center aisle to where I was sitting on the far side a few rows back. He leaned over, wrapped his reassuring arms around me gently, and whispered, "Here's a hug from Nancy."

— Connie Kaseweter Pullen —

58

And Peepers, Too

Impossible situations can become possible miracles.
~Robert H. Schuller

L iving in an attic apartment had felt like an adventure following my divorce. My daughter moved with me, from the quiet,
little house in the woods where I had spent the previous twenty
years. There was no elevator in my apartment building, and the
last flight had thirteen steps, but I was healthy and soon noticed the
climbs were helping me lose a few pounds. The tenants renting the
first and second floors were friendly, good neighbors. And the drive
to the school where I worked was now less than a mile.

Four years later, my daughter was commuting back and forth from
college on weekends, those nice tenants were gone, and I was battling
cancer for the second time. Now those steps to my attic apartment
seemed like a mountain.

It was time to buy a house of my own. I started praying that I
would find the right place. My wish list was short. First, I wanted three
bedrooms on one floor so my daughter would have her own room
when she came home, and my aging mother would have a place to
stay when the time came. I also hoped for one full bath plus a second
half-bath to make it convenient for visitors. Finally, as an afterthought,
I prayed it would be close enough to water to hear the "peepers" in
the spring. The last request embarrassed me. I had only asked for this
because the mating calls of the frogs in our pond were something I
missed from my home in the woods. I told God the peepers were not

really necessary.

Soon, my daughter and I were checking out every house in the area as she urged me to "think small" to make upkeep easier. We cruised back streets, screeching to a halt when we saw For Sale signs. We hadn't found the right house, and then my aged car broke down. It would have cost so much to fix that I had to buy a new car. That would put the house search on hold for a year or two.

A few months later, a co-worker stopped at my desk and asked if I was still looking for a house. "Not 'til I get the car paid off," I answered. "Why, do you know of a nice one?"

Her mother had died a year or so earlier, and I suddenly regretted asking.

"My brother would like to settle Mom's estate," she said. "It's hard for me to let go. She lived down the road from me on the corner, and we spent a lot of time there. I still stop in after work just to check things out."

Something nudged me, but I felt it was just the old desire to check out another house. At lunch, I mentioned it to a friend, and before I knew it, we were in the car heading to see the house. All we knew was that it was "on a corner" and "down the road" from our co-worker. Since there was more than one house on a corner to view, we were soon laughing at our foolishness. But then I saw it and I knew it was the one, because it was the house I had pictured in my daydreams: a cream-colored, ranch-style home with wide windows framed with brown shutters and a yard that would be easy for me to mow.

A few days later, my co-worker opened the front door and ushered me inside. There was a kitchen, living room, three bedrooms and a bath, all on one floor. She opened the door to the cellar and went down ahead of me. At the bottom, she stepped aside, and I was looking into a tiny bathroom complete with a shower.

It was the house I had prayed for, but I knew it was above my price range. I had no desire to go into debt while I was fighting my cancer.

"I love it," I admitted. "But I know I can't afford it."

"Make an offer," she countered.

When I told her what I could afford, she said she would call her brother and let me know.

The next day, my offer was accepted.

With the help of my daughter and numerous friends, we moved in that fall.

That house was on the top of a hill, and below it were the Rails to Trails bike and walking trails. When spring came, as I carried out the trash late one evening, I heard an unexpected sound at the bottom of the hill, near the trails. It was the peepers.

I had forgotten my request. God had not.

— Fay A. Yoder —

59

More Than Coincidence

A sister is a gift to the heart, a friend to the spirit,
a golden thread to the meaning of life.
~Isadora James

My little sister Mary was an exceptionally beautiful girl with thick golden hair, sparkling blue eyes and a spitfire personality. She was nearly five years younger than me, so during our childhood she would tag along while my other three siblings and I were outside exploring and playing in our neighborhood along the shoreline in Queens, New York.

As we matured and settled into our respective careers, family life and motherhood, we became especially close and often travelled together. Mary became a registered nurse whose specialty was wound care for patients who were recovering from surgery or other serious ailments at home.

Then, at age fifty-nine, Mary was diagnosed with lung cancer. As the big sister, I felt a special responsibility to be very present for my little sister. Throughout the year, with strong support from other family members, I accompanied Mary to her cancer treatments and many medical appointments.

Before her diagnosis, we had booked a Caribbean cruise to celebrate Mary's sixtieth birthday, which we had to cancel due to her scheduled treatments. Instead, we managed to take a fall cruise to Canada. We had a great time visiting the New England ports of Boston and Portland on the way to Saint John and Halifax. Despite having difficulty walking,

Mary enjoyed the cruise immensely as a welcome respite from her medical treatments.

After arriving back to New York City's harbor, we looked forward to the winter holidays. Our family had always celebrated Christmas in a big way. It was a magical time when we were children, complete with a large real Christmas tree, surrounded by a model train set and piles of presents. The festivities were topped off with a special feast on Christmas Day. Mary continued these holiday traditions with her two sons, and it was her favorite time of year.

The Christmas before she passed, we shopped together and picked out our Christmas cards. We lamented that this tradition was waning, with many folks preferring to send greetings via social media or abandoning Christmas greetings altogether. Mary was old school when it came to sending greeting cards and never forgot a birthday or occasion for our large extended family.

Mary survived until May 2016, bravely fighting her illness with grace and dignity. That first Christmas without her was especially hard. As each Christmas card arrived, I was reminded there would be none from Mary, who had never missed sending a holiday greeting. Then one evening, while I was putting out the trash, I noticed a heart-shaped card embedded in an evergreen bush. It was bright red and decorated with glitter and drawings of treats. But, most startlingly, it was addressed simply to My Big Sister.

Some skeptic might say the card could have blown there from a neighbor's yard, but I know it was more than coincidence. It was a message from my little sister Mary letting me know she was okay and would always be with me.

Tenderly, I packed the card away with the other greeting cards that Christmas, and every holiday season since I've looked at it as a reminder of this special message from heaven.

— Patricia Beach —

60

The Prayers of a Child

*The prayer that begins with trustfulness and passes on
into waiting will always end in thankfulness,
triumph, and praise.*
~Alexander Maclaren

After a year of trying and some medical intervention, I conceived my son in June 2008. The doctors had told me I had a one-in-a-million chance of getting pregnant, so of course I prayed like crazy that nothing would go wrong with my pregnancy. I did everything I was supposed to do, and I was not worried at all once I passed the first trimester. I also knew without any doubt that I was carrying a boy. I started referring to the baby as "him" from the very early months. My friends all told me I was crazy, but I knew.

Our son Carter was born in February 2009. He was perfectly healthy, and we had no complications with the delivery. The doctors told us to enjoy him because we'd never be able to have another one. I thanked God constantly those first few weeks of my son's life; I felt so incredibly awed by our miracle boy, especially since I turned thirty-eight a month after his birth.

When Carter was two years old, we took him to see *The Nutcracker* ballet. He was enthralled. About halfway through the show, he looked up at me and said, "Mommy, I want to have a baby sister so I can name her Clara." I smiled and gave him a hug. I told him it was a very sweet wish, but I doubted very much that we'd be having another child. I explained to him that, at the age of forty, it was very unlikely that God had another child planned for us.

Carter started praying. For almost two years, he prayed daily, earnestly asking God to send him a baby sister. My husband and I would smile at each other, feeling a pang in our hearts that Carter's fervent prayers would very likely never come true. After all, we were not even trying for a second child; we had discussed it and decided it wasn't a good idea. We felt our little family of three was complete, and we'd be selfish to try for a second child, possibly putting that unborn child at risk due to my age. We felt blessed already to have our healthy son.

When I was about to turn forty-two, we got a huge surprise. I was pregnant. My husband was in shock, but then we both jumped into each other's arms and danced around the house, thanking God for the chance to become a family of four! I knew it would be a girl this time; I was as certain of her gender from the start as I had been of Carter's. Immediately, Carter began praying in earnest again. This time, his prayers usually went, "God, please let me have a healthy baby sister." I prayed right along with him every time.

My second pregnancy was just as uneventful as my first except for the very last month or two when my blood pressure went up, and I had to go on maternity leave a month earlier than planned so I could rest. But in September 2013, I gave birth to a perfectly healthy daughter. My son, who had prayed her into existence, was there with his daddy to cut her cord after she was born.

My son was in awe of his baby sister from the start, and, of course, he got to name her. Clara is just as enamored of her "Bubba," as she calls him. They are now nine and four, and best friends in a way that I could never have imagined given their age difference. I am so incredibly thankful that my son's prayers were answered, and that we now have our truly complete family of four.

— Stephanie Schiano Wallace —

61

Merlin's Miracle

Dogs are miracles with paws.
~Susan Kennedy

etey guards our storm door. His silky ears pop up, and his bright eyes shine as I approach the house. His tail wags furiously when I bend down to accept his kisses.

He has lived with us for only two weeks, yet he already rules the house. The couches and the bed we swore were off limits are already among Petey's favorite spots.

Chewed twigs and paper-towel rolls litter the family room, but we're not in any hurry to clean them up. And I've learned to fall asleep faster after taking him out for his middle-of-the-night potty breaks.

My husband and teenage daughters had wanted a puppy, but I hadn't. I found house-training our first dog a real headache, and I didn't want to deal with a pup's incessant chewing. I wanted an older dog so those problems would be behind us.

I'd grown accustomed to living with our thirteen-year-old Wirehaired Dachshund, Merlin. He slept a lot and rarely got into things he shouldn't.

But poor Merlin was diagnosed with a baseball-sized tumor on his spleen and was gone six months later. I couldn't imagine life without his sweet spirit in our home. I wrote journal entries to him every couple of days as immense grief colored my daily life.

We visited animal shelters several times that fall, but we never found a dog that interested us. The holidays and cold weather temporarily halted our efforts.

I still thought of Merlin daily, but my journal entries became more sporadic, and my memories held less pain. I began to ask Merlin's spirit to help us find just the right dog. I didn't understand why we were having such a hard time finding a new dog. After all, our hearts were open and we loved dogs.

As the days grew longer and spring flowers bloomed, we renewed our hunt. A Basset Hound stared mournfully at us, but my husband, Mark, said she would drool too much. I could barely control a male mutt as I walked him around the shelter yard. I played briefly with a female Chow at another shelter, but she wasn't our answer either.

Mark and I decided to visit two more locations the following weekend. We never reached the second one. The Humane Society had assembled a dozen dogs of different sizes, shapes and colors at a local pet adoption event. They yapped, barked, whined and climbed all over each other as they frantically jockeyed for human contact.

Mark spotted the pup first. White and gray, gangly and seemingly overwhelmed by his more aggressive sister, he rested happily in Mark's arms. When the pup snuggled into the crook of my elbow, all my arguments for an older dog melted away instantly.

We had never seen such a mellow puppy. We couldn't tell his breed, but we knew we wanted him.

A volunteer asked questions about our yard, our house and other family members. We signed the appropriate papers and headed home. We would pick up the pup several days later, after he was neutered.

Our daughters came with us. They took turns carrying Petey as we chose a collar and a new water bowl, and then they giggled while entertaining him in the back seat.

When we got home, we all played with and held Petey. He bounced after toys, dove into our laps, kissed our faces enthusiastically and sniffed everywhere. Smiles and laughter filled the room. I had forgotten how much fun a puppy could be. Maybe we had been ready for a puppy after all!

As I placed Petey's paperwork on the table, I spotted the official name of his coloring — Blue Merle. Hairs stood up on my neck, and I silently thanked Merlin's spirit, which I was now convinced had indeed helped us find our wonderful new dog.

— Lisa Waterman Gray —

A Christmas Miracle

The believers in miracles accept them (rightly or
wrongly) because they have evidence for them.
~G.K. Chesterton

The Christmas holidays were approaching, but I wasn't in the mood for merry-making. My soul mate had just passed away, and this was the first holiday season in my adult life that I would be spending without him. And now my wedding band that we'd crafted together was missing.

When we had become engaged right after World War II, nobody we knew had any money, including us. Still, my thoughtful fiancé managed to scrape some funds together to buy me an engagement ring. It was just a thin, simple gold band that would be classified more as a friendship ring today. Nevertheless, I was thrilled with that ring and literally wore it out; it actually fell to pieces one day. I even saved those bits, hoping to repair the ring in the future.

When we got married, we splurged on thicker gold bands for the wedding. I forgot about the pieces of my engagement ring until I was cleaning out a utility drawer years later and found them lying in the bottom.

After taking the remnants to a jeweler, we were told that he could melt down the pieces with some additional gold to form a new ring. He even had a vibrant red stone he could add to make it more beautiful and romantic. We were enchanted with the idea and commissioned the work.

When it was finally ready, I was just as thrilled to wear it as I'd been with my original ring. We'd scrimped and saved all of our lives to pay for our house, our children's education and to finance our business, so we never treated ourselves to an extravagance like jewelry. This ring made me feel like a teenager again, while my husband was thrilled to see the joy that it brought me.

So, losing that special ring right after losing my husband felt like a double whammy. I wracked my brain, retracing every step, with no luck. I considered myself fortunate, however, since I hadn't left the house that day, so it had to be close by. Yet I had puttered around everywhere, including doing lots of digging in the garden. I'd read accounts about people using a metal detector to find jewelry. I wondered where I could find one.

I forced myself to drag out the Christmas decorations anyway. My husband had always loved the holiday season and all of its trappings, so he would have wanted me to carry on with the festivities. I kept looking for the ring as I pulled out the decorations. And then, I laid down a grid pattern and methodically searched every inch of the house. I even probed in silly places where it was unlikely to have fallen or rolled.

I began to look suspiciously at my cats. They loved to play with shiny objects, and goodness knows they'd swallowed enough of them. They also could easily have found the ring and knocked it into some obscure place, like under the fridge. I even checked their litter box.

My daughter-in-law has always been helpful, and this time was no exception. Donna helped me clean and decorate the house and she continued the search for the ring. She's quite a sleuth, so if anyone could find the ring, she would. Along with the physical help, it was great moral support.

Christmas Day arrived, and Donna's gifts to me included a lovely new ring, similar to the one I had lost. It was a kind gesture, but it wasn't the same as having my old, sentimental band back. While I now had something solid filling that empty spot on my finger, it only served to remind me of the loss.

Later that day, I quietly sipped some cocoa alone in my rocking chair, thinking of my dear husband. Every time I rocked, there was a slight twinkle underneath the tree. The Christmas lights were being reflected by something in the baseboard that had been obscured earlier by the presents we opened that morning.

Setting aside my cocoa, I crawled under the tree for a closer look. Lo and behold, there was my ring, wedged into a crack between the floorboards and the baseboard. I could hardly believe it. It was like a final surprise Christmas present from my husband, left under the tree for me to find.

There, sitting on the floor by the twinkling tree while holding my precious ring, the full impact of my heightened emotions hit me. I began bawling like a baby. My wailing sobs brought the rest of the family running, and they managed to calm me down enough to see the joy in the occasion.

That was the most emotional and memorable Christmas of my life. Because it was so bittersweet, it will be etched in my memory forever. I had a little bit of my husband back that Christmas Day, and it felt like he gave me that ring all over again.

— Denise Del Bianco —

Finding Peace

Walk Me Home

There's no other love like the love for a brother.
There's no other love like the love from a brother.
~Author Unknown

I sat at my kitchen table for two hours, working on something that should have taken me a quarter of that time. Writing usually comes easily to me, but writing my brother's eulogy was complicated.

Casey had died in a car accident. He was with his roommate, Kyle, a friend of ours, who also died. They were both twenty-eight. I happened to be working that particular evening.

I'm a firefighter, and we respond with the ambulance to medical calls. I wasn't on the first unit to respond, but we were asked to assist. As I pulled up to the scene, the ambulance carrying my brother to the hospital sped past us.

As I got the details of the accident, I suspected my brother was in that ambulance, and I went to the hospital to confirm. From there, I had to place the call to my parents.

My parents, my brothers Matt and Tom, and a few other family members made it to the hospital before Casey died. He was still technically alive when they arrived, being worked on in the ER, but with little hope of survival.

When it was over, we gathered in the room to pray and say goodbye. I went home to wake my fiancée and our two-year-old daughter. I didn't want to wake her to this news over the phone; I wanted to do it in person.

We went up to my parents' house and gathered in the way the immediately grief-stricken do — sitting around in their living room, talking, laughing, crying, stunned. Eventually, we went home in the early morning.

As we left, I remember the sound of my mom crying from the back of the house. It was barely human, like a wounded animal, the saddest sound I'd ever heard in my life.

The rest of the week was a blur, leading up to Kyle's memorial service on Thursday, with Casey's funeral Mass to follow Friday morning.

I had made up my mind not to bother with a eulogy. I thought it would fall to me by default, being the oldest. Our youngest brother, Matt, asked us if he could do it, though, and I had no objections, happy to be free of the burden.

At Kyle's memorial, I cried openly. Kyle was the youngest of four, with three sisters. Each of his sisters spoke at his service, and that more than anything changed my mind. I would have to get up and speak, along with Matt and Tom, for Casey's service the next day.

So I sat at my kitchen table and tried to transfer what was in my head to the page. It was going slowly, though. I knew exactly what I wanted to say, but it was so hard to physically write it down. It was just another thing that made it all real, and not some bad dream. But that awareness didn't make it any easier to push through.

Eventually, I did finish, somewhere around 1:00 a.m. I had to be up early to get ready in the morning, and I had some minor errands to take care of. Getting to sleep quickly was a major priority. I knew that if I went to bed right then, though, I'd lie awake for hours. The only night I'd been able to fall asleep at a decent time had been the first night after Casey's death, and that was the day I spent getting drunk and feeling sorry for myself. I didn't think that was a great option at this point.

So I went for a walk around my neighborhood. I strolled down the middle of the street, aimlessly, trying to wear out my mind and body so I could lie down at peace for just a few hours.

I was roughly three-quarters of the way through my walk, headed back toward my house, when I came to a particularly well-lit spot. I saw my shadow, looming, elongated in the distance. Then, two distinct shadows appeared on either side of my own shadow. I don't want to make this into more than what it was, but it was beautiful, pure, and filled me with emotion.

My shadow, in the middle, was definitely and clearly my own. The other two, though, were not. They didn't look anything like mine, and they didn't react like mine. Together, it looked like a group of three people was walking and laughing. This lasted the final two blocks I had to walk home.

I didn't want to let go of that moment. I just wanted to keep walking and stay in that bubble. I knew that this was all I was going to get though, and it was going to have to be enough. Feeling overjoyed and completely content, I went inside and fell asleep within minutes. And for the first time all week, I slept peacefully.

I got up the next day and made it through the funeral. I gave my eulogy, and I think it was pretty damn good. I thought about telling that story, but I didn't. I held onto it, wanting to keep it for myself at that time. I shared it with my cousin Sean that night at the reception. And later on, I told my wife, because that's the kind of thing husbands share with their wives.

My brother and my friend are both dead, and I'll never see them in this lifetime again. But I know that we'll see each other eventually, and we'll finish that walk.

— Dan Boyle —

64

The Silver Van

Dreams are today's answers to tomorrow's questions.
~Edgar Cayce

My husband opened his eyes and looked over at me lying next to him in bed. "Not you again."

"Not me again?" I smiled teasingly, not wanting him to feel bad about the words he'd just uttered. "You mean you're not happy to see me?"

"Yes, I am, but I thought I was going to heaven."

Larry had been sick for a year with metastatic prostate cancer that had spread throughout his entire body. He was in excruciating pain and had been praying for God to take him home. As much as I dreaded the thought of losing my beloved husband, I'd finally reconciled myself to the idea that it was time to let him go.

When I asked him what he meant about going to heaven, he continued in his weak voice: "I was in the back of a brand-new, shiny silver van. There were windows, but it must have been nighttime because I couldn't see out. There was a little girl in there with dark, curly hair who was giggling and jumping around. I was so happy until a voice said that I had to go back because it wasn't my time. I guess I must have been dreaming—but it seemed so real."

"Was it God who told you it wasn't your time?" I asked. My curiosity was piqued; this seemed like more than a dream.

"No, it was a man's voice. But I know it wasn't God!"

After a few moments, I got up, made myself a pot of coffee, and went to the bathroom to wash my face and brush my teeth. When I returned to check on Larry, he was sleeping. I knew his time was nearing, and I spent most of that day sitting next to the bed, holding his hand and staring at him. I wanted to preserve his image in my mind.

That was the last real conversation we had, because Larry was in and out of consciousness for the next two days. On the third day, when all five of our children were home and gathered at his bedside, he passed away. Our dear hospice nurse showed up just in time to share in Larry's passing. After giving us a little more time with him, she placed a call to our local mortuary.

What we witnessed thirty minutes later was astounding!

A brand-new, shiny silver van pulled up to the house — the exact one Larry had described from his dream. It had dark tinted windows, which explained why he hadn't been able to see out of them.

The following day, I shared our story with the owner of the mortuary, and she told me that they had recently purchased the new silver van to replace the black one they'd used previously. She also said that the little girl with dark, curly hair whom Larry described from his dream sounded exactly like her young daughter who often rides in the van. I was stunned!

Larry's so-called dream of his journey to heaven had come true! Witnessing in real life exactly what he'd described in detail a couple of days prior gave me the needed assurance and peace that my husband was finally where he wanted to be.

— Connie Kaseweter Pullen —

65

The Gift at the Grave

No matter where I am your spirit will be beside me.
For I know that no matter what,
you will always be with me.
~Tram-Tiara T. Von Reichenbach

The first challenge of this emotional day was to find the gravestone with my father's name. The field was massive and peppered with nearly identical markers — rectangular, dark gray stones that lay flat on the ground.

I was twelve years old, and this was the first time I had visited his grave since his funeral the year before.

I didn't see my father as much as I would have liked since my parents divorced shortly after I was born. Despite that, my father knew about my deep interest in frogs. I can't remember a time that I didn't love frogs. My father always gave me little gifts that were frog related: a seashell with a frog painted on it; a frog figurine; a necklace with a frog charm.

After trekking through the maze of gravestones on a sunny day, there it was — the stone marking my father's final resting place. I gasped — not because I was seeing my father's name etched on a gravestone for the first time, but because a tiny green frog was sitting on the stone, right by my father's name.

I was astonished and happy and sad at the same time, and I started to cry. I crouched down to get a closer look at the frog, half expecting him to hop away, but he didn't flinch. The frog was calm and unbothered by my presence, as if he were expecting my arrival.

I scooped up the little creature and held him in the palm of my hand. We looked at each other as if we were having a silent conversation that only he and I could understand. When I finished crying, I set him down gently. It felt like the right time to say goodbye.

The frog hopped away, disappearing into the blades of grass, knowing his job was done. My father had given me his final gift... and I was at peace.

I whispered, "Thanks, Dad."

—Amanda Mattox—

66

The Familiar Fisherman

Having a fishing rod in your hand is merely an excuse
to explore out-of-sight depths and reveal mysteries
that previously only existed in dreams.
~Fennel Hudson

"**W**hy don't you join us? We're camping at Rock Creek for two weeks, and your dad would love to see you guys." The offer from Mom was just what I needed. I hadn't camped in years, and I missed it.

"Tell him that sounds great. Laura and I will meet you there. And I'll ask for a few extra days off from work." I wrote down the campground location and other details. Excited, I started laying out what my wife and I would need for the upcoming weekend: tent, sleeping bags, fishing gear, and our camp box, which always remained at the ready, stocked with camping equipment. Thank goodness for understanding supervisors; mine gave me the entire week off.

On our way down Highway 395 from Reno to Rock Creek, we passed all my favorite locations on the backside of the Sierra Nevada mountains: Lundy Lake, June Lake, Big Springs, Deadman's Creek, Mammoth Lakes, Hot Creek, Owens River at Benton's Crossing, Convict Lake, and Crowley Lake. I had fished them all with Dad.

My father enjoyed several hobbies — rockhounding, panning for gold, and digging for lost treasure — but none were like fishing. For him, it was the main reason for being outdoors. No matter where we camped or hiked, there were always trout to be caught — rainbows, brookies, browns, and golden — and we hooked our limits of each.

Dad could catch fish when nobody else did. But, like most anglers, he kept his best techniques to himself. One time, however, while fishing at Hot Creek, a "fly-fishing only" river, I think he revealed one of them. That day, Dad landed one brown after another; I didn't get a single bite. So I asked him to show me the fly he used. After he reeled in, he held it up for me to inspect. It looked the same as mine, but his fly had a worm hooked on the end. "Well, what d'ya know," Dad said. "My hook must have dragged the bottom or something." He just grinned and tucked the fish into his knapsack.

During the Rock Creek camping trip, we fished every day, sometimes at several different locations. Dad had recently finished a round of cancer treatments, and he wanted to hit as many spots as possible. After fishing three lakes on the June Lake Loop, all in the same day, I finally spoke up and told him I was tired of fishing all the time and wanted to do something else. I have regretted that comment ever since. He packed up his gear, and we headed back to camp. We never fished together again. Dad didn't say much, but I know I hurt him.

His cancer didn't stay in remission very long. He died soon after that trip. I was devastated. He had only wanted to share his last few months with his son, doing what he thought I wanted to do. Would it have hurt me so much to have fished a few more times with him? I wanted to take back my selfish suggestion, but for whatever reason, I never did. He went to his grave without hearing my apology.

I continued fishing, but my heart really wasn't in it anymore. I became more of a spectator, watching and teaching my children how to fish. I spent most of my time untangling their lines, fixing broken tackle, and baiting their hooks. The fun had gone out of fishing.

Then one day, I thought I saw Dad or someone who looked like him at Trillium Lake in the Mount Hood recreation area. The man fished on the dam where the dirt road crossed between the lake and stream outlet. He used the sidearm method of casting, not overhead like the other anglers. He bottom-fished, too, while everyone else used a bobber. The man wore a straw cowboy hat, tipped down to keep the sun out of his eyes, so I couldn't see his face. But he sure resembled my dad, even from that distance. He wore a khaki shirt with his sleeves half-rolled up and some khaki pants. A tan knapsack sat close by, not a tackle box like the others. No chair or stool either; he stood holding his pole. As soon as he cast out, he hooked one fish after another, while everyone else barely got a nibble. All these traits — his clothing, his hat, even his fishing style — belonged to my dad.

The next time we fished Trillium, I noticed the same person, dressed the same way, fishing in the same exact spot. Maybe the glare off the lake distorted my view, but it sure looked like he nodded in my direction a couple times. I decided to walk over and meet him, but by the time I rounded the corner and started down the road, he had disappeared. I hurried over to the nearby parking lot, thinking he went to his car. I scanned all the vehicles — nothing. I even checked the men's outhouse. I didn't see him anywhere. Where could he have gone so quickly? The area only had one exit. Then a thought crossed my mind. *Dad, was that you?*

I've seen this person a few other times, once at Lost Lake and once on the opposite bank of the Sandy River near Welches. He is always in the distance, wearing a straw cowboy hat. He is tall, husky, and walks slowly with a long stride. In each sighting, he wears those khaki pants and shirt, holds a fishing rod, and carries a knapsack by his side.

One time might be a coincidence, maybe even two, but not several sightings. I really believe it was my father. I'm not sure how all this eternity stuff works, but somehow Dad was allowed to return to the physical world for a few brief encounters. I think these appearances had a divine purpose: to let me know that Dad no longer held my insensitive remark against me. In fact, maybe he never did. Either way, I felt encouraged and hopeful that death is not the end, but the beginning of something better. One day, I will find out for sure, but none too soon, I pray.

I've heard heaven has a river that runs pure and clear. It might even have fish. If so, I plan to cast my line in and try for a limit. No doubt, Dad will already have his.

— Charles Earl Harrel —

67

Flying with Butterfly Wings

Beautiful and graceful, varied and enchanting,
small but approachable, butterflies lead you to the
sunny side of life. And everyone deserves
a little sunshine.
~Jeffrey Glassberg

I was holding my mother's hand the night she took her last breath. In the days that followed, I found myself feeling deeply hurt and confused. I had devoted myself to caring for her, and now that was over. I couldn't help her anymore, and I felt a terrible longing to know if she was okay. I desperately wanted to know that her pain from the cancer was over and that she was no longer afraid.

On a crisp mid-winter day, I opened the front door to the magnificent sight of a giant swallowtail butterfly resting on the inner frame of the door. I stopped and stared, only inches from its beautiful, blue-spattered wings.

Suddenly, a memory of my mother came to me with such force that I felt as though I was physically shaken. We had been out to lunch and were getting back in the car when a butterfly landed unexpectedly on my mother's head. I attempted to communicate to her the presence of her little guest. However, I was laughing so hard I couldn't find the words. She finally spotted the butterfly in the reflection of the glass and shooed him off. We laughed together until tears of joy rolled down our cheeks. I smiled at the memory and went on with my day, giving no further thought to the butterfly.

But that night, I had a dream.

In the dream, my mother was standing in a field, and I was watching her. Then, she suddenly disappeared. I turned around in circles, frantically trying to find her. Then I noticed it: a single butterfly bouncing with each flap of its wings.

I woke up longing to see my mother again. I got dressed in a hurry and walked outside to take my two young sons to school. I reached out to unlock the driver's door, and found a giant, blue-speckled butterfly was perched on the handle. I gasped as peace washed over me. Now I understood the butterflies and the dream. It was my mother. She was letting me know she had made it home and was no longer in pain. She is now, like the butterfly, spreading her wings and flying free in the most beautiful fields in heaven.

Her wings were ready; my heart was not.

—Jenn P.—

68

Untied

You will find that it is necessary to let things go; simply
for the reason that they are heavy. So let them go, let
go of them. I tie no weights to my ankles.
~C. JoyBell C.

It began with a dream and ended with a vision. For months, my husband and I had been looking at potential building sites for our dream home. I'd envisioned a two-story house on a hill overlooking a gurgling stream and trees — maybe even mature fruit trees. My husband wanted a place with a pasture for raising horses and, perhaps, a few cows.

Then one day, while driving to work, we saw a new sign: LAND FOR SALE. A few days later, we met the owner, and he took us on a walking tour around the thirty-four acres. There was a small creek running through the woods. A gentle breeze carrying the aroma of ripe peaches wafted through the air as we walked around the property. It was love at first sight.

There was even a peeling, weathered red barn hidden behind the trees. The barn was a bonus we hadn't expected. The property was everything we'd hoped for — and more.

We hadn't planned on building immediately, but that didn't stop us from enjoying our new purchase. It became our weekend retreat. My husband bought a 1948 red Ford tractor with a bush hog and spent hours tinkering with his new toy. While he mowed the grass and puttered in the barn, I took long walks, sketched out each room of our future home, and gathered pecans and peaches. Those were wonderful times, and as I reflect on them, I think of that period in my life as almost perfect. I felt complete. It was the two of us, and our newest addition to the family: the land. We'd become caregivers, new parents coddling a wonderful, new love. We replaced acres of wire fences and built a wooden walking bridge across the stream. Now our sweat and blood were mixed in with the dirt.

But before we had a chance to build, tragedy struck. My husband was diagnosed with a rare, incurable brain disease. In a five-year-period, he went from running marathons to being strapped in a wheelchair. A few days before he died, we held hands and talked. "Go on with your life when I'm gone," he said.

Those were painful words to hear, but I tried to follow his advice. It was difficult and I suffered from anxiety attacks. But as the months passed, I began building a life without him, with the exception of one problem: I'd lost all desire to build a home without my partner, yet I couldn't part with the land. I'd drive out there and walk around, but even that was difficult. Without being mowed, the grass was taller than me. The fruit lay rotten and spoiled on the ground. Horseflies buzzed around me, and I feared snakes and other critters were hiding in the overgrown grass.

Our dream property became my albatross. It was holding me back. I started imagining problems that the land would cause. I worried trespassers might get hurt and sue me. I paid the taxes, but I avoided the land. Then one night I had a dream, perhaps a vision.

In the dream, I was lying on a gurney, and my arms and legs were strapped down. I couldn't move. I heard a door open behind me, and I turned my head in the direction of the sound. My husband walked up to me, but didn't say a word. First, he released the straps on my legs, and then he undid the straps on my wrists. He smiled at me — that gorgeous, beautiful smile — and then he turned around and left. I heard a door close.

I woke up shivering, trying to focus on where I was and what had happened. I knew it had been a dream, but it felt real. I lifted the pillow to my face and smelled his scent. I rubbed my wrist where the tight straps had bound me. Was it only my imagination, or were red marks slowly disappearing? I knew why he had visited. He'd brought a gift. He'd given me permission to release him and the land.

Shortly after the dream, I sold the property, and that allowed me to enjoy what we had there. Just a whiff of freshly mowed grass or a bite of a juicy, sweet peach brings back wonderful memories of a very special time with my husband.

—Donna Crisler—

Prisms of Peace

When it rains look for rainbows,
when it's dark look for stars.
~Oscar Wilde

I hadn't talked to my mother in four years when I got the call that she was in the ICU and she wasn't going to make it. At that point, I let go of my disappointment in her struggles with sobriety, and I visited her every day.

No matter how prepared you think you are, it is never easy to say a final goodbye to a loved one. I was lucky to have so many second chances in her ICU room over the course of that week to say my last farewell.

Ultimately I decided that it was okay for her to go. It would be selfish to think otherwise. At the exact moment that I came to accept this, my middle child ran into the room and told me to hurry outside. There, I saw the most vibrant rainbow I had ever seen in my entire life! It was an enormous full rainbow, and it seemed to speak to me. Struck by its beauty, I felt peace radiating from it. I knew I had made the right choice in my heart to let her go, and that everything would be okay.

I felt lucky to have received such a magnificent sign, but the rainbows didn't stop. My mom spent a total of ten days in the hospital. From the day of our first rainbow to the day of her funeral, I saw ten rainbows. I was overjoyed and thankful for each and every one, but I was especially happy to receive the one on the day of her funeral.

From that day forward, I saw at least one rainbow every week.

On a few occasions, my friends texted photos of rainbows. No matter how or in what way, the signs always came. My heart would soar at the sight of them. I had several conversations with God and said that I would understand when the rainbows stopped. I told him I had seen enough, and I would be forever grateful. Yet they still appeared.

As an only child, cleaning out my mom's cluttered home was the worst. Wandering room-to-room and seeing memories was like walking through a museum of my old life… a life that I would never live again. The pain was unbearable. But I also found so much that explained my mother's valiant attempts to turn around her life; and it was gratifying to find her AA card and church group materials and know that she was trying so hard.

When I closed the door for the last time, I got the exact message I needed! My mom always told me that things happen in threes and sure enough, I was sent three different rainbows that afternoon! God once again had turned my sorrow into joy!

In the midst of all of this upheaval, I changed job assignments at the elementary school where I was working. I was moving from second to fifth grade. I would have a new classroom and new curriculum. I was consumed by doubt and stressed about all these changes.

But then, the day before the new term, I walked outside the school building and saw a huge rainbow. I couldn't help but laugh! Immediately, I felt at peace. I hopped in my car and started driving in the opposite direction of the rainbow toward home. I was a little sad that I couldn't gaze at the rainbow on my drive when I happened to look out of my side window. Unbelievably, another rainbow! An hour later, I got a text from a friend about a rainbow sighting in a completely different direction than the last two. I saw another… and then another. I saw a total of five rainbows that day, the day before I started teaching fifth grade! It was truly remarkable, and I'm not sure I would believe it if someone had told me that story.

I felt a little ridiculous telling people about my rainbows. It was neat at first, but then it seemed a bit much. I took pictures to document them. I hoped people believed me, but I also knew it sounded like I was "reaching" for signs.

However, the rainbows were continuous. I received at least one a week for exactly six months after my mother's death — June seventh to December seventh — and it snowed the following day! Snow is extremely rare in southern Louisiana.

Were those rainbows only for me? Certainly not. Signs from heaven are for everyone to claim as their own. For me, those rainbows were six months of miracles that I really needed.

— Misty McLaughlin Stantz —

70

Hands from Heaven

Tears shed for another person are not a sign of
weakness. They are a sign of a pure heart.
~José N. Harris

When I called the ambulance that morning, I thought my husband was having a heart attack. At the ER we learned he had a large blood clot in his lung.

From his hospital bed, he motioned for me to come closer. He had already talked to each of our three grown children privately. Now he had words for me.

I leaned in close to Mike, straining to hear him speak over the beeps and blips of the machines monitoring his heart.

"I'm thinking I may not make it out of this place," he said weakly in my ear. "If I don't, I want you to know I want you to have a happy life."

I cupped my hand over my mouth as I choked back sobs. His words hit me hard. I knew he was trying to make it sound like his death was just a possibility, but something told me his words were final. Minutes later, he was gone.

For the first few weeks after his passing, the business of Mike's death consumed me: the life-insurance paperwork, the bills, and all the arrangements. On top of that, less than a month into widowhood, my basement flooded. A few weeks later, I stepped through a puddle in the kitchen floor as I reached for a coffee cup. I looked up at the ceiling. My roof was leaking!

Mike was gone. I didn't have time to fall apart. But my house was!

Finally, after managing my home through one crisis after another, I set out to do things my husband wouldn't agree to when he was alive. I replaced the living-room furniture, ordered a new queen-size mattress operated by a remote control, and installed new garage-door openers. With those projects behind me, I brainstormed a remodeling plan — anything to keep me busy.

But keeping busy did not make me forget my husband. He was always on my mind. When I sat down to watch TV, I couldn't believe he wasn't napping in his recliner next to me. When I looked out my kitchen window at the birds swooping in on the rustic birdhouse, I missed catching glimpses of Mike tending to the flowers in the yard.

I was so focused on adapting to life without Mike that I pushed my emotions as far back as I could. My days were sprinkled with sadness but devoid of tears. At the end of the day, everything was a blur of activity. Sleep came easily because I welcomed the escape from my new reality. And then, one night, I had an unusual dream.

I was looking down on a woman who was sitting in a chair in an empty room. Her head was lowered. Her face was buried in her hands. Suddenly, I wasn't looking down at her — I WAS her. I was stuck in grief. I couldn't get up from the chair.

"Mike is gone. I am so sad and alone," I lamented.

Suddenly, I felt a presence in the room. Something told me it was Mike. I didn't see him. I sensed only his hands, huge like a giant's, looming large and powerful in front of me. He reached for my hands ever so carefully. I was moved by the love and tenderness with which he handled me, as if he were picking up a butterfly by its wings. He eased me up from my chair, and I stood. He released me, and I started walking forward.

I woke up from my dream with tears streaming down my face. I remembered every detail. For days, I relived it. Over and over, I felt Mike's gigantic hands lifting me to my feet. Just the thought of his touch triggered a waterfall of tears but I didn't stifle them. I knew I had to release my pain into the light of day. I needed to let go.

It has been more than a year and a half since my husband passed away. I am still grieving. But now, I don't bury my feelings. I let the fresh tears spill out, and I let them carry me to wherever I need to be.

There is a saying that explains this: "Crying is how your heart speaks when your lips can't explain the pain you feel." I have learned that if a heart cannot express its brokenness, one's chance for happiness falls through the cracks. Tears are the medicine that puts a heart back together. My husband needed me to know this. His last wish for me was that I have a happy life. He wanted it for me so badly that he reached down from heaven and took matters into his own hands.

— Teresa Anne Hayden —

71

A Word Whispered to a Toddler

Grandchildren are the dots that connect the lines
from generation to generation.
~Lois Wyse

My father died four years ago at the age of eighty-one. I wish I could say he went peacefully in his sleep, but he didn't. Parkinson's disease and dementia whittled him away to nothing, physically and mentally, during his last five years. He was so frail, he broke his hip in four places, spent three agonizing weeks in a hospital where every possible mistake was made, and developed aspiration pneumonia. The broken hip became an afterthought. His throat was so devastated by botched tube placements, he lost the ability to talk and couldn't even say goodbye when he died.

When he was young, he was an athlete and reserve policeman in Belfast, Northern Ireland. He immigrated to America at twenty-eight and became known in the Southern California Irish community as a singer, storyteller, event emcee, and peace activist. During the 1970s, when "the troubles" in Northern Ireland were at their worst, he was interviewed on radio and television talk shows and contributed articles to the *Los Angeles Times* and *Belfast Telegraph* condemning the hatred and terrorism in his hometown. Because of his outgoing personality, the change his brain diseases caused in him were shocking to everyone who knew him. Friends who visited him often left in tears because so little was left of the man they remembered.

I lived in his hospital room during the last three weeks of his life, monitoring the staff, praying, talking to him, playing his favorite music, and doing everything I could to make him comfortable. Despite his health problems, I wanted him to live. I wasn't ready to let go. Finally, it was determined he could not survive without the aid of machines. He had always said he didn't want that, so I gave them permission to start the morphine drip that would end his life.

Family and close friends filled the room. I sat in the corner, completely crushed. My best friend, Dean, held my father's hand and asked him if he was ready to meet Jesus. He nodded yes. He prayed with him. When they finished, Dean said, "Mark, he wants you." I looked up and saw my dad reaching for me. I rushed to him and took his hand. He still couldn't speak, so he pulled me to him with the little strength he had left and gave me a kiss.

Even through the haze of five years with those diabolical brain diseases and the drugs flooding through him, he had the clarity of mind to know his life was ending. That kiss said everything that he couldn't say and meant the world to me because many times during his final years, he couldn't even remember I was his son.

I hugged him and cried. He stroked my hair. He was the one dying, but he wanted to comfort me. I continued to hold him as the morphine took his consciousness, and for most of the next twenty-four hours until his big heart finally let go and his body went cold. I prayed through my tears for passage of his soul into heaven.

I was angry at the hospital, at myself, and at God. I couldn't understand why such a good man had to suffer so horribly if God knew he would die anyway.

My daughters were one and three years old when he passed. Sometimes, it was hard to hold back tears in their presence, as if my despair became more pronounced when measured against their sweetness. One day, my elder daughter, Marli, looked at me and asked, "Are you sad, Daddy?" I held her and said grown-ups need to cry sometimes, too. I didn't want her to know about death yet, so I told her that her grandpa moved back to Ireland. She still asks me when he's coming home.

Sleep was difficult, but exhaustion always took me eventually. One night, however, sleep was impossible. I lay awake all night talking to my father, thanking him for all he had done for me, apologizing for mistakes, and praying he was whole again in heaven. I had lost my brother, my only sibling, twenty years earlier. His death was the worst pain my father ever felt, so I also prayed they were reunited.

The next morning, I woke and prayed, "Dad, I need to know if you're happy and free from that broken body. Please send me a sign."

I lay in bed listening to my wife cooking breakfast in the kitchen and my daughters playing in the living room. The morning sunlight started to expel some of the darkness in me. My older daughter came in, stood by my bed and asked, "Daddy, what does the word 'claim' mean?"

With my last prayer still fresh in my mind, I was startled. If I would associate one word with my father, it would be that one, because he owned an insurance claim adjustment company for most of his adult life. He was always talking about claims.

I asked her where she had heard that word.

"Emma keeps saying it," she replied.

I rushed into the living room, sat down with my younger daughter, and said, "Emma, who said claim to you?"

I'd like to report she said "Papa John," the name my girls called my father, but she was playing with a toy and had already moved on. I watched her play and wondered why my toddler, who was just starting to speak, would repeatedly say that particular word less than five minutes after I asked my father for a sign that he was okay. And why would my older daughter care enough to come into the other room and ask me what it meant? It was the only time she had ever done that.

I concluded that it was a message from heaven so I could finally have some peace. Or maybe my father, who had always come through for me in life, found a way to be there for me again by whispering a meaningful word he knew into the innocent, receptive ear of my child.

Whichever it was, since that morning, my pain has been lighter. I know my dad is okay, and that relief has allowed me to stop torturing myself. He was a happy man despite his own losses, and I would not be honoring him by dwelling on the hospital's mistakes and the pain he endured. He wanted me to be happy, too. And he wanted me to live.

— Mark Rickerby —

72

A Song from Beyond

Music is well said to be the speech of angels.
~Thomas Carlyle

"We're really living it up here," my husband used to say with a large, satisfied smile on his face. Julie had the good fortune of being able to retire from his podiatry practice at age sixty-two, and soon after we moved into a new townhouse in southern Florida. Everything about the community was inviting, and Julie loved the warm weather. He was simply happy to sit at the large bay window by our kitchen table, surveying the cherry blossom tree. But with his kindness, positive nature, and sweet laughter, he soon drew a large group of friends to him, who joined us in the pool, at card games, and during occasional day trips.

Being alone with my husband was my favorite part of retirement. We both felt we were in the prime of our lives. We shared a new grandchild, trips to the beach, and a love of nature and music. Before we went to bed, we sometimes lifted the lid of the music box Julie had given me to hear Debussy's "Clair de Lune." The gift symbolized not only our mutual love for music, but our deep love for one another.

Neither of us realized that our wonderful life would change drastically for the worse three-and-a-half years later. The first sign of a problem was when Julie was unable to swallow a carrot he had just chewed. He succeeded in dislodging what was left of the carrot and wasn't worried at all. I urged him to see a doctor, but it took three-and-a-half months of persuading for him to see a gastroenterologist. His diagnosis — stage III esophageal cancer that had spread to his stomach — was devastating.

Having had so many in my family die — including my mother and grandmother — before I reached age eleven, I became almost obsessed with the question: "What happens after we die?" I hoped that we were allowed somehow to continue on. Believing this would help me to make sense of my early losses. It also gave me hope that Julie and I would not be parted permanently.

Years earlier, I had suggested that my husband and I make a pact. I told Julie that if he died before me, he should send me a sign that he was okay. Of course, if I predeceased him, I would provide the same courtesy, although I'm not quite sure it was a courtesy he wanted! Nonetheless, mostly to humor me, Julie agreed.

But now that the possibility of an early death was more of a reality, I only spoke about life and my husband getting well. Julie chose the traditional chemotherapy route, designed to destroy the cancer and save his life. When I read about the curative value of drinking freshly made juice several times a day, I kept my husband on a steady juicing regimen, seldom leaving his side.

Within a year and a half, Julie had improved to the point where the doctors could no longer detect cancer. I threw him a "return to wellness" party in our condominium clubhouse. Julie still looked gaunt, but he was alive. I cried through much of the celebration as friends and family surrounded us with their love and good wishes.

In time, Julie's hair, which had fallen out, began to grow in — endearingly curly this time. His body filled out, and he even felt well enough to take a cruise. One evening on the ship, my husband, who had resumed his love for eating, began to choke on his food. Once again, he was unable to swallow. Immediately after we returned home, his physicians prepared to surgically implant a feeding tube. I remained full of hope despite some nagging doubts. Julie also agreed that it didn't matter what concessions he had to make. The important thing was life itself.

When the surgeons opened my husband to insert the tube, there, in places the CT scans and MRIs had been unable to detect, hid an insidious colony of cancer. The surgeons quickly sewed up my husband. The doctors would try to make him comfortable, but there was nothing they could do to keep him alive.

For the first several weeks after his death, I was a sobbing mess. I often let out a primitive howl that sounded like a wounded animal; my hurt was so deep.

I knew I had to do something to get myself back on my feet, so I pushed myself to attend a bereavement group. The pain I felt was still needle-sharp, but at least I had begun to get my sobbing under control.

Several weeks later, upon arriving home from a meeting, I was greeted by the sound of "Clair de Lune" coming from the music box Julie had given me. I ran into the bedroom and looked at my dresser to see if I had left the lid partially open. The top of the music box — the part that released the musical mechanism when open — was shut tightly. There was no rational reason for the music to be playing!

As I remembered my pact with my husband, my eyes began to tear. My husband had indeed found a way to let me know he was okay. Tears fell as I first looked down at the music box and then up to the ceiling. "Thank you for waving hello," I said.

In case I had further doubt that Julie was sending a sign, the fire alarm in my home went off twice the following week. A friend of mine who was an electrician was unable to find a short in the wire. I could almost hear the sweet sound of my husband's laughter from the other side. I thanked him again for coming, but this time I told him he needed to return to where he belonged — to move forward on the path he had let me know really does exist.

I managed my way through my grieving after that and even did new things. This once-shy woman went on to teach English abroad and become the leader of a large bereavement group. I still miss Julie and feel sad that he died young, but I am proud of the independent life I made for myself. I'm ninety now, and when my own time comes, I hope to leave this world with grace, comforted by the knowledge that Julie and I will be reunited.

—Mary Bader Schwager—

Heavenly Guidance

73

Love Taps

God could not be everywhere,
and therefore he made mothers.
~Rudyard Kipling

My mother would wake me up only once on school mornings. If I failed to get up, and she came back and caught me asleep again, I was in big trouble. After I got in trouble a few times, I learned my lesson. The instant I heard her coming back down the hall I would leap from my bed, my heart pounding. Over time, I became almost phobic about being caught sleeping when I was supposed to be awake. This continues even today.

When my stepfather died, Mom moved in with us. Memaw became a second mother to my little daughter, Sara. She let her help cook and taught her how to bake. They played video games with each other, confided their secrets, and became great friends. Although we all lived in the same house, the two of them shared a life that didn't include me, as I had to work outside the home. They developed an unbreakable bond.

Over the years, Mom maintained her habit of waking me, claiming she just wanted to make sure I didn't oversleep. The only thing I'm more phobic about than being in trouble is being late, so I didn't mind. She soon realized that the mere sound of her voice at my door, no matter how soft and caring, still sent me flying out of bed, bordering on a heart-attack level of panic.

She tried several other methods to wake me peacefully and finally settled on a much softer approach. After stepping quietly into my room, she would put her first two fingers together and lightly tap twice on the back of my hand. That's all it took. I wouldn't fly out of bed in a full-blown panic, but my eyes would pop open immediately, and I would stare at her smiling face until I could get my bearings. This actually woke me even faster than calling out my name, and the panic was much less intense.

When Sara was fourteen years old, my mother died shortly after being diagnosed with cancer. I was lost, but Sara was inconsolable. It was very difficult getting through the funeral, the estate sale, and dealing with all of Mom's affairs after she died. But Sara was going through a loss just as intense, yet beyond her capability to handle. She wanted to move into her Memaw's bedroom, and although I had second thoughts, I thought it might help her grieving process. Over time, it did. The only problem was that her bedroom was now at the opposite end of the house from mine. Unless she or I screamed, we couldn't hear one another.

One night, several months after Sara moved into her memaw's room, I was awakened from a deep sleep by Mom's two-finger double tap on the back of my hand. As always, my eyes flew open, and I expected to see her standing there smiling. But, of course, I was alone. According to the clock it was 3:30 a.m.

I knew I had felt my mother's tap on my hand, but I convinced myself I had only dreamed it. Closing my eyes, totally unable to fall back to sleep, I thought of her gentle "love taps," as she called them. She had demonstrated her love in so many ways. My thoughts drifted to how badly I missed her and how much I still needed her.

As I was taking a stroll down memory lane, I felt it again: two double-fingered taps on the back of my hand. This time, I bolted up from the bed and stared wide-eyed into the dark room. I was certain that I hadn't dreamt it. I was not sleeping. The clock now displayed the time as 3:43 a.m., thirteen minutes later than the first taps. Slowly, I crept through the dark house, half-expecting to see my mother at any moment. Everything seemed surreal until I discovered Sara in her bathroom. She was sick, pale, and vomiting.

Shocked, I asked her, "Why didn't you call out to let me know you were sick?"

She replied, "I did, but I guess you couldn't hear me."

When I asked her how long she had been sitting on the bathroom floor, she answered, "Maybe about ten or fifteen minutes. I'm feeling much better now."

I helped her get up and walked her back to her bed. As she climbed back into bed, she looked up at me and asked, "Mom, how did you know I was sick?"

Looking into her eyes, I caressed her pale cheek and replied with a smile, "Your Memaw woke me up."

— Ferna Lary Mills —

Home for the Night

Pay attention to the feelings, hunches, and intuitions
that flood your life each day. If you do,
you will see that premonitions are not rare,
but a natural part of our lives.
~Larry Dossey, MD, The Power of Premonitions

I t was 6:15 p.m., and I was headed home after a hectic day at work. I lived in a twelve-unit apartment building on a busy street. The building was old, inexpensive, and a friendly place to live.

I liked Wednesday nights and typically did the same thing each week. I would spend a relaxing evening with my next-door neighbor. Little did I know that there was a complete stranger, not far away, planning to make this one of the most atypical nights of my life.

Parking across the street, I saw my neighbor, Steve, standing outside the front of our building, looking around.

"Hey, Steve," I said casually, walking up to him. "What are you doing home tonight?" Steve was a bartender at a popular pub, and Wednesdays were very busy nights. He usually worked and partied at night and slept during the day.

"I haven't gotten much sleep the last few days," he said, "so I called in sick again tonight."

"Again?"

"Yeah, I've stayed home for the past two days and nights," he said in a strange voice. This didn't sound like Steve at all. He was usually very upbeat, frequently making people laugh with his wild stories.

"Are you okay?"

"I'm not sure," Steve said, lowering his voice. "I feel like something bad is going to happen. I just can't figure out what it is."

After a few more minutes of conversation, I headed up the stairs to my third-floor apartment. I turned on some music, quickly changed clothes, and heated up leftovers from the previous night.

Wednesday was "beer night" with Mary. She was eighty-two, lived alone, and hadn't left the building in almost a year. She needed a walker to even get around her apartment. Without an elevator, she couldn't get down the stairs anymore. Fortunately, Mary's cousin brought groceries and other items to her every week.

Mary and I shared the same fire escape off our kitchens, so our back doors were only about ten steps apart. After dinner, I knocked on Mary's kitchen door, and we had a beer together. We talked about everything and nothing, and laughed at the silliest things. We had become good friends.

It was getting late, and I went back to my apartment to get ready for bed. I closed my bedroom door, opened the window, and turned off the lights.

I was in a deep sleep when I awoke suddenly. There was a noise. Whatever it was, it wouldn't stop, and I got out of bed quickly. I reached over to turn on the lamp, but nothing happened.

As I opened the bedroom door, a wall of heavy smoke hit my face. I gasped for air and began coughing immediately. Without thinking, I flipped on the light switch, but again nothing happened. The room was pitch black. I couldn't see anything in front of me and could hardly breathe. The constant pounding and yelling was coming from my back door. Making my way toward the kitchen, I saw the beam of a flashlight through a window and heard a lot of noise outside on the fire escape. As I got closer to the kitchen door, I recognized the voice. It was Steve.

"The building is on fire," Steve yelled through the door. "Don't go out your front door into the hall."

"How bad is it?" I asked, quickly opening the door. The fresh air hit my face, and I took a deep breath.

"It's coming up the stairwell fast. You've got to get out NOW!" Instinctively, I reached into the kitchen drawer to grab a flashlight before stepping outside.

"Does Mary still live next door to you?" Steve demanded quickly. "I haven't seen her in a long time, and no one is answering the door." Briefly, I told him about Mary, and that she couldn't get down the steps by herself.

"Are you sure?" he asked incredulously.

"Yes," I said adamantly.

Mary still hadn't opened her back door. Steve clamored down the fire escape to get some help while I waited for Mary. Finally, I heard her coughing and the slow tapping of her walker coming across the wooden floor. When she got the door open, she was out of breath and very shaken. I helped Mary out onto the fire escape and briefly told her about the fire.

Mary was terrified and trying hard not to cry. She knew how steep and narrow the fire escape steps were going to be for everyone. Three men came back up the fire escape with Steve.

Steve explained which two men would carry Mary down the steps. The plan was for Steve to walk in front of Mary, shining his light on the steps. The fourth man would walk behind all of them, using my flashlight to also light up the steps.

The five of them slowly started making their way down to the second-floor landing. The two men carrying Mary were breathing heavily and struggling to hold on to her without falling. They finally made it to the second floor and took a short break. They were halfway there!

Without a light, the steps were too tricky for me to walk down by myself. I sat on the top step with my feet on the one below and slowly scooted my way down the steps, one at a time. I was more than halfway down when people began cheering and clapping. Mary and the men had made it safely to the ground level! Steve then came back up the steps with a flashlight and helped me the rest of the way down.

Steve and his buddies were our heroes that night. Steve had invited his friends over for a late-night poker game. About 2:00 a.m., they were playing cards at the kitchen table when the light fixture began to sizzle. Shortly afterward, the power went out. Steve stepped out into the hallway and saw fire below on the first floor.

Steve's premonition kept him home that night, and divine intervention saved our lives. Steve and his friends woke everyone up and helped all of us get out in time. They also called 911 and kept the building from being severely damaged. The fire was deliberately started in the basement, near the furnace, and the fire department ruled it arson. No one was ever arrested.

The building was repaired and cleaned. The landlord installed smoke detectors throughout the building and secure locks on the basement door. Mary moved to a safer place where she could live on the first floor. We held a celebration for Steve and his buddies, realizing more than ever the importance of having a strong sense of community with our neighbors.

— Barbara Dorman Bower —

The Mass Card

We cannot destroy kindred: our chains stretch a little
sometimes, but they never break.
~Marquise de Sévigné

My father's brother Leroy was my favorite uncle. From a very young age, we had a special bond. Uncle Lee was always willing to hang out with us kids, whether it meant playing video games or roughhousing on the lawn. He was always happy to sit at the kids' table with us at holiday dinners. Our time together was filled with silly jokes, funny stories and general laughter.

As I became a teen, the relationship grew, and I found he was easy to talk to and confide in. All teens should have someone who can listen as well as he did, and not judge their thoughts and feelings. Uncle Lee had a way of easing the pain and angst of growing up.

When I became an adult, I didn't see Uncle Lee as often. He had his family, and I had mine. Over the years, we grew apart. Soon, it seemed we never spoke.

He died unexpectedly when I was in my late thirties. It was sudden, sad and the resolution of a life filled with drama and pain. I felt we'd said our farewells years before, and there was nothing I hadn't said to him in life that I would say to him in death. So I opted out of attending a very emotional funeral.

When my parents returned from the ordeal, I was given three Mass cards — one for me and one for each of my children. I put them in a wallet inside my desk.

I never forgot where I put them, but I didn't look at them again until several years later.

My daughter and I love camping, and this particular Friday we'd packed up the car and were heading out to a cabin at Brendan T. Byrne State Forest. My Dodge Magnum was loaded to the brim with supplies we'd need for the weekend. With everything organized and ready to go, we hopped in the car.

We live in a lake community and have to pass over a bridge to leave. I was so used to it that it never fazed me. But as we crossed the bridge, I felt something in the steering change. I had no control of the vehicle. The car was going toward the edge. I pulled the emergency brake and, when that didn't work, my fingers automatically went to the electronic switch that would open the back window next to my daughter. I knew if we ended up in the water, I wouldn't be able to roll down the windows and get her out.

Fearfully, I prepared for the worst, yelling, "Hold on, honey!"

My heart was pounding as I clutched the steering wheel. I braced myself and thought through my plan. I would push my daughter through the window so she'd be visible to a passerby. I probably wouldn't make it, but at least she would be saved.

And then the car stopped suddenly, like someone was standing in front of it. It jerked hard, rocking us back and forth. I was only a half-inch away from the barrier.

I breathed hard, realizing I'd been holding my breath the entire time. I turned to look at my daughter, who was as white as a sheet.

"Are you okay, Mommy?"

I could only nod, swallowing hard. Then the tears of relief came like a flood. I had been prepared to accept my fate only seconds before, and here we were, unharmed.

Even the tow-truck driver didn't understand how we managed to stay on the bridge. He scratched his head as he looked at the broken tie rod.

The car was repaired that next week, but I could never drive it again. I started to panic at the sheer thought of even being inside it. My husband went behind my back and purchased a new minivan for me. It was a very thoughtful and welcome gift.

I said my goodbyes to the Magnum as I emptied the glove box of its contents. It was being traded in, and I'd never have to look at it again.

It was then I found a Mass card at the very back of the glove box. I began to tremble and then cry. Suddenly, I knew who had been looking out for my daughter and me. There is no doubt Uncle Lee was standing in front of my car, refusing to let us go over that bridge to an uncertain fate.

Later, when I checked my desk drawers, all three of the Mass cards were where I'd left them. I questioned family members about the card; every one swore they hadn't put it in my glove box.

— Nicole Ann Rook McAlister —

76

Grand Advice

A dream which is not interpreted is like
a letter which is not read.
~The Talmud

I didn't know my grandparents well. They lived in England, and I lived in Canada. I visited them only a few times, but I remember once taking a photo of my granddad. His slender body and long arms stretched wide, just begging for an embrace, and my grandma sat beside him with the largest smile on her face. It was one of my favorite memories and the only photo I own of my grandparents together. My grandmother hated getting her photo taken, but she had made an exception that time.

My granddad passed away when I was nine, and my grandma died when I was in my teens. I kept that special photo of the two of them tucked in an old photo album.

One night, when I was in college, I crawled into bed exhausted, and I had a vivid dream.

I saw a picture — the exact picture of my grandparents that I took when I was nine. This time, though, it wasn't a picture; it was real. My granddad pulled me in with his long arms, and I sat on his lap. I could feel the strength of his arms around me. I could sense the warmth of my grandmother's small hands on my back as she embraced me. They explained to me that my mother had cancer, and I began to cry uncontrollably. They rubbed my back and told me that she would be okay — that everything would be okay.

I awoke to a pillow soaked in tears. I was crying hysterically…

from a dream. It had felt so real, like a real visit, and it scared me. I tried to return to sleep, but I couldn't.

I called my mum as soon as I could. It was a difficult conversation because I couldn't stop sobbing. She tried to console me, telling me it was just a dream, but I could tell from her voice that she was concerned, too.

Three months later, my mum went to the doctor for a sore throat. She seldom went to the doctor, and never because of something as trivial as a sore throat. But something didn't feel right, and my dream had scared her. That day, the doctor confirmed that she had cancer. My grandparents had been right. But at least they had said she would be okay.

My mum has been cancer-free for over fifteen years. She is strong and living life to the fullest. That visit changed both our lives. My mum might not be here today if my grandparents hadn't found a way to send me the message. Not a day goes by that we don't say "thank you" for that dream that changed everything for us.

—Nicki Wright—

77

Grandpa's Approval

He who has gone, so we but cherish his memory,
abides with us, more potent, nay, more present
than the living man.
~Antoine de Saint-Exupéry

My dress — white, beaded and beautiful — is hanging on the door. My maid of honor, my best friend since third grade, is sleeping in my bed, resting before the duties she'll perform tomorrow. I lie there restlessly. I am eagerly anticipating my life with my husband and anxious about it at the same time.

I close my eyes, and I am in my grandfather's living room. The smell of the wood stove tickles my nose, and I breathe deeply. I can almost taste the creamy macaroni-and-cheese dish my grandmother will undoubtedly have baking in the oven. I hear the tinkle of the bell that hangs from my grandparents' Siamese cat's collar.

I smile. There is my grandfather, sitting regally in his overstuffed chair, wearing a train conductor's hat, red suspenders, and a loving smile. His head bobs up and down slowly, as it has for my entire childhood, and he appears deep in thought as he listens to my groom-to-be. I can't hear what they are saying, but I know it must be about me when Grandpa turns his head to meet my eyes. He inclines his head a bit, as if to say, "So this is the one?" I nod, eager for his approval.

He looks back at my love, takes his hand with the firmness of a much younger version of himself, and shakes it, before covering their clasped hands with his other hand in a gesture of love and respect.

With the wood stove crackling at my back, I sit watching them chat like old friends, laughing as men do, gesturing occasionally as they tell their stories. I feel safe, loved and sleepy.

I open my eyes and I'm back in my bedroom. My maid of honor is snoring softly. My wedding dress catches my eye, and the faint smell of wood smoke lingers in the air. It's my wedding day, and my grandfather — whom I loved, respected, and lost three years prior — had visited my dreams, met my groom, and approved.

I smile and shake my best friend's shoulder. "Wake up, wake up! I'm getting married!"

— Tia Ruggiero —

78

Bon Voyage

What we have once enjoyed deeply we can never lose.
All that we love deeply becomes a part of us.
~Helen Keller

For many years, I visited my daughter Emily in California over our spring breaks when she was in college. Luckily, most of the time, her schedule coincided with my middle-school teaching calendar.

My sweet mother always called me the night before I would fly out to see Emily. Mom would tell me special things to tell her, remind me of things not to forget, and tell me to have a safe trip. I was also reminded to tell my daughter, her only granddaughter at the time, that she loved her.

My daughter got a job in California after graduating, so I still managed to go and see her on my spring breaks. Mother would still always call the night before I got on the plane.

I loved knowing that I was always going to get a call the night before I left. Mom and I talked on the phone so often that she always knew my plans.

Several years later, my sister, brother and I moved my parents from North Carolina to Colorado to be with us as their health started to fail. After Dad passed, Mom wound up living between my sister's house and mine. We shared many hours of fun as we fixed her hair, took her shopping, and shared fond memories of our childhoods with her and Dad.

But then, my mother fell and broke her hip. Within three months, she was gone. We were heartbroken. No more loving phone calls, no more funny stories that Mom was so good at telling, no more of her yummy tea cakes.

A few months later, I was getting ready to fly out to see Emily in California for the first time since the funeral. I was madly packing my bag as I did laundry and tried to figure out what the weather would be like in Los Angeles.

I stayed up late packing. I crammed a bunch of cash in one of the side pockets and placed my traveling clothes next to the open bag.

When I finally finished around 2:00 a.m., I collapsed into bed and tried to grab a little sleep before my early-morning flight. As I drifted off, I remembered how my daughter had told me not to stay up all night packing and getting ready, as I was well known to do.

Suddenly, my phone rang and startled me out of my sleep. I mumbled "Hello," and I was shocked to hear my mother's voice say, "Hi, Bev. I just called because I knew you were flying to California to see Emily, and I wanted to wish you a safe trip."

"Mom!" I screamed. And without even realizing it, I added quickly, "Mom, what's heaven like?"

"It's nice; it's really nice," she said. "But they keep us awfully busy... and I have to go now."

With that, I woke up. The phone was not in my hand, but I had heard my mother's dear, sweet voice as clearly as if she were standing next to me.

"Oh, Mom, I miss you, miss you so," I murmured to myself with my heart bursting with both joy at her message and then sadness that she was no longer with us. Excited, exhausted and in kind of a daze, I fell back to sleep eventually.

I had a wonderful time with Emily in California, and when I got home I told my sister and brother in person about my incredible phone call from Mom. We all cried a bit.

Some may say it was just a dream, but it didn't feel like one.

I'm pretty sure that Mom was sending me off to California with her normal loving call.

— Beverly Hood Schultz —

79

Worth Listening

We have two ears and one mouth so that we can
listen twice as much as we speak.
~Epictetus

Sleep was a long time coming one night in May 2010. After tossing and turning for hours, I finally gave up. I flipped on my nightstand lamp and grabbed my Bible, asking God to speak to me personally through whatever passage I randomly opened it to. I often did this, and more times than not, I stumbled upon something that really hit home — a pertinent and helpful message for whatever situation I was facing.

The first thing that captured my eye when I opened my Bible was a pink commentary box at the bottom of the page. The commentator said that King David had not been where he was supposed to be when he was tempted by Bathsheba, and if he had been where he should have been — on the battlefield with his men — instead of lagging behind at his palace, he would have been spared a whole lot of trouble.

After reading this, something in my spirit stirred. A voice in my head told me that I needed to go the next morning to a place where I volunteered approximately once a month.

I didn't want to. I had been busy over the weekend, and my house was a total wreck. I worked as a nurse three days a week, and the following day was one of my days off. I had planned on spending it in my pajamas, catching up on laundry and de-cluttering my house... and my mind.

The prompting wouldn't let up, though. *Don't be like David. Be at the right place at the right time* was what I was hearing. But this made no sense. Couldn't I just go in the afternoon after getting caught up on some sleep?

I'm ashamed to say that I bargained with God, wanting proof that it was His voice I was sensing. I wanted to make sure I hadn't fabricated all this in my mind. *Unless You somehow confirm that this is really You, I'm going to sleep late. And if I volunteer, it will be in the afternoon,* I thought.

The next thing I knew, I was awakened by my phone. It was only 7:00 a.m., so I was nervous as I answered the call from a family friend. It turned out she just wanted my mother's new phone number. Really? Who calls someone at 7:00 a.m. unless it's a life-threatening emergency? That seemed like my wake-up call from God, so I got up!

I stumbled to the coffee pot. "What are you doing up so early?" my husband asked as he headed out the door for work. I recounted the entire story. He nodded his head, but he looked at me as if I were crazy. And I was starting to wonder if that was a fair assumption.

You'll understand why in time. This time, the voice might as well have been shouting in my ear; that's how real it was. I was washing my hands at the kitchen sink when this assurance swept over me, resonating through every cell of my body. Knowing for sure that this was bigger than my imagination, I was now fully surrendered and at peace as I finished getting ready.

Along my forty-minute drive to my destination, I came across some ominous black clouds. Since it was May in North Carolina, the first thing that popped into my mind was a tornado. Maybe that was the reason for all this... Maybe a tornado was about to touch down on my house, and God wanted me out of there. My heart flip-flopped. The rest of my drive was spent praying for protection — for my house and, most importantly, my family who lived nearby.

No more than thirty minutes had passed since I began my volunteer work when I received a phone call from my husband. He raced to tell me something that left me speechless. "Our house has been broken into. ADT just called and said the alarm is going off. The police are on their way."

My heart felt like it stopped and then started up again at ten times its usual pace. Being a former cardiac nurse, I feared I was experiencing ventricular fibrillation — a fatal heart rhythm. *Whoa, God, You weren't kidding when You told me I would soon understand why!*

As crazy as it sounds, the first emotion I felt was awe-filled joy — definitely not the typical reaction one would have after hearing her house had just been broken into. I was completely amazed that God was looking out for little old me.

Of course, my husband and I were concerned about our house. But more than anything, we were completely "wowed" and thankful. And my husband no longer thought I was crazy for following that voice.

Who knows what would have happened if I had been at home, especially had I been asleep in our back bedroom when the break-in occurred?

This experience is one I will never forget. What I gained from it far outweighed the cost of our insurance deductible and the hassle of replacing our front door and the television that was stolen. When I'm going through hard times, all I have to do is ponder this miraculous encounter. I am instantly comforted and filled with peace.

After this life-changing ordeal, I vowed to never, ever dismiss that voice... no matter how strange the message.

— Mandy Lawrence —

80

My Shooting Star

*Every morning you have two choices: continue to sleep
with your dreams, or wake up and chase them.*
~Author Unknown

I still remember the moment I realized I was going to dedicate my life to public service and become a firefighter. Waking up in the hospital after the first of my five facial reconstructive surgeries as the result of a traumatic assault, I heard the surgeon say, "Not only are you lucky to be alive, but you owe a special thanks to the fire department, hospital staff, and police officers who helped work as a team to save your life."

The next several years, I devoted every free moment to furthering my firefighting career. I spent long hours studying for my EMT license while working a full-time job. I also joined a volunteer fire district. My biggest support system and advocates in achieving this dream were my then girlfriend, now wife, and my mother. However, with this specific line of work, there was an even bigger advocate — my Uncle John. A veteran, he was very proud that another family member was pursuing a field to serve the community.

Having been unexpectedly relocated in my teens due to my dad's job change, I benefited from a new relationship with my uncle, who lived in the same town. Because of the distance from our hometown, he became the only family at our holiday meals, spent countless hours with me discussing my education, showed me the town in his cool red sports car, and rarely missed one of my soccer games. Once I left that state to attend college, Uncle John would faithfully text, call and e-mail me, asking about my job search. I applied to more than twenty departments around the state and had several face-to-face interviews, but I never made it past the initial stage.

Uncle John was the only person I could call and vent to, regardless of the time of day, and he would say the most uplifting things to reassure me. He told me to keep pushing forward, and that he believed this was my calling.

Tragically, we lost Uncle John more than three years ago, and I began to give up on my dream of becoming a firefighter. At that point, I had a steady job working for an advertising agency, and I was getting married in the fall. Life was changing.

One night, I was sitting on the couch deleting voicemails on my phone when I saw the name "Uncle John" on an old voicemail. I deleted every voicemail on my phone except his. I listened to it... listened again... and listened a third time before the goosebumps started in. That night, I began updating my certifications and completing applications again.

Eventually, I submitted an application that led to repeated interviews. On the morning of the final interview, I pulled into the fire station, looked up in the still-dark sky and took some deep, calming breaths. And then I saw it through my windshield—a shooting star that flashed across the skyline. I was startled at first because I had not seen many in my life, but I didn't think much of it.

It wasn't until I was leaving the interview that I started to think about the shooting star and how cool it was to witness it. Then I got goosebumps. Something inside me knew immediately that these goosebumps weren't because of the weather; it was Uncle John's way of saying that he was with me and was proud of me.

I called my mom on the drive home and talked to her about what had just happened. I didn't usually believe in that type of connection, but in that moment at that point in my life, I knew that I had connected with Uncle John.

I now work full-time for a fire department in Missouri and have my uncle to thank. He kept pushing me to pursue my calling, and he was certainly with me that morning. Even though Uncle John isn't here to share this success with me, I know he is looking down with a big smile and a thumbs-up!

Every time I see a shooting star, I pause and say, "Thanks, Uncle John."

— Thomas Schonhardt —

81

The Hot Seat

Insight is better than eyesight when it comes
to seeing an angel.
~Eileen Elias Freeman,
The Angels' Little Instruction Book

I had to move. A developer had bought out our block to build a new department store. I found a one-bedroom, one-bathroom, garage apartment with a living room and a tiny kitchen that would suffice until I could find a bigger place.

The location was convenient, and I made a deal with the owner that I would upgrade the place if he would charge me only one hundred dollars per month for the entire time that I lived there. I bought better appliances at a salvage store, replaced the fake wood paneling with drywall, built a new closet, and carpeted the floors.

The utilities were included in the rent, so it was a good deal for me. I was twenty-two years old, working two part-time jobs, and I was trying to save enough money to buy something someday.

The only problem I could find with the apartment was the hot spot in the floor. Every time anyone sat in the recliner in the living room, the floor in front of the chair got hot. I went under the apartment into the garage to make sure there was no logical reason for the heat. I surmised that the hot-water pipes or perhaps some electric cords were under the floor in that spot, but they weren't.

One day the landlord's daughter Julia stopped by to see what I had done with the place. She said that her brother had lived in the apartment when he graduated high school. He promised to fix up the place, but he didn't. Instead, he signed on with the local fire department and it took most of his free time. Unfortunately, he died from smoke inhalation after fighting a fire.

Julia told me that she loved what I had done to the apartment and couldn't wait to see it when I was finished. Like me, Julia couldn't understand the hot spot in the floor.

Then one morning, at 5:00 a.m., Julia knocked on my door. "You are going to think I'm nuts," she said, "but you have to get the things that matter most to you and come outside."

She seemed so serious and frightened that I didn't bother to ask her why. I started throwing things out the door to the ground while she gathered them and put them farther away from the building.

The fire department showed up. "Where's the fire?" the captain shouted.

"There's no fire," I said.

"Well," the captain said, "we got a call just a few moments ago. The caller told us to get here as soon as possible."

Suddenly, the water heater exploded, and the garage caught fire.

I asked Julia how she knew to warn me and was shocked when she said her brother had told her that the water heater had a short in it. "I was washing my face, and when I turned on the hot water, I heard Jimmy's voice. I looked up and saw his face in the mirror, as if he was standing right behind me. I turned to see if he was really there, but he wasn't."

Julia went on to say that she wondered if she was imagining things, but she remembered that mysterious hot spot in my living room. She believed that Jimmy had been trying to warn me with the hot spot. She even believed that Jimmy had called the fire department. She said that she hesitated to knock on my door because it all seemed so far fetched.

"I'm glad you did," I said, as I stood there watching the thousand dollars' worth of labor and materials I had paid for burn up.

After the fire went out, Julia's dad said to me, "Don't worry, we have good insurance."

The insurance company paid to rebuild the apartment and even for me to stay in a motel until it was finished. The apartment turned out better than I could have made it on my own, and the landlord stuck by his agreement with me! I continued to pay just $100 per month.

But the real miracle was that Julia's dead brother had sent her a message to save me. But isn't that what firemen do?

—Joyce Carol Gibson—

82

Look Left

If you can heed only one piece of advice from the
universe, make it this… Pay attention. Do this and
everything else will fall into place.
~Bryan E. Wright

I was distracted by the music rising from the back seat of the car. "Honey, can you turn that down?"

"Sure, Mom," Lainey mumbled, yet complied.

It was a sunny Saturday, and I was overjoyed to be taking my fifteen-year-old daughter to the theater. We shared a special bond, and going to musicals together was our guilty pleasure. How lucky I was to have a teenager whom I not only adored, but who also enjoyed spending time with me. Not being a fan of driving on the Denver freeways, I typically drove white-knuckled and felt the need to stay vigilant. I was not going to let twenty minutes of discomfort on I-25 ever stop us from enjoying our special time together. And this morning was no different.

Suddenly, a heavy sense of foreboding crept over me, leaving me with no option but to acknowledge its existence. I didn't want to scare Lainey or have her question my sanity, but I suddenly needed complete silence while I drove.

"I don't know, babe, I just get the feeling that something isn't right with the traffic here. I need to pay attention. Please turn off the music."

From the driver's seat, I surveyed my surroundings. My focus suddenly became myopic to only those things closest to us, and my other senses dulled as I felt my fight-or-flight reflexes kick in. I noticed the sun was sitting low on the winter horizon, making visibility a little more challenging than usual. Traffic on the freeway was heavy, and drivers were traveling too fast as they jockeyed for position and wove between lanes. Nothing too unusual was happening around me, but I couldn't shake the feeling that staying on high alert was required.

I pulled into the right lane to prepare for entering the off-ramp and breathed a sigh of relief. From here, the rest of the way would be city streets and easier driving. The sense of foreboding lifted. It must have been a false alarm, I thought. I was just nervous about driving in fast traffic.

On the off-ramp, we eased our way up the hill to the intersection and stopped at a red light. We were the first car in the left-turn lane. As we waited for the light to turn green, traffic exited the freeway and backed up behind us.

The traffic light turned green, and time stood still.

I clearly heard the words, "Look left," as if they had been spoken by an unseen man in the passenger seat next to me. I kept my foot on the brake while I complied and looked left. I saw the driver of the car approaching the intersection to my left. When his light turned from yellow to red, he made the reckless split-second decision to run the red light. I saw the look on his face as he gunned the accelerator and the stunned look on the face of his passenger as they entered the intersection. I slammed my hand on the horn to warn the driver to my right not to enter the intersection, as he was in a left-turn lane as well.

I yelled, "Lainey, don't look!"

Unfortunately, the driver to my right did not respond to the blaring of my horn and pulled into the intersection just as the bad driver ran the red light. Glass shattered and steel crumpled as the two cars collided. A third car was hit as well and was rolling backward toward our car. I quickly pulled into the intersection to avoid being hit by that car and we snuck around the accident scene to the left and got out of there unscathed. As I checked the rearview mirror behind me, I saw other drivers had exited their cars to assist the injured motorists.

Lainey and I were both extremely shaken. How easily we could have been the first car into the intersection. Our hearts went out to all the injured parties.

Who was that male voice that warned me to look left? I am not exactly sure, but I do believe in angels. I believe that the sense of foreboding encouraging my vigilance on the freeway and the commanding voice was an angel or form of divine intervention. Whatever it was, I am deeply humbled and grateful!

—Ruth Anderson—

83

Mom to the Rescue

Mama always said life was like a box of chocolates.
You never know what you're gonna get.
~Forrest Gump

My sister's voice sounded frantic over the phone. Between tears and hiccups, she told me the whole sad story. After she bought her wedding dress six months earlier, it went into a closet. When she tried it on two weeks before the wedding, she found to her horror that she had gained weight. A friend offered to alter it but she had done a terrible job and now the dress had puckered seams.

An image of Mom at her sewing machine popped into my head. She would have known how to fix it, but she had died four years earlier. Unfortunately, neither Lynn nor I inherited her sewing talents.

"Can you find another seamstress?"

"It's too late! I'm just going to have to find another dress."

I recalled the dress she had bought and how great it had looked with her dark hair and tan. This would be the wedding of her dreams. After struggling through nearly twenty years of unhappiness with her first husband, she had found the courage to divorce. Now, two years later, she was marrying a man who adored her.

"I remember watching the movie *Forrest Gump* and seeing that feather float down," she said when she called to announce their engagement. "I have this special feeling that the universe is watching out for me, the way it did for Forrest Gump."

Although Lynn and I were five hundred miles apart, we spent hours on the phone talking about the wedding. A cousin had offered her beautifully landscaped back yard for the ceremony.

"I want to plan every detail of this wedding," Lynn said. "I was so young and scared the first time around that I just went along with other people's ideas."

She found the right flowers, music, food and, of course, the wedding dress. She and her fiancé wrote their own vows and made sure her two teenage boys were included in the ceremony. Everything floated into place as if the magic of the *Forrest Gump* feather still hovered above her.

But now she had no dress just days before the wedding.

"Don't worry, Sis, we'll find an even nicer one," I said.

My words were encouraging but they didn't match my spirit. It had taken a week of exhausting shopping to find the first dress. My sister was picky and this would be quite a challenge.

Three days before the wedding, we set out on our mission. In store after store, Lynn tried on all sorts of dresses. Nothing looked right. The dresses were too frilly or too plain, too short or too long, too frumpy or too fancy.

"I wish Mom were here to tell me where to find a decent wedding dress," she said. She sat down suddenly, putting her face in her hands. "And I wish she could be here to see the wedding."

"Yes," I said. "Mom loved weddings. She was good at shopping, too." We both smiled, remembering how Mom would bring us into the dressing room with her, and then send us back and forth for new sizes, different colors, and more choices.

We dragged ourselves out of the store. Lynn looked as defeated as I felt. It was nearly closing time, and there was only one more place to try, at the other end of the shopping center.

"If I don't find a dress here, I'll have to drive into the city tomorrow," she said as we parked. "How can I take time to do that with everything else that has to be done?"

I let the question go unanswered. Instead, I took her hand. As her "Big Sis," I really wanted to come through for her.

"Sis, don't be discouraged. You know Mom and the universe won't let you down — look at how happy you guys are together. You'll find something in here, I'll bet!"

"I hope so." Her voice sounded gloomy. "Let's get this over with." We got out of the car and walked to the store entrance. Then she stopped so abruptly I nearly ran into her.

"Look!" she said, pointing down. There, right in front of the gleaming glass door, was our Forrest Gump white feather. She bent to pick it up, and I saw tears trickling down her cheeks.

"This is from Mom. I just know it!" she said. "She's here, and she's guiding us."

Dumbfounded but excited, I simply nodded. We hurried into the store. Lynn headed straight for a rack and chose a single dress to try on. Twenty minutes later, we emerged with a majestic, ankle-length white silk moiré, more beautiful than the first dress and a perfect fit. A matching shawl flowed across her shoulders and gave her an almost ethereal look.

Had it been there all along? Or had our mother's loving spirit come to the rescue?

On Lynn's wedding day, as I stood proudly next to her and watched her glowing face, I held my bouquet and a little something extra I had tucked into it: the white feather I'd picked up at the store entrance.

"Thanks, Mom," I whispered. "Glad you could make it to the wedding."

— Maril Crabtree —

Angels Among Us

84

Running with Clarence

Being a daddy's girl is like having permanent armor
for the rest of your life.
~Marinela Reka

"My daughter's a marathon runner." That's how my dad, in the final months of his life, described me to people. I'd worn many hats in my six decades — traveler, mother, businessperson, writer — but the one my father saw as key to understanding me was my runner's hat. Dad was a keen observer and he'd always understood that my marathons — and the training, setbacks, and perseverance that went into each one — were, for me, bigger than the events themselves. Being a "marathon runner" was the way he distilled the entirety of my life into a description of the kind of person I was.

It was spring, and I told Dad I'd signed up for my favorite October race and would start training in June. "This will be our marathon," I told him. "You'll be out there with me." He flashed a beautiful smile and nodded his head. Through the rest of spring, my family watched this man we loved slip slowly from us as cancer took over his body.

Day One of training was scheduled for June fifteenth. I'd been staying nights at my parents' condo, keeping watch on Dad from a twin bed next to his so my mom could get enough sleep to handle the day shift. On June fifteenth, Dad passed away. The wind chimes outside his room played a distinct melody as he passed, and I knew he was free and at peace. I put on my sneakers and ran in the rain.

Through months of training, he was with me. Round holes in the clouds were portals through which I talked to him. Balls of sunlight gleaming through gaps in the leafy tops of trees were him sending me energy. Wind chimes along my running routes played vigorous notes, even in a slight breeze. Whenever my thrice-sprained ankle made my foot drag rather than bounce, he'd remind me that every forward step was a gift.

When the gun went off on race day, I spent the first miles finding a workable rhythm. This was my fourteenth marathon, and I was no longer fast or young. Finishing, for me and for Dad, was the goal. I had yet to go over the five-hour mark in a marathon, so if I could finish under that for one more year, it would be a bonus. It was at Mile 3, the point where I usually begin to calm down and ease into a mental and physical pace I can sustain for many miles and hours, that I became aware of an old runner with a smiling face and white hair tucked under a white visor. He was running near me, wearing a red, white, and blue tank top and neon-pink knee socks. "I'm a veteran," I heard him say to another runner. He addressed her, but looked at me. My dad was a veteran. Were this man's pink socks for Breast Cancer Awareness Month? My mom is a two-time breast cancer survivor.

After about seven miles, it dawned on me that this man was always nearby. I've often fallen into a synchronous pace with other runners and gone for miles, even whole marathons, within yards of them, occasionally nodding silent acknowledgment of our progress while each runner stayed focused on his or her individual effort. This was different. The old veteran in the patriotic singlet and pink socks seemed to be watching, sometimes even waiting, for me.

I decided that Dad had put him there. By Mile 10, my brain was calling the old runner Clarence, after George Bailey's guardian angel in *It's a Wonderful Life*. His eyes twinkled, and he manifested no signs of the fatigue, pain, or intense introspection that most of us in the middle of the pack wear for twenty-six miles. Clarence's pink socks and visor-topped mop of white hair became my beacon. *Where's Clarence?* There, just ahead, waiting at the water stop until I appear. *Where's Clarence?* There, just behind, not close enough to make me expend energy conversing, but close enough to let me know I'm not running alone. On the bridge that marks the race's halfway point, Clarence appeared off my left elbow.

"What're you looking for, a 4:45?" he asked me, the first time he'd spoken to me directly.

"I'm just looking to finish, but I'd be glad to break five."

He wished me luck.

Miles ensued, pain increased, and the finish line inched closer. I didn't see Clarence from just past the halfway mark to about Mile 20. I was hunkered down deep inside my body and brain, willing myself to keep moving. My splits were encouraging. Whenever I'd cross a timing mat on the course, I'd realize I was doing pretty well.

I crossed Mile 20, which I consider the you-did-it point. If you can make 20, you can summon whatever it takes to bring it home. At Mile 20, Clarence appeared for an instant, again off my left elbow. "You're gonna crush five, honey," he said. Then he disappeared. Not ahead, behind, nor to the side — just nowhere.

I crossed the line at 4:37. As I came down the chute, the announcer said my name and hometown. I cried, thanked the volunteers for my medal and heat blanket, and hobbled through the finish area. I looked up to see Clarence to my left, smiling. Unlike the rest of us, he wore no heat blanket. "I couldn't have done it without you," I said to him. "Thank you."

"You're welcome." He smiled and jogged away.

I called to him: "What's your name?"

"Brian." Then he was gone.

The announcer was calling out finishers' names. He called the name Brian S., from my hometown. I recognized the name and knew Brian S. was a young man, about my kids' age. But I realized the race results would be online when I got home, and I could learn the name and hometown of the guardian that Dad had recruited to run with me. Our three names — mine and the two Brians — would be near each other.

I found my name at 4:37. The name above mine was my town's Brian S. Age: 25. Finish time: 4:37. There were no other Brians. I read scores of names both above and below mine. None were Brian. A shiver of love and wonder shot through me.

Then I saw that my and Brian S's split times — at the six points on the course where time was recorded — were virtually identical. Dad had orchestrated everything, right down to ensuring I'd have reason to study this page so I would see these numbers and know beyond doubt that he'd been there through every footstep.

On the course, people would have seen a young man and sixty-something woman running near one another. I saw no young man, just a vibrant veteran in pink socks.

We'd finished together. And we'd crushed five.

— Lori Hein —

85

A Cousin's Love

Cousins are friends that will love you forever.
~Constance Richards

I spent my childhood in the kind of picturesque small town you only see in the movies these days. We played in creeks, decorated our bicycles for parades through town, gathered in friends' yards for impromptu baseball games, and counted our cousins among our best friends.

The cousins I was closest to were a sister and brother who were older than me by four and five years. They didn't seem to mind the age difference. I was just the "kid sister" who tagged along everywhere.

Cheryl played Barbies with me and even let me play with the Mystery Date game she got for Christmas one year. I insisted on going to dance class like she did, and she tried to help me with the steps, but I was a terrible dancer.

Kenny was more of a big brother than a cousin. He kept an eye on me, and even babysat for my younger brother and me on occasion. While Kenny was tall for his age, I was short and skinny for mine, and he called me Squirt. I hated that nickname, and I would beg him not to call me that. Some days, he would feel generous and call me Munchkin instead. That wasn't any better.

The autumn after I turned twelve, we moved to another state and I didn't get to see my cousins anymore. May rolled around, and so did my thirteenth birthday. The phone rang that day, and a deep male voice said, "Happy birthday, Donna."

"Hey! You didn't call me Squirt or Munchkin!" I was thrilled to hear Kenny's voice.

"Well," he replied, "you're a teenager now. I guess I need to stop treating you like a kid."

Kenny went on to talk to Mom after that, and said he would visit us. He would come after his graduation from high school in a couple of weeks.

I thought I'd never be able to wait for those two weeks to pass, but then, five days later, Kenny was killed in an automobile accident. No one would ever call me Squirt again.

Twenty or so years rolled by. I was headed to my younger son's preschool to drop him off for the day. He was in the passenger seat beside me, buckled into his booster seat. We had the green light, and I was just about to go through the intersection when a deep male voice suddenly shouted from the back seat.

"Watch out, Squirt!"

I slammed on the brakes and came to an almost immediate stop just as a huge dump truck ran the red light and barreled through the intersection. It narrowly missed my car. I checked on my son and almost instantaneously looked in the back seat to see who was in my car.

No one was there.

I pulled through the intersection and then off onto the shoulder, trying to gather myself. I was shaking, and my poor little boy was as white as a sheet. We had just missed being very seriously injured and quite possibly killed.

"Are you okay, baby?" I gave my son a little hug while I tried to make sense out of what had just happened.

"Who said that, Mommy?"

"Who said what?" I asked distractedly.

"Who said, 'Watch out, Squirt'?" I couldn't believe it. Had he heard it, too? I wasn't sure what to tell him, so I said we must have had a guardian angel watching over us that morning, and then we continued on to his preschool.

After I dropped off my son, I sat outside his preschool in the car for a few minutes, going over everything. If both my son and I had heard it, then it must have happened. I didn't imagine it, right?

And that's when it hit me. That deep voice had called me Squirt. I hadn't heard that in over twenty years, but I knew who it was.

Kenny had saved our lives.

As the realization that Kenny had reached out from beyond the grave to save us washed over me, I began to cry. I sat in that parking lot and cried for all of the years I had missed with Kenny, and then I cried for the joy of knowing that he had been there all along, watching over my sons and me, keeping us safe. Kenny had always been more like a big brother than a cousin, and now he was my guardian angel.

"Squirt" never sounded so good.

—Donna L. Marsh—

86

One Wing at a Time

We are each of us angels with only one wing,
and we can only fly by embracing one another.
~Luciano De Crescenzo

The October air was crisp and invigorating. What a day to be alive! I walked faster as I approached the main entrance to the hospital. My client Jerry was being discharged after an overnight stay for a minor procedure on his foot. I had come to bring him home.

For some reason, this antsy, contentious man and I bonded instantly. Following a disastrous succession of cleaning ladies, my neighbors Lori and Ted asked if I would be interested in taking the job. Since Jerry knew me, he thought it was a brilliant idea. According to Jerry's sister, he viewed me not as a housekeeper but rather a friend who regularly came by — to tidy up.

I entered Jerry's room, expecting to hear the usual litany of complaints: the hospital TV didn't have enough channels; the food was the pits. A woman with a clipboard stood at the bedside scribbling notes. Her ID tag read: Social Services. The housekeeping staff bustled about, preparing the bed for a new patient. Jerry was dressed, slouched in his wheelchair.

"We gave him extra pain meds to keep him comfortable," the social worker told me without looking up from her writing. "He'll be groggy for a while." There was a soft buzzing sound I couldn't place. Some newfangled monitor, I guessed. Then I stole a glance at Jerry.

He was snoring. The social worker handed me a small white bag. The pill bottles inside rattled like maracas.

"So," I asked her, "the car service is picking us up?" The social worker seemed puzzled by my question. Then she gave a start.

"Oh, I'm terribly sorry," she replied. She had forgotten to order a car.

Oblivious to the drama unfolding, Jerry dozed peacefully. His clothing and personal items were now hanging in plastic bags suspended from two metal poles on the back of the wheelchair. The social worker tried her best to give it a positive spin. "Cabs pass by down front all the time," she said with a wan smile. "It'll be easy." She had also forgotten that the avenue in front of the hospital was a no-stopping zone. I imagined taxis whizzing past, slowing down but unable to pick us up. Not a good outcome. A staccato of beeps shrilled from her pager.

"I have an emergency," she said as she hurried away.

You and me both, sister, I thought.

Outside, I pushed Jerry's wheelchair on a half-block of cobblestones, looking for a cab. The road went uphill too, so it seemed like Jerry and his swinging bags of possessions weighed a thousand pounds. Utterly defeated, and furious at the social worker, I tried not to burst into tears. I let the wheelchair roll to a bumpy halt. "Dear Lord," I breathed an exhausted prayer, "please…" Seconds later, I heard a quiet voice.

"Excuse me, ma'am? It looks like you could use some help."

A rough-hewn stranger, who had suddenly appeared by my side, reached out, calmly taking the handle of the wheelchair. "I got this. We're good." He fell in step with me. I glanced at him. He was not a young man, judging from his long grey hair tied back in an elastic band. His brown leather jacket had seen better days. Suddenly, I noticed his left arm, hanging in the sleeve. The strength with which he steered Jerry's wheelchair and cargo was impressive, especially with only one arm.

"Are you from around here?" I asked.

"No, not really," he answered, with a faraway smile. "You might say I'm just passing through. Traveling alone." I took comfort from this mysterious man's strength. We walked, the sound of our footsteps tapping on the pavement, and then crossed the street. It was a short distance, but time seemed to expand, stretching into a kind of healing interval. We approached Jerry's building, an upscale apartment house.

I turned to this mysterious stranger who had materialized out of thin air and said, "Buddy, you have been an absolute angel." I reached for my purse. "Here," I said. I opened my wallet, intending to hand him money. "You saved me, big time. C'mon, buy some coffee and a sandwich. If you hadn't shown up when you did, I'd still be out there."

"That's not necessary, ma'am." He quietly waved away the money. "But you could pray for me." We stopped at the ornate glass front doors. José, the doorman, saw me. I looked away for just a moment and then turned back. The stranger had disappeared.

"Did you see that guy who was just here with us?" I asked José when he got closer.

"What guy?" he said. "I didn't see nobody. Just you and Jerry. You must be beat from pushing that chair and everything. Did you push that all the way from the hospital?" José shook his head in admiration. I glanced around, and then shrugged. He propped the door open. Jerry began to stir as we rolled down the hallway to the elevator.

"What's going on?" he groused when the doors opened. "I'm cold." For once, I was glad to hear the familiar, cranky tone. It meant Jerry was back to his old self.

Who was that man with the injured arm? A divine messenger? Or merely a helpful stranger? What mattered was his assistance, his gracious heart, when I needed it most. To this day, I still wonder. Perhaps there is a new protocol in heaven. Some angels earn their wings one at a time. If so, that's just fine with me.

— Cindy Legorreta —

87

Heaven Pays a Visit to the ER

You are not alone. Your angels are by your side.
~Author Unknown

I watched him bounce down the hallway. It was 11:30 on a Wednesday night in the emergency room of a prestigious Chicago hospital. As I stood there, I wondered why he was so happy. He was amazingly light on his feet, and there was something about him that was a bit familiar. The rest of the ER was quiet and somber, with not too much going on. But there he was, walking toward me while pushing a gurney, with a spring in his step almost as though he had wings. He was aglow with joy, shining in the semi-darkness.

As he approached me, he extended his hand and introduced himself. "Hi, there!" he said. "My name is John, and I'm here to take Marge." My eighty-eight-year-old mother had been ill and was going to have a CAT scan. John was here to take her downstairs. The doctor had encouraged me to go home and get some sleep, so I gave Mom a kiss on the forehead, making sure she knew that the picture of Dad, who had passed away nine months ago, was lying next to her head. They had been together for almost seventy years, and I knew how much she missed him. I looked at her and said, "I love you, Mom!" Then I patted the photograph and said, "Don't worry. Dad's here." She looked off into the corner for some reason, and she said, "I know."

When I got close to home about an hour later, my cell phone rang. It was a doctor from the emergency room who had just started his shift. "Hi, Gail," he said. "How are you?" We exchanged pleasantries, and then he asked me where I was. I explained to him that the doctor on call had told me to go home and come back in the morning.

"Well," he said, "I don't want you to speed or get in an accident, but you need to come back to the hospital. Your mother has an aneurysm, which has burst."

My heart felt as though it was lodged in my throat. "Is she dead?" I asked frantically.

The reply was no, but he also said that he was not sure how much time she had left. I turned the car around and headed back to the hospital.

Entering through the emergency-room door, I suddenly felt a sense of tranquility that I could not explain. When I was quickly ushered into a side room, I knew she was gone. I was told that she had not died alone, though. They attempted to comfort me, explaining that a group of nurses, doctors and the chaplain had gathered around her, held hands and prayed. She had passed away peacefully as she slept.

But the funny thing is, I knew she wasn't alone. My mother had looked into the corner and said my father was with her. And that surprisingly happy man had bounced down the hallway with a big smile on his face. He had taken my hand and introduced himself as John. He had reassured me that he was there to take Marge. And John was my dad's name.

— Gail Gabrielle —

88

The Voice

Everyone was born with a guardian angel.
Guardian angels brighten our journey of life
with divine love, protection, peace, healing,
grace, strength and, miracles.
~Lailah Gifty Akita

My mother, sister and brother were asleep when I got home, and it was eerily quiet. I decided to hit the sack early because I couldn't bear the creepy calmness of our house. I took a shower to help me get sleepy, and then I slipped between my crisp sheets, smelling fresh from the dryer sheets that I keep underneath my pillow. I was off to La La Land.

I've always had vivid dreams, but on this occasion I had an experience that felt far more real. *I was surrounded by total blackness. There was nothing visible around me, and there was no gravity. I was literally floating through the blackness, and the air was very thin. Although I was levitating through this void, there was no sense of fear or panic. I felt at peace and relaxed even though I was alone. I heard nothing — not even the sound of my own breathing. There was no wind. Suddenly, out of nowhere, the silence was broken, and a voice said, "Wake up."*

I opened my eyes and found myself still lying in the same position that I started in, sheets and blanket neat and tight. I heard the voice again: "Get up." I was trying to process what it meant. "Get up!" was repeated with more urgency, so I hopped out of the bed. When my feet hit the floor, I felt a bit off-balance, and I noticed a dull throbbing in my head. I crept slowly to my mother's bedroom and announced, "Mommy, I have a headache."

My mother, who was still asleep, replied groggily without looking up, "Just open the window." I leaned up against her door and wondered to myself, *What does opening a window have to do with my headache?* But I obliged. We lived in a split-level apartment where the bedrooms were on the lower level, and the living room, kitchen and dining area were upstairs. There was a window right above my bed, but that voice was in my ear again. "Go upstairs."

Unsteadily, I climbed the stairs, planning to open the window right at the top of the steps. I made it halfway up but then tumbled backwards. I heard the thuds as my body banged the walls and bounced down the stairs, yet I didn't feel a thing.

The ruckus awakened my mom, and she got up to check on me. She, too, had a dull headache and dizziness. Something was definitely wrong. My mother, who stood 4 feet, 11 inches tall and weighed barely 120 pounds, dragged me, my sister and brother, one by one, outside to our fire escape. It was still late at night.

In the morning, a neighbor found us lying there in the sun and asked if we were okay. I could barely open my eyes, and I couldn't hear his voice very well either, but I did hear the piercing cry of sirens in the background.

We were whisked away on gurneys, with white sheets draped over our limp bodies. I was in and out of consciousness but do remember bright lights, beeping machines, the murmurs of doctors and nurses, and the discomfort of an oxygen mask attached tightly to my face.

Later that day, we learned that we suffered from carbon monoxide poisoning. The attending physician informed us that had we stayed in our apartment through the night, we would have died.

I can only attribute our escape from death to that persistent voice that gave me direction. It made sure that we got to safety. All I can think is that my family has a guardian angel.

— Angel Morgan —

89

Beacon of Flight

You should never feel alone. There's always someone
to turn to. It is the guardian angel
who is watching over you.
~K. Sue

Despite my second-grade teacher's announcement to be seated, I stood in the back of the classroom. I wasn't going anywhere. Besides, I had a valid excuse. I was waiting in line to use the pencil sharpener. This was the 1960s. In those days, each classroom had one industrial-sized pencil sharpener bolted to a countertop. Ours was in the back corner of the room. My desk was located in the first row of desks in front of the teacher's desk.

"Just five more minutes," Miss Winters announced. "You should be seated at your desks, have your books out and be ready for Reading."

It was even my favorite subject. But no matter, I would just stay there.

"Go ahead." I motioned to Jimmy Wilson, my fellow classmate who stood behind me in line. He tightened his grip around his two fistfuls of pencils.

He looked at me, and then down at his fistfuls of pencils. Then he turned to look behind him at the big wall clock hanging on the wall over the door.

"You sure?" He looked down at his pencils again. "I'm gonna sharpen all of these. ALL OF THESE," he emphasized.

"Yeah," I smiled. "That's okay. Go ahead."

"You're not gonna have time, ya know." He scurried past me to the pencil sharpener. "Oh," he smirked. "You think she's not gonna yell at you because you're the teacher's pet."

He was quickly sharpening his third pencil. "One more minute," Miss Winters reminded us.

I neither made eye contact nor glanced in her general direction. I stood with my arms crossed, focusing on Jimmy Wilson sharpening his pencils at a quickened pace.

"We'll take a few extra minutes today," Miss Winters announced. I heard papers ruffling. It sounded like she was redistributing them into piles on top of her desk.

I glanced toward the seated students. Some had turned to look toward me as I stood in the back of the room. Several even motioned for me to hurry up and sit down.

"Okay, that's an extra three minutes. We'll take two more." Miss Winters' voice was strained.

I uncrossed my arms. I felt embarrassed for Miss Winters having to stretch the rules to accommodate what appeared to be my stubbornness. I might need to sit at my desk to save face for her. But my desk had become this forbidden zone in my mind.

"C'mon, Bieber, take a seat," one of my classmates prodded.

I shook my head.

"Why not?" my classmate asked.

I shrugged my shoulders. "I dunno."

Jimmy Wilson shot past me, darting to his seat.

I didn't even move toward the pencil sharpener.

"Okay, time is up," Miss Winters announced.

For a split second, I doubted my instinct. I was about to take a step toward my desk, but was distracted by a loud *dink* and *splaaaaasssshhhh*.

Hundreds of glass shards lay shattered across my desk and chair.

A black bird had flown full speed into the large classroom window.

Miss Winters, in near hysterics, screamed and ran to the back of the room to hug me.

"Oh, my. I wondered why you didn't listen to me. But if you had, you'd have glass in your pretty little face and hands." She was frantic now, her words spoken very quickly.

I stood frozen, and I looked to the girl seated in the desk behind mine. Miss Winters ran over to check on her and then the boy seated to the right of my desk.

The girl seated behind me had something in her eye. She started to cry.

"Gayle, please go get Mr. Meyers (our school principal) and Miss Griffin (our school nurse)," Miss Winters directed the girl seated closest to the door.

"Biebs," Jimmy Wilson shouted over to me. "How'd you know?"

"I didn't." I shrugged.

"You must have." He was amazed. "You always listen to the teacher, but today you didn't."

And the truth is that I didn't know.

I only knew for certain that a calming spirit was impressing upon me not to go near my desk that sunny afternoon in second grade.

— Diane Moore —

Divine Messenger

A little faith will bring your soul to heaven,
but a lot of faith will bring heaven to your soul.
~Author Unknown

Christmas was only a few days away, but there was no joy in my heart. I'd made sure we had a pretty tree, a wreath on the door, the house lit up, cookies baked and presents wrapped, but none of it had made a bit of difference. All of it seemed meaningless with my mother in her final stages of cancer.

She lay just a short trip down the hall from that beautifully decorated tree. *If it weren't for the kids, I wouldn't have bothered,* I thought. I'd put up a good front for the kids, and been pleasant to all the friends and relatives who'd come to visit, but inside my heart was breaking. I knew we were down to a matter of days. The question was only whether it would be before or after Christmas.

Checking in on my mom, I saw that she was awake. Lately, she'd been sleeping more and more. As I sat carefully on the edge of the bed so as not to disturb her frail body, she took my hand and said, "I'm not afraid anymore."

We'd had conversations about this. Her faith was strong, and she had no doubt that she'd see Jesus in heaven. What bothered her was, as she said, "the getting there." Was it instantaneous? Did one head toward the light? Would someone be there to guide her? Other than saying I was sure God had a plan, there wasn't much I could say. It wasn't like anyone I knew had gone all the way to heaven. So when she said her fear was gone, I asked immediately what had changed. Her answer astounded me.

"An angel comes at night and comforts me. He's a big, black man with beautiful, white wings. He picks me up and rocks me. I know now that everything will be fine."

My cynical, doubting self immediately thought, *Yep, cancer has definitely gotten to her brain.* Of course, I smiled and told her how nice that was, but I didn't believe a word of it.

That evening, I gave her the usual pain medications and dragged myself up to bed. It was only 10:00 p.m., but I was mentally, physically, and spiritually exhausted. I slept deeply for a good four hours until a noise awakened me. Some weeks earlier, I'd installed a baby monitor so I'd be able to hear her if she needed me. There was no voice, but I could hear a strange, rhythmic sound. Grabbing my robe, I hurried down the stairs. Softly opening my mother's door, I gazed at her sleeping form huddled under the blankets.

Turning my head toward the sound, I beheld the platform rocker that was in the corner of the room. My mouth literally dropped open as I watched it gently rocking back and forth, back and forth. My logical brain was screaming that this was impossible. That old, heavy platform rocker just didn't move on its own. One could jump up and down beside it, and it wouldn't even twitch. It took feet planted firmly on the ground and a bit of a push with one's legs to get it going. Plus, it always stopped the instant someone got up. Yet here it was, rocking away.

I couldn't see anything, angelic or otherwise, but I had no doubt a big, black man with white wings was sitting in that chair rocking my mother's spirit. I must have stood there a good five minutes watching that chair. In that time, peace was restored to my soul, and I found my faith again.

My mother passed away a few days later on December twenty-third. Glad that she was free of pain and in heaven, I was sad for myself. I chose to sleep in her bed that night so I could experience the familiar smell of her. Lying sleepless in that bed, the room was filled suddenly with the overwhelming scent of roses, which were my mother's favorite flower. At the same time, the chair began to rock. It probably didn't last more than a minute, but I knew that God's newest angel had come back to tell me everything really was all right.

— Terri Sharp —

Angel in the Attic

Angels descending, bring from above,
Echoes of mercy, whispers of love.
~Fanny J. Crosby

It was the summer of 1999, and I had recently moved into an old farmhouse in upstate New York. I was outside building some raised-bed vegetable gardens when a car pulled into the driveway. A thin, pale, thirty-something woman got out, walked over and introduced herself as Vicki, a past resident of the house.

Vicki explained that she had lived in the house during the late 1960s and most of the 1970s with her mother and numerous siblings. Apparently, the happiest times of Vicki's life had been in that old house. And she told me she had used the spacious attic as her secret hideaway whenever she had a bad day.

Vicki walked with me around the yard and reminisced about her childhood experiences: birthday parties, backyard campouts, raking leaves with her sisters, chasing fireflies near the gully in the summer twilight. She noticed some old clamshells under the huge pine trees in the side yard and explained that her mother hosted a family clambake every Labor Day, and everyone always threw the shells out there. I had been wondering where all those clamshells came from.

When she got ready to leave, Vicki became very emotional, and I invited her to stop by anytime. She promised she would visit again.

She seemed nice, I thought as I watched her drive away. *A little odd, but nice. Though I doubt she'll ever stop by again. She was probably just being polite when she said that.*

The next day, I met one of my elderly neighbors at the post office, and I told him about my visitor. He'd been a lifelong resident of the area, and he remembered Vicki and her family. He explained that he had recently heard that Vicki had been diagnosed with a terminal brain tumor. The doctors hadn't given her much time.

Unfortunately, the doctors had been correct. A few weeks later, just before Labor Day, I was saddened to see Vicki's obituary in the local newspaper.

It wasn't long afterward that strange things began to happen around my house.

Occasionally, I would hear shuffling sounds from up in the attic. I was worried it was squirrels looking for a warm place to stay on cool autumn nights, but every time I went up there, I'd find the boxes of Christmas and Halloween decorations undisturbed and orderly with no sign of rodent invasion. What had I heard up in the attic?

That fall, my old cat, Claude, began frequently seeing something around the house. He often stopped and stared, watching something invisible move across the room. Was it just because he was a crazy animal, or could Claude actually see something or someone that I wasn't able to see?

One dreary, rainy morning, as I was scrambling to get ready for work, I couldn't find my keys. I had no idea where I had left them; they could be anywhere — on my desk, in the drawer, on the nightstand. I gave up looking and grabbed a spare set of keys off the key rack by the back door as I headed out to my car. When I got home that night, after an exhaustingly long day at work, my keys were in the middle of the kitchen floor. They hadn't been there that morning — I would have tripped over them. Someone had found my keys for me.

For years, I hadn't been sleeping well. Insomnia, bad dreams, and restlessness always seemed to keep me awake. My doctor had prescribed low-dose sleeping pills, but even those didn't seem to help much. However, that fall, I somehow unexplainably reclaimed a regular nightly seven hours of uninterrupted slumber. Whatever was happening around my house had an extremely positive, restful effect.

For my mother's birthday that year, I decided to invite my family over for a big dinner. I'm not a great cook, but I had found a recipe for slow-roasted beef, supposedly giving the meat extra flavor and tenderness. I put the gigantic roast beef in the oven late on the evening before the dinner at what I thought was a low temperature.

When we got up the next morning, I found the oven door wide open. I checked the oven carefully and discovered that I had actually set the temperature way too high. If the door had not been opened during the night, the expensive roast beef would have been ruined. Who had opened that oven door to save the roast?

Then, one very scary night in early October, about 11:30 p.m., a small but violent storm — the meteorologists called it a microburst — moved through my area.

I was sound asleep but woke to a crash of thunder. Half awake, I stumbled to the window, trying to peek around the curtains, but could see nothing in the darkness except lightning flashes.

At that moment, a woman's soft voice whispered over my shoulder, "Storm warning." I spun around. No one was there except for me; the room was empty.

Another crash of thunder roared, and I didn't hesitate another moment. I grabbed the flashlight off the nightstand, scooped up Claude, who was cowering in the hallway, and headed down to the basement.

The wind was howling as rain slapped against the windows. Thunder and lightning seemed to surround the house. (I found out later that the National Weather Service had issued a severe storm warning for my area about thirty minutes earlier.) Just as Claude and I stepped through the basement door, I heard a gigantic crash and felt the house shake.

Later, when the storm was over, I discovered the crash was one of the giant pine trees in the side yard toppling over and smashing into the wall of my bedroom. If I had been standing there by the window when it happened, I'm sure I would have been crushed along with my dresser and nightstand.

Whose voice was it that I heard that stormy night? I'm sure it was Vicki, my guardian angel who inhabits the attic — finder of lost keys, saver from burnt roasts, sleep supporter, and natural-disaster protector.

Apparently, when Vicki stopped by to visit that day, she wasn't just being polite. When she promised to come back and visit again, she really meant it.

—David Hull—

92

Listen

The guardian angels of life fly so high as to be beyond
our sight, but they are always looking down upon us.
~Jean Paul Richter

All of us have routine tasks in our lives — things we do so often, we can almost do them with our eyes closed. My mornings are usually very predictable. My housemate/ business partner and I usually start our day around 7:00 a.m. As soon as we are both dressed, we begin our morning drive. The travel route is always the same. Kathy, a retired police officer, who drove a patrol car for years, always does the driving. She still knows the timings of the lights and often takes off just seconds before they turn green as I hold onto the armrest. Still, our drive is always full of laughter and lively conversation.

Our first stop is to pick up a freshly baked French baguette and croissant from the local bakery. The employees know our order and often have it ready by the time I get to the counter. Next is the local coffee shop, where I am always greeted by name as they prepare our standard order of a large English breakfast tea and a small coffee. The next stop is to our favorite section on a hill in a nearby park. We sit under a large tree and enjoy a view of the river beneath us. There, we pray and then discuss our plans for the day.

Everywhere we go is within a ten-block radius. The grocery store, the bank, the post office and the drugstores are conveniently located on the main street. The last stop is always the mailbox store. Our mail and packages are sent there so we can offer uninterrupted sessions at our healing center. So, every day, after we gather our mail, we drive directly to the center.

On this day, we were talking and laughing as we approached the red light at the intersection after the mailbox store. Then we both stopped talking suddenly. This time, Kathy did not take off a few seconds before the light changed. In fact, she sat as the light turned green. The driver behind us started beeping his horn. Still, Kathy did not move, and I did not say anything. Within seconds, we heard a loud, rumbling sound, and a huge flatbed tow truck came barreling through the red light, with another car racing behind it. The truck and car were traveling so fast that we both gasped. The car behind us was suddenly silent. No one moved.

Kathy and I looked at each other, and then she slowly drove us through the intersection, pulled over in the next block and parked the car. Both of us had tears in our eyes as we sat in the car, processing what had just happened. As I handed her a tissue, she said, "A voice told me to wait, not to move. I am so glad I listened."

"I am grateful, too," I responded.

She began a prayer of gratitude, and I joined in. We knew that day, in that moment, we were protected and had a purpose.

— Sheila Quarles —

Chapter

10

How Did That Happen?

93

Miracle on Lake Travis

Believe in miracles. I have seen so many of them
come when every other indication would say
that hope was lost. Hope is never lost.
~Jeffrey R. Holland

In April 1995, my wife Debbie and I headed out with our three-month-old daughter to our favorite camping spot: a clearing on a large cove overlooking rugged beauty and awe-inspiring homes perched on seventy-foot cliffs.

Debbie, an avid reader, was happy to curl up under the majestic oak trees with her books. Our daughter was a delightful baby who truly enjoyed the peaceful, outdoor setting. I spent the mornings and evenings fishing. During the days, we took walks in the woods, swam in the clear, cool water, and enjoyed our idyllic time together. During the evenings, we cooked my day's catch of fresh fish over an open fire and then lay together in the hammock watching the stars.

As our week neared its end, Debbie decided to take the baby home and give me an extra day alone for a marathon of fishing. We packed up most of our gear, leaving me the bare necessities, and Debbie and Kayla left. I had no idea at the time that it might be the last time I would see them.

I hit the lake before dawn that glorious Sunday morning. The sun was shining brightly, and the fish were plentiful. After a long day of fishing and swimming, I was ready to head back when I noticed hundreds of crappie crashing against the west edge of the cove. I had to have one more shot at them! I started up my outboard motor and headed across the 2,000-foot-wide lake at full speed.

Then I felt something pulling at my leg. I glanced down and saw that my foot was caught between my fishing rod and the line. As I leaned over to free my leg, I hit the tiller handle on the motor, forcing the boat into a sharp turn. The jolt knocked me into the water. The motor was still turned, causing the boat to circle me. I tried to grab the side of the boat as it circled me, but it was moving too fast. I began to feel desperate, realizing that I was at least 1,000 feet from either side of the lake in 100 feet of water with no life jacket.

Suddenly, shockingly, the motor straightened out, and the boat took off down the lake, leaving me stranded. I tried not to panic and prepared to swim for the bank. The wind was blowing briskly, causing small waves to cover my head at times. I was in pretty good shape, but for some reason, I wasn't making any progress. I could barely move my left leg, and I was desperately out of breath.

About halfway to the bank, I realized I was not going to make it. I was exhausted. I couldn't breathe. I couldn't move my leg. The lake was empty. I slipped under the water, furiously fighting to stay afloat. Suddenly, I had the awful awareness that I could die. I slipped under the water again, praying to God to give me the strength to go on. It was no use. My arms and legs ached to the point that I could no longer move them. I knew it was the end. I said silent goodbyes to my wife and baby daughter and asked God to watch over them.

As I managed to break the surface once more, I was thrilled to see a boat speeding toward me. I was shocked when I realized it was my own boat. For a horrifying moment, I thought that it was coming back to finish me off, but then I saw two men on my boat, waving and shouting. With one last burst of strength, I shouted, "Help me!"

The boat pulled alongside me, and the men lifted me into the boat. I was gasping for breath. As we reached the bank, I finally noticed with horror that my shorts were shredded and barely hanging on my body. Three deep gashes were just below my hip. I realized that when I had fallen into the water and the boat had first circled me, the propeller blades had actually run over me, causing the severe wounds. The frigidness of the lake had kept me from bleeding out.

As we waited for EMS, my rescuers told me how they had come to my aid. George Miller and Grady Walker were construction workers who had been working on a new home on the cliff inside the cove. They had not been scheduled to work that Sunday, but they had chosen to anyway. Taking a break, they'd noticed my boat driving in circles, but they had thought someone was just playing around on the lake. Even after they saw me and realized I was in trouble, they knew they had no way to come to my rescue. That's when the true miracle occurred. George and Grady heard a crashing sound on the bank below. They looked down and saw that my boat had driven itself onto the shore!

After the boat amazingly straightened out from its spin and headed a quarter-mile down the lake, it made an unexplainable ninety-degree left turn into the country-club harbor, then drove itself past dozens of expensive yachts and pleasure boats without touching any of them, before turning to the left again, and finally crashing onto the bank below where the men were working. It was a miracle!

Taking advantage of this amazing opportunity, George and Grady dropped their tools, ran down the steep bank and hopped onto the boat. Quickly, they pushed it back into the water, hopped on board, and headed straight back for me, saving my life! George said it seemed that someone had been driving the boat. I said, "Yes! God was driving the boat!"

My wife met me at the hospital. She and the doctor were amazed by my experience. The gashes in my leg required nearly sixty stitches. There is no doubt that if the boat had not made its miraculous trip to the shore and the construction workers had not come to my rescue, I would have drowned in the lake.

A few days later, Debbie and I went back to Lake Travis to seek out my rescuers. Again, they told us their version of what had happened, and we all agreed that a miracle had taken place.

About six months later, I received a sad phone call from George's wife. She told me he had died of pneumonia. She'd found the thank-you note we had given him and called to give me the sad news. I said another prayer, thanking God for extending George Miller's life, allowing him to save mine before God called him home.

— Michael Evans —

94

Written for Love

When two people are meant to be together,
they will be together. It's fate.
~Sara Gruen

O
n Sunday, October 9, 1994, I was dragged to a Detroit Lions
football game by my father. His buddy had bailed on him at
the last minute, and my mother had other plans. So, that left
me.

I was seventeen years old, and I brought two things with me
to the game: my signature brand of teenage sarcasm and an issue of
Seventeen magazine — because that's how we passed the time in the
era that pre-dated smart phones. I could have thought of a million
and one places I would rather have been that day.

Only ten years later would I come to realize the significance of
this date and how it would change my life forever.

I had always loved to write. When I was eight, I "published" my
first lifestyle magazine, a creation comprised of an entire roll of Scotch
tape and two steno pads I pilfered from my dad's home office. To this
day, the three issues are still in my possession. They, along with several
issues of *The Explorer*, the high-school newspaper for which I was
editor-in-chief, are tucked inside a box in the basement.

Many years later, in 2000, I found myself living more than 900
miles from home in South Carolina while I worked as an on-air reporter
at a CBS affiliate. Often anxiety-ridden and homesick, I grew ever more
dependent on the act of writing as a much-needed cathartic release.

I wrote an entire children's book one afternoon in the time it took to down three lattes at my favorite café in Five Points. The next day, I illustrated a makeshift cover and printed a prototype copy at a local Kinko's. It pacified me to hold a hard copy in my hands. In the months that followed, I queried countless literary agents.

I was certain my book would become The Next Big Thing. But when, over time, the ratio of rejection letters to junk mail became 3-to-1, I relinquished hope, and my lone copy took its rightful place in the dark, dusty abyss under my bed with my other past writing ventures.

Fast-forward to the fall of 2004.

I was back home in Michigan and working for my local government-access channel as a content creator, which meant that a typical day could include myriad tasks — including taking photos of a meet-and-greet between the mayor and a local resident at City Hall. She had, ironically, just published her own tome about her tenure as a den mother at my college alma mater. She brought her publisher with her that day, and at the end of the meeting, something occurred to me: I was inhabiting the same airspace as a book publisher.

This chance may never come again, I thought.

I pushed aside my apprehension and literally chased down the publisher in the parking lot. I told her I had written a children's book and asked whether she'd like to read it.

"Sure, I never turn down an opportunity to read new work," Marian said. Then she gave me her business card and invited me to her office the next evening.

On cloud nine, I floated to my car and swore I heard cherubs playing harps in the clouds above.

This could be the turning point, I thought. *This is going to change everything.*

And it did — but not nearly in the way that I had believed.

Twenty-four hours later, with my dusty prototype in hand, I waited nervously for Marian in the cozy lobby of her office. I tried my best to ignore the fact that my stomach was doing flip-flops as I perused the framed book covers that lined the walls. When Marian finally greeted me, I felt in my bones that everything I had written up to this point had led me to this precise moment.

And it had — but, again, not nearly in the way that I had believed.

About five minutes into our chat — before I had even handed over my book — Marian made my head spin with a question straight out of left field.

"Are you single?" she asked.

Flabbergasted, I managed to reply in the affirmative. "But... why?"

Marian scurried off and returned with a photo in hand. There were three people in it: Marian, Football Hall of Famer and former Detroit Lions running back Barry Sanders, and a man I didn't recognize.

"Scott," Marian said as she pointed to the man I didn't know. "His name is Scott Conover. And I think you two would be perfect together. He's a client of mine. He also wrote a children's book — after he retired from the NFL. He played with the Detroit Lions from 1991 until 1996."

I would later realize that Scott was indeed on the field — as a starting offensive lineman — during the game I attended with my father back in 1994.

But I hadn't connected the dots during my sit-down with Marian. All I knew was that I had zero aspirations to date an NFL player. Weren't they all flirtatious partygoers? I mean, I didn't know any personally. But that's what I had come to believe. No, thank you.

When I politely declined, Marian persisted. She told me that Scott was a graduate of Purdue University, had a passion for philanthropy, had never been married and didn't have any children — although he wanted to someday. An avid reader, he'd founded a children's foundation in an effort to promote and encourage literacy among underprivileged youth.

Marian continued, "A fundraiser is planned for his foundation next Saturday. Black tie. You should come. I'll tell him you're my guest."

Well, gee, I thought, *perhaps I should at least meet him.*

And so I did.

On Saturday, October 9, 2004, ten years to the day after I watched him play at the Pontiac Silverdome, I came face-to-face with the man who, after a three-year courtship, would become my husband on July 7, 2007. (Sidebar: We were married by the mayor — who had since become a judge — whom I had met on that fateful day at city hall.)

Was this all just one giant coincidence? I prefer to believe there are none.

I do, however, believe in a higher power who arranges circumstances and happenings in a way that defies logic.

Today, eleven years of marriage and two beautiful children later, Scott and I still regale our friends — and each other — with the grandiose plans we envisioned for our respective books. Scott had once set his sights on a nationwide book tour; I had hoped for soaring book sales and my name on a bestseller list.

In the end, our books produced none of the above.

But they were written to bring us both a love we never knew was possible.

And what could possibly be greater than that?

— Courtney Conover —

95

Face-to-Face with a Miracle

Life is funny... We never know what's in store for us,
and time brings on what is meant to be.
~April Mae Monterrosa

It had rained all summer. The fields were soaked, the basement was damp, my flowers were beat up, and I was weary. Fortunately, my husband of thirty years and I were leaving on a flight for the sunny beaches of Los Angeles.

Being farm people who didn't fly too often, we had arrived two hours early for our flight. As we waited, my attention was drawn to a woman sitting in a yoga pose. She was beautiful — with a fresh manicure, sparkling diamond ring, fashionable platform sandals, and a red carry-on bag. Her facial features seemed familiar to me — the lips, the structure of her nose, the color of her toned skin. I started to shake slowly from the inside out, wondering silently if she was the birth mother of our twenty-six-year-old daughter. The adoption had been private; we had been blessed to be the ones chosen.

She closed her laptop, packed up her belongings, and headed to the ladies' room. I knew it was her, as only a mother knows. I turned to my husband and said, "I'd swear that is our birth mother." He went to talk to her, and confirmed that she was indeed our daughter's birth mother!

Then our flight started boarding. My legs were shaking as I went through the motions of moving forward because I really wanted to stay with the woman. We were about to board the same plane and would likely be separated by rows and rows of seats. And we had a lot to talk about.

We boarded and discovered that we were, indeed, seated quite far apart. I wondered if I should try to find an empty seat next to her. Or perhaps she would come back and seek us out? On the other hand, maybe she didn't want to talk to us at all!

I was so eager to be near her and thank her, to fill her in on the last twenty-six years. But I did nothing. I tried to reassure myself. If it was meant to be, she'd reach out to us when we landed at LAX.

Soon, the announcement came for landing. We were trapped in the back of the plane, stuck behind all the people slowly disembarking ahead of us. It was so frustrating. What if we lost our chance?

But when we emerged from the jet bridge, there she stood, waiting for us. Emotions flooded all of us, and she rested her shaking hand over her mouth. I remember asking if I could have a picture with her and promising not to share it on Facebook. As we clung to each other, fighting back tears, a sense of love clouded my thoughts and vision. I don't remember many of the details of the conversation that followed. I do remember saying "thank you" repeatedly.

She insisted on giving us a ride to our hotel. Before I knew it, a car was edging through the traffic and making its way to the curb. Oblivious to what was happening, a young gentleman jumped out to open the trunk. She introduced him as her fiancé, David. Then she proceeded to tell him that she'd offered to take us to our bed and breakfast. He was agreeable, but looked a bit perplexed. I'm sure he must have been thinking, *Where did she meet these two?* We merged through rush hour and set off for the unknown again.

At this point, she said to him nonchalantly, "Do you remember the baby I told you I gave up for adoption?" He nodded, and she said, "These are the parents who adopted my baby!" With that, he darn near drove off the road as he glanced to the back seat where Jim and I sat cozily. He started asking questions.

"Where did you find them?"

"How did you know it was them?"

And again, we all concluded, it was meant to be!

I don't remember the route to our destination. In fact, I had to pinch myself to make sure I wasn't dreaming.

It was time to say goodbye, but we'd had an encounter that I will cherish the rest of my days, as I stood with this brave woman who had changed the course of my life. I had come face-to-face with my miracle, and now it was time to move on. We hugged. We cried. We thanked each other. We shared a most perfect love story in the form of our daughter.

—Denise Wasko—

A Taste of Heaven

Do you think the universe fights for souls to be
together? Some things are too strange
and strong to be coincidences.
~Emery Allen

My friend Susan and I were running errands on a deliciously sunny day in early spring when we decided to stop for ice cream. There was a great little place near her house that had quite an extensive menu. They offered dozens of flavors that could be scooped onto cones and topped with anything from rainbow sprinkles to brownie chunks, various soft-serve tastes to combine into an incredible array of sundaes and, of course, all the standard fare: banana splits, milkshakes, malts, and ice-cream sodas.

After some deliberation, Susan chose butter pecan in a waffle cone, and I went for the chocolate vanilla twist with toasted coconut. As we sat finishing up our frozen treats, Susan's mother Agnes called to ask if we would mind stopping by her house to pick up a box of donations she had ready for the Salvation Army.

"Why don't we surprise her with an ice cream?" I suggested after Susan told her we'd be right over.

"She'd love that!" Susan replied. "But I wonder what we should get her… She likes just about everything they have here."

The two of us got back in line and looked at the menu, considering all the possibilities. We were still debating when we reached the counter, where we overheard a lady's voice behind us mention chocolate milkshakes. We couldn't quite make out the conversation, other than something about how a chocolate milkshake would be just perfect.

"That's it!" Susan said, and ordered a large one to go.

The clerk filled our order, Susan paid for it, and the two of us went back to her car.

Just before driving off, we noticed a woman walking toward the far corner of the parking lot. We only got a quick glimpse of her before she disappeared behind the building, but for that moment Susan and I were transfixed.

"Did you see that lady?" Susan asked, pointing to the spot where she had just been. "She looked a lot like Linda. I mean, really looked like her."

I had thought the same thing myself when I saw the stranger. She bore a striking resemblance to Linda, Susan's older sister who had died of breast cancer four years earlier. With the same hair color and body type, she even walked with the same carefree stride Linda had before the illness overtook her. Or maybe talk of Agnes and this lovely spring day had us feeling nostalgic for the loved one we wished could be here with us now.

The drive to Agnes's place took about fifteen minutes. When we arrived, Susan rang the bell, but no one answered. She gave the door three hard raps.

"Mom! Are you there? It's us!"

A few seconds later, Agnes appeared in the doorway looking a bit bleary eyed.

"Sorry, I must have dozed off. I hardly ever do that in the middle of the day," she said as she opened the door for us. "I was having the strangest dream. Your sister Linda was here, and we were having chocolate milkshakes."

— Miriam Van Scott —

97

The Easter Island Statue

The best place to seek God is in a garden.
You can dig for him there.
~George Bernard Shaw

Daniel was teaching in the United States when his father died. His father had gone into the hospital for a standard heart procedure and died on the table. As home was New Zealand, Daniel could not afford the sudden expense to return.

Several years after this occurred, Dan and I met. Not only did he love me, but he bonded closely with my five-year-old son. After a whirlwind romance, we decided to move in together and start a life as a family.

We had a truckload of boxes and possessions emptied into the center of the living room of our first apartment. My boxes were labeled meticulously as to which room they were for and the order in which they should be unpacked. Daniel's items were mainly an unlabeled pile of laundry baskets and boxes.

One of the first things I noticed in Daniel's messy pile of stuff was a small granite statue.

"What's this?" I asked as I lifted up the Easter Island–style stone head.

"Dad gave it to me after he visited there. It was a souvenir. Where did you find it?" Daniel examined it. "It's the only thing I have left of his. Funny, I don't remember packing it."

"Then we should put it right up. I know just the place," I replied as he handed it back to me. I placed it on the living-room window ledge. "It will be like he's here with us."

We moved several times after that. Somehow, that little statue always ended up in one of the first boxes I'd unpack, even if the box was labeled to be opened last.

Finally, we decided to buy a three-story log cabin in the Pine Barrens of New Jersey. That little statue showed up first as always, regardless of being packed in Box 12. Again, the statue took a place of honor in the living-room window.

We were only in our home a month when Hurricane Irene hit. Many unpacked boxes were still in our bottom level. Being in a lake community, we had a tremendous amount of flooding, and the drain on the street in front of our home overflowed. We woke up to no power and three inches of water in our basement. Daniel injured his back trying to lift a heavy box and was hardly able to move.

After several phone calls, our insurance agent informed us we did not have flood insurance. We were on our own.

I was still nursing our eight-month-old daughter at the time. I handed her to my eleven-year-old son and began the hard work ahead of me. I used a neighbor's shop vac after the power came on and we began to clean up, ripping up three rooms of carpeting and carrying up what belongings could be salvaged.

Everything was in disarray, and that little statue got lost in the shuffle. It was three years before I found it again.

After two years of hurricanes, I finally got the opportunity to start my garden, which consisted of mostly pots and a few raised beds.

One day, as I was going through my pots and pruning, I found that little statue.

"Did you put him here?" I asked my husband, a bit spooked by the sudden appearance of the statue.

"No," my husband said with a smile. "But my dad did always love his garden. He must be giving his approval."

Neither of our children admitted to putting it there, but there it remained.

Fast-forward two years later. It was spring, and my daughter and

I were preparing to head out to the garden. Almost all our yard has been transformed from white sand into a green herbal paradise.

It was a Sunday morning, and Daniel was reorganizing his study when he shouted from the downstairs, "Hon, did you put my dad's statue outside my study on the bookshelf?"

"No! The last time I saw 'him' was in the garden," I replied. And then I wondered if I'd ever get used to my father-in-law moving that statue around, making sure he remained part of our life!

— Nicole Ann Rook McAlister —

98

At Last Sight

Deeply, I know this, that love triumphs over death.
My father continues to be loved, and therefore
he remains by my side.
~Jennifer Williamson

When my father died, it was a relief. He had struggled with lung cancer and it had been so hard to see him unable to breathe. I didn't cry when he died, because I knew that living longer would have only prolonged his suffering.

So I remained dry-eyed even though I no longer had someone to rescue me when I walked into the pool convinced I could walk on water. I no longer had someone who said he loved me even though he had to listen to the horror of me playing the flute. I no longer had the clever man who only pretended to hold up my bike as I rode it on my own without realizing it.

I didn't cry when I picked out that God-awful black hat and marched up to the altar to share my recollections of the man he was. I didn't cry when I bent over his casket to say goodbye. I didn't cry when my mother refused to allow my precious stuffed monkey to be buried with him.

There were no tears when I had to get a job because my father had been the breadwinner, and there wasn't much bread to be won after death.

No, I saved all of my tears for my second year in college. By that time, my friends had forgotten about my pain. They remembered vaguely that I was without a father. And I did my best to ignore that fact, too, preferring to imagine him at home 500 miles away with my mother and brother.

He couldn't call me, I lied to myself. He was too busy. There were lots of babies born in August and September. He was home. I was at school.

I didn't cry until my sophomore year when I saw him for the first time since his death.

Medical Ethics 101 was one of those classes that sound amazing in a departmental write-up, the kind of class one envisions will entail lively discussion on the pressing issues of the day.

It was anything but.

The conversations were stilted. No one wanted to share. The discussions were as uneventful as a middle-school dance with boys on one side and girls on the other. But there were no gender lines in Medical Ethics, just those who wanted to debate and those who didn't. And the professor sat firmly on the latter side.

It was just an average Friday of biding my time in a class I was hoping would produce an easy A to balance out my C in Econ. My curly-haired, ex-hippy professor slogged through yet another uninspiring topic, sidestepping the potential for lively debate by showing a video of a medical conference. My mind was on spring break and how, while all my friends were off to warm locales, I would be venturing home to a house now occupied by (only) two other people — hardly somewhere I wanted to be.

I was starting to doze off. The last thing I wanted to do was watch a video in which middle-aged medical professionals talked about end of life. But then, three rows behind one of the panelists from Jefferson Medical College, I saw my dad. He wasn't taking notes like everyone else. Instead, he was staring directly into the camera.

The video switched angles and another panelist was shown, but I continued to watch intently. For the next hour, I saw my father twenty-seven times. Most of those times, he looked directly into the camera like he had looked at me hundreds of times over breakfast right before flashing me a smile.

That class gave me something nobody else could — one more hour with my dad.

Years later, I would tell this story to my twin sons, who would ask if I ever told the instructor and whether she had given me a copy of the video. I shook my head with tears in my eyes.

They may not understand, but to bring my professor into it and to ask for the video might have shown me something I didn't want to see. Maybe it wasn't my father. Maybe it was just some other middle-aged guy with white hair in a suit. To ask might've pointed to a reality I didn't want to accept.

So I saw it for what I wanted it to be. I chose to believe.

For one final hour, I was in the same room as my dad again.

— Christina R. Green —

For Good But Not Forgotten

When you open your mind to the impossible,
sometimes you find the truth.
~From the television show, Fringe

In *Chicken Soup for the Soul: Miraculous Messages from Heaven*, I shared a story about my late cousin Morgan, who died of pancreatic cancer at age sixty-two. Morgan was one of those vibrant, generous and positive souls who had an almost otherworldly "life force" about him.

So I guess I shouldn't have been all that surprised that, a year or so after his passing, Morgan's wife Jennifer and their two adult kids, Adam and Alana, appeared as guests on the television show of noted medium John Edward. But I must admit I was totally blown away by the reading itself, especially the part where Mr. Edward stated confidently that the last piece of music my cousin heard before he left this world was a certain song from the Broadway show, *Wicked*.

It was indeed a recording of a song from that musical, entitled "For Good" (on which my wife was singing) that was played for Morgan on the night he died. Nobody except Jennifer, my wife and me would have even been aware of the details of this very private moment, and it turned out that Jennifer didn't even know that "For Good" was from that particular show. So, trust me, nobody could have shared that nugget of information with John Edward except Cousin Morgan himself!

Now, let's move the calendar up a decade or so (during which period, well, let's just say Morgan had made his presence known on more than one occasion). My wife Dana and I had just watched a show we enjoy called *Better Things*. Both of us had been totally captivated by the little girl who plays the youngest daughter on the show. It's not only that she's cute as a button and a remarkably mature and talented actress for her age, but there's something kind of magical about her — an "old soul" to a degree I've rarely seen in a kid this young.

We have a collection of butterfly-winged angel fairies in our living room. I had actually remarked to Dana on that Friday night, "If I could pick one face to place on one of these angel dolls, it would probably be *this* kid's!"

When I woke up the next morning, I went to my e-mail and hurriedly scrolled the headlines of the notes I received. I say "hurriedly" because Dana and I needed to get ready to leave for Long Island to visit my late Cousin Morgan's family at his longtime home in Massapequa. We were headed there to celebrate Morgan and Jennifer's son Adam's fortieth birthday. Dana and I hadn't seen the whole wonderful Glatzer crew for at least a year and a half, so this was going to be a truly special occasion. Anyway, one of the e-mails I received was from Dana, and the headline read: "You're not going to believe this!" I clicked on it to find a video of that young actress from *Better Things*, at age eight, in her first ever public singing performance from 2015.

Oh, wow… She's a singer, too? I said to myself, thinking that was the main point of Dana's e-mail. Then it hit me what song she was singing in that first public performance. Yes, it was that song, "For Good," from *Wicked*. It was the one Dana had recorded for Cousin Morgan, the last song he listened to on the night he passed away. And she was singing it as a duet with Kristin Chenoweth, the person who had performed it in the original *Wicked*! So cool!

But then I happened to read the notes under the video. This otherworldly little girl with whom we had so been fascinated? Turns out her father is none other than psychic John Edward himself! Yes, the same John Edward who gave Morgan's family that reading on TV and, somehow, knew the last thing Morgan heard before he died was that song from *Wicked*. Mind-blowing indeed, but also very reassuring about whatever the world is which lies beyond!

Two hours later, we were on the train to Long Island to meet up with the rest of my late Cousin Morgan's family. Boy, did I have a story to tell them! I happened to check Facebook on my phone, and up came that annoying "People You May Know" feature. The first name that popped up was a woman with a first name I hadn't heard or seen in decades: Fritzi. I just shook my head and looked toward the heavens. Fritzi? Yep, that was Morgan's *mother's* name!

— Gary Stein —

My Mother's Namesake

Miracles come in moments. Be ready and willing.
~Wayne Dyer

I was in San Francisco, attending a few work conferences and my boss was staying across town. After the drive in from the airport, it became clear that the hotel I was staying in wasn't exactly in the best part of town. It was, however, beautiful, and it was still filled with lush Art Deco décor. In fact, I don't think it had ever been updated.

The elevator groaned as it reached my floor, and groups of backpackers shoved past me, speaking quickly in foreign tongues. When I got to my room and started unpacking I noticed the iron-colored stains on the fabric headboard of my bed. I decided it might be best to just keep my clothes in the suitcase this time. I didn't feel at all comfortable in my room.

I decided to leave the hotel and explore a bit. Naturally, I had packed heavier clothing than what was needed. The days were warm, but I was relieved to find the nights were cold. I stepped out onto the sidewalk that first evening with nervous excitement. The city was lit up beautifully. I was happy that I had worn my new coat. It was floor-length. Vintage. 1930s. Black velvet.

A week prior to the trip, a friend from my dart league had stopped me downtown. "You're just the person I'm looking for. My mother has been cleaning out her closet, and I have some clothing there I think you'll just love. I'll bring you this coat. It just *screams* your name."

I forgot all about it until a few days before I was set to leave when Sue found me again and handed me the coat. I just about fell over from excitement. The coat was just like new. The label inside said, "Himelhoch, Detroit, MI." A nice vintage label. Looking at the size, I knew it would be too small, but I slipped it on anyway. I couldn't believe it. It fit like a glove.

At this time in my life, I was heavy into vintage clothing. I wore things with moth holes in the lining, and I pin-curled my long, auburn hair and wore tiny hats made of nothing more than pipe cleaners and flowers. If it was old and worn, I probably owned it, even daring to use lipstick that was long past its expiration date and rouge that probably should have turned to dust. This coat was a stunner. I wanted to *live* in it. It fit in just the right places. It had a beautiful, wide lapel, puffed sleeves with tight arms, and a tiny, pleated waist.

I daydreamed while I wore the coat. I could be a young Hollywood starlet heading to her big premiere, or maybe a typist in a newspaper office. I could be anyone in this coat. Greta Garbo herself would be jealous, and I was confident in it. That's exactly why I wore it on my trip. I also didn't want to let it out of my sight for fear it might disappear.

I walked around San Francisco alone a lot that week. I didn't know a soul, but I did enjoy the conferences. I explored without the aid of GPS or a map. I even found the house that was filmed for the TV show *Full House*. Danny, Jesse, Joey and the girls weren't there.

I explored as much as I could. And when I'd get nervous walking at night, I'd tug the coat just a little bit tighter around myself, straighten my shoulders, and walk on with a smile. I felt invincible.

The trip went well, and when I came home, I showed everyone the photographs. I also showed my mother the coat. She, who made almost all of my clothing growing up and whose mother worked as a seamstress, was fascinated with it. Deep down in the lining, we found something unusual. A tag had been stitched in at the bottom of the coat. It was almost undetectable. I certainly hadn't noticed it before. The name "Eva" was sewn there.

"Where did you get this coat?" my mother asked. "Why is my name inside?"

"I don't know, Mom. I'll ask my friend Sue. She gave it to me. I don't have her number or anything."

The next week, I ran into Sue again. "Sue, the inside of the coat says 'Eva.' It's just... my mom's name is Eva. Is that your mother's name?"

"No. My mother's name is Maxine," she replied. "My grandmother's name was Eva. I guess it was hers when she was young."

"May I ask her maiden name?"

"Truax. Eva Truax. My mother is Maxine Hill."

I was startled, to say the least. "My aunt's name is Maxine. She's my mom's sister. I'm pretty sure my grandmother was a Truax, but then I could be wrong."

I phoned my mother with Sue still standing there. She was just as excited as I was. "Eva Truax? You're sure?" she sounded surprised.

"Yes, I'm sure. The coat belonged to Eva Truax," I replied.

"Well, I'll be danged. That's my Aunt Eva. I was named after her," replied my mother. I'd been wearing her aunt's coat all along. It turns out, she even shares Aunt Eva's middle name.

The coat I treasured so much had come full circle. I had no idea that Sue was my cousin. As far as I knew, she was just a friend with great taste and a kind heart. My mother had a namesake. That's something else I had never heard.

My family's history opened up before me. My mom and Sue got together in person and had a great time reminiscing. At family functions, cousin Sue is now with us.

Someone sent that coat my way. It was more than just coincidence. It was more than just happenstance. It was heaven-sent.

— Amanda JE Phillips —

The Radio That Couldn't Be Stolen

Life is a series of thousands of tiny miracles.
~Mike Greenberg

When I was seventeen, my friends and I were surf bums. There's no point in candy-coating it. We were sand-loving, wave-crazy, hedonistic, adrenaline junkies who were perpetually sunburned and determined to never grow up. We couldn't wait for the school bell to ring so we could get back to the beach and surf some more, and then play volleyball under the lights of the pier until it was too dark to continue.

One summer morning, my friend Matt and I were playing two-man volleyball at a beach in Malibu, California. Wedged in the sand at the edge of the court was a medium-sized transistor radio playing a Beach Boys cassette tape. There was nothing special about this radio. In fact, it was a wreck. I'd gotten it secondhand from my father as a child and had put a lot of wear and tear on it since. The antenna was bent, the speaker cover was dented, the plastic housing had been cracked and taped back together, and it was plastered with stickers on every side. It wasn't worth much when it was new, and all the damage over the years had rendered it worthless.

We were playing two other beach bums who challenged us and getting overheated when a snow-cone vendor passed by on the road above the volleyball court. We called time-out, and the four of us went to buy some. We were only gone a minute. When we came back, we discovered our radio was missing. Matt and I were so annoyed that we abandoned the game and vowed to find it. It was like losing an old friend. We walked the beach listening for radios. It was no easy task because it was the middle of summer, and the beach was packed. When we heard music, we followed it to the source. After three or four "investigations," we found our radio entertaining a group of younger kids.

I snatched it from them and said, "I'll take that, thank you!" Their mother yelled "Hey!" and instead of chastising the children for showing up with a radio none of them had brought, she proceeded to chew us out! But when we suggested calling the police to referee the argument, she became a lot friendlier, even offering us money for our trouble (and to keep her little angels out of juvenile court). We returned victoriously to the volleyball court with an extra five dollars.

On the way home that night, we stopped to see a movie in Hollywood. We parked on a side street near Grauman's Chinese Theatre. When we came back out, we found the window broken and the radio stolen again! Oddly, nothing else was taken. Our surfboards were still in the back of my friend's pickup. Even banged up as they were, they were much more valuable than that old radio. Our wetsuits were still inside the car, too.

"Oh, well," I said with resignation. "It looks like we were destined to lose that radio today."

Matt wanted to file a police report to submit with an insurance claim for his broken window, so we went to the nearest police station a few miles away. They took our report, and we left. We drove up Cahuenga Boulevard several miles away from where the car was broken into. I was casually looking out the window when I saw a guy walking along the sidewalk and holding a radio to his ear that looked remarkably like ours! I turned to Matt and yelled, "Stop! I think I just saw our radio!"

"What?" he replied. "You're crazy. That's impossible!"

He wasn't in a very good mood after sitting on pieces of his broken window and getting blasted by wind through the now-empty opening.

I talked him into going back, and we pulled up alongside the man. There was no mistaking the bent antenna, dents, taped crack and, most of all, the stickers.

Matt said, "I can't believe it!"

Not knowing what to expect from this thief, we decided to put on a show of force. Matt was a bodybuilder, and I was kind of a karate kid in those days. I had a throwing knife under my seat. We pulled into a driveway in front of the man and blocked his path. I got out, held the throwing knife up with one hand, extended the other hand palm-up, Bruce Lee-style, and yelled, "Radio! Now!"

I must have been a sight. Matt stood menacingly behind me. The thief looked at both of us wide-eyed and said, "Here, man! Take it! Take it! Don't throw that knife at me!"

He had no idea it was all a bluff. I had never thrown a knife at anything but a wooden board and had no intention of throwing one at him over a radio. But our young egos and sacred honor wouldn't allow us to drive away and let some stranger walk away with our trusty, beloved, music-making pal. As the saying goes, you never leave a man behind.

Matt demanded two hundred dollars from him to fix his broken window, but he said, "I didn't break into your car! I just bought the radio for five dollars from some guys at the corner! I swear!"

He seemed sincere and was so terrified that I started to feel sorry for him. Matt wasn't quite so forgiving. He yelled, "Buying stolen property is a crime, too, you know!"

"I know, man! I'm sorry!" the man pleaded.

His fear drained all the machismo right out of me. I handed him the five-dollar bill the mother of the beach delinquents had given me earlier and said, "Here's your money back. Let's go, Matt."

Matt looked at me like I had lost my mind but got into the car.

We drove home listening to our radio and wondering what Twilight Zonian force made it possible to find that radio in two crowded locations twice in one day, particularly miles away from where it was stolen the second time. It was the same needle in two different haystacks.

In those days, we didn't just live on the earth; we lived *in* it. We cavorted with nature, romped with dolphins and seals, and surfed those waves as if they were living, thinking creatures playing joyfully with us. We collected shells and marveled at their wondrous designs. We celebrated sunsets. As we talked and laughed about our good fortune on the way home that night, we wondered why we deserved such divine intervention in a world full of people with much bigger problems. We speculated that God had helped us get that old radio back twice because He appreciated us as much as any artist does those who savor and revel in his masterpieces.

— Mark Rickerby —

Meet Our Contributors

Monica A. Andermann lives and writes on Long Island with her husband Bill and their little tabby Samson. Her writing has been included in such publications as *Guideposts*, *Ocean* and *Sasee*, as well as many other *Chicken Soup for the Soul* books.

Dr. Ruth Anderson is an international best-selling, award-winning author and ordained minister. Founder of Enlightened World, Ruth is devoted to making a difference in the spiritual lives of others. Her passion is to serve as a conduit between the spiritual and physical realms, educating others along the way.

Patricia Beach is pursuing her passion for writing following a diverse career in transportation management. Pat holds a Bachelor of Arts in English from St. John's University and a Master's in Construction Management from NYU/Polytechnic. She enjoys writing poetry as part of the Farmingdale Writing Group.

Barbara Bennett wrote *Anchored Nowhere; A Navy Wife's Story* about the family's twenty-six moves over seventeen years in five countries. This is her second contribution to the *Chicken Soup for the Soul* series. She is currently working on her first mystery. She enjoys crafting, volunteer work and being Grandma Uber to her five youngest grandkids. Her oldest is in the Navy.

Rachel Bliss is enrolled at Keuka College to earn a bachelor's degree in Social Work and will graduate in 2020. She is married and has a two-year-old daughter. Rachel started writing at age seven and has dreamed of becoming a published author. She hopes to write inspirational works that help others find healing in life's struggles.

Barbara Dorman Bower is a CPA and is retired from the financial services industry. This is her third story published in the *Chicken Soup for the Soul* series. She enjoys having the time to explore her creative side, and likes to travel with her husband as often as possible.

Dan Boyle is a firefighter/EMT from Butte, MT. He is married to Ashley, and has two children, Madison and Ben. He enjoys swimming, basketball, cooking, and reading. He hopes to write more often, on a variety of subjects, in different formats.

Dr. Sally Willard Burbank, an Internist from Nashville, released a book for families of dementia patients called *The Alzheimer's Disease Caregiver's Handbook: What to Remember When They Forget*. Her first book, *Patients I Will Never Forget*, shares funny and inspiring stories and is sold online. Learn more at www.sallywillardburbank.com.

Jacqueline Gray Carrico has contributed stories for two previous *Chicken Soup for the Soul* books. She is the mother of a grown son who will soon be married. Jacqueline is a dedicated nurse who often finds inspiration from her patients. She enjoys refinishing furniture in her spare time.

Eva Carter has a history in finance in the telecommunications field. She is a frequent contributor to the *Chicken Soup for the Soul* series. She enjoys writing, photography, working out, traveling, and going out to dinner with her husband, Larry.

Pam Carter earned her Bachelor of Arts degree from Bellarmine College in Louisville, KY. She and her husband, Rick Jeffries, are retired and live in Mount Washington, KY. They also enjoy spending time at their second home in Tampa, FL.

Brenda Cathcart-Kloke lives in Denver, CO where she enjoys writing and sharing inspirational stories. Several of her stories have been published in *Chicken Soup for the Soul* books. Her other interests include oil painting and spending time with her family.

Cj Cole lives on the lower Eastern Shore, home of the Chincoteague Wild Ponies, and has served the shore as a radio personality and advice columnist for more than fourteen years.

Sara Conkle is a wife, mother, grandmother, and nurse. She has worked in the field of Hospice and Palliative Care for two decades. She lives in Ohio and enjoys writing and reflecting about her experiences. This is her second contribution to the *Chicken Soup for the Soul* series.

Courtney Conover is a mother, writer and certified yoga teacher who always believes in miracles. She and her husband, a former NFL offensive lineman, reside in Michigan with their two young children, and they always root for the Detroit Lions. Learn more at courtneyconover.com, Facebook, Instagram, and YouTube.

Gwen Cooper received her B.A. in English and Secondary Education in 2007, and completed the Publishing Institute at Denver University in 2009. In her free time, she enjoys krav maga, traveling, and spending time with her husband and Bloodhound in the beautiful Rocky Mountains. Follow her on Twitter @Gwen_Cooper10.

Maril Crabtree grew up in Memphis and New Orleans but calls the Midwest home. Her essays, short stories and poems have been published in numerous journals and literary magazines. She believes in unexpected blessings and lifelong friendships. Learn more at www.marilcrabtree.com.

Donna Crisler enjoys writing short mystery and children's stories. When not writing, she's either reading, gardening, traveling or working hard to improve her bridge skills.

Denise Del Bianco is a retired widow living in her hometown, Bischwiller, France, after traveling the world with the love of her life, Pietro. After meeting in France he and Denise raised two children in Italy and Canada. She enjoys cooking, reading and cuddling her furry grandkids. Her twitter handle is @DeniseBecht1.

Wendy Newell Dyer is a member of the Passamaquoddy tribe of Maine. She graduated from the University of Maine at Machias in 2003. She has three sons and three grandsons. Wendy enjoys writing, running, hiking and mountain climbing on the coast of Maine. Read her blog at wendynewelldyer.wordpress.com/.

Linda Eiffert is a retired mother of three and has two grandchildren. In her spare time she enjoys gardening, all types of crafts, including rehabbing old and used furniture for interior decorating.

Carol Chiodo Fleischman is the author of the children's book *Nadine, My Funny and Trusty Guide Dog*. She lives with her husband and current guide dog in Niagara Falls, NY.

Gail Gabrielle is pursuing her passion of writing after teaching special education for many years. She is an avid reader, enjoys sketching, working out, and is an advocate for both autism and animal rights. She has three adult children who are the loves of her life and inspire her each and every day.

Joyce Carol Gibson, author of *Salvage Yard of Souls*, enjoys writing. The publication of her book in 2016 by Brighton Publishing Company exposed law enforcement corruption in her community while she worked for the local sheriff. Afraid she would be harassed for her book, she was surprised to be praised by fellow officers.

Julia Gousseva was born and raised in Russia but now lives in Arizona with her husband and her son. She writes fiction and nonfiction stories, mostly set in Russia.

Longtime freelance writer, **Lisa Waterman Gray**, enjoys finding the mystery and magic in life — whether at home or while on the road. She has described great food and terrific travels through the U.S., Quebec and Italy for publications from USAToday.com to *The Kansas City Star*.

Christina R. Green discovered she wanted to be a writer at seven but it wasn't until she was in her late thirties that it became her career. She's the author of the upcoming book *West of You*. When she's not writing, she's on the Internet planning her next adventure with her twin sons, Hayden and Grayson, and their dog Scoobie.

Terry Hans is drawing on forty-five years as a Dental Hygienist to compile a collection of humorous stories from her side of the hygienist's chair. Terry has two accomplished daughters and four athletic grandsons. She enjoys traveling and cheering at her grandsons' sporting events. Terry and her husband live in Willow Spring, NC.

Charles Earl Harrel served as a pastor for thirty years before stepping aside to pursue writing. His stories, devotionals, and articles have appeared in numerous magazines and anthologies. He is also a five-time contributor to the *Chicken Soup for the Soul* series. Charles enjoys camping, hiking, and painting landscape scenes.

Teresa Anne Hayden is a writer living in Cayce, KY. Her greatest treasures in life are her three children, seven grandchildren and her Catholic faith. This is her fourth story published in the *Chicken Soup for the Soul* series. Learn more at teresahaydenwriter.com.

Lori Hein is a freelance writer and author of *Ribbons of Highway: A*

Mother-Child Journey Across America. Her work has appeared in numerous publications and several *Chicken Soup for the Soul* books. Learn more at LoriHein.com.

Kaitlin Hodnett graduated from Louisiana State University at Alexandria with a Bachelor of Arts in English. She was voted one of Louisiana's Best Emerging Poets in 2018 through Z Publishing House. Living with a chronic illness, she turns to writing as an escape from reality, and as an outlet for her unwavering faith.

Julie Rine Holderbaum is a high school English teacher in Minerva, OH. She writes frequently about issues affecting public education for the Ohio Education Association. She enjoys yoga, reading, and spending time with her family. She also writes more personal pieces on her blog, which can be found at thethrillofthehill.blogspot.com.

David Hull is a retired teacher who enjoys spending his days reading, writing and working in the garden. He also enjoys spoiling his nieces and nephews. He's had many stories published in *Chicken Soup for the Soul* books. E-mail him at Davidhull59@aol.com.

When not writing, **Jeffree Wyn Itrich** is usually found quilting, rehabbing furniture, painting, and gardening. As a recent transplant to Texas, she takes great pride in her Texas heritage, going back four generations. She's working on her Texas accent and her pecan pie recipe.

Mary Potter Kenyon graduated from the University of Northern Iowa. She is program coordinator for Shalom Spirituality Center in Dubuque, and author of seven books, including one on creativity to be published in 2019. She speaks and does workshops on writing, grief, and creativity. E-mail her at marypotterkenyon@gmail.com.

After decades of working as a registered nurse, **Linda Kinnamon** realized she had too many experiences of heaven to keep them to herself. *Alchemy of the Afterlife* is her award-winning memoir of these heavenly encounters. When she's not writing, Linda loves exploring the mountains of Colorado. Learn more at lindakinnamon.com.

Nancy Julien Kopp lives with her husband in the Flint Hills of Kansas. She writes essays, fiction for kids, memoir, poetry and more. She has stories published in twenty-one *Chicken Soup for the Soul* books. She loves to play bridge, travel, and enjoy her children and grandchildren. Read her blog at www.writergrannysworld.blogspot.com.

Mary Elizabeth Laufer has a degree in English education from SUNY Albany. As a Navy wife, she moved thirteen times in twenty years, working as a substitute teacher, library assistant, and private tutor. Now that her children are grown, she devotes most of her time to writing.

Caroline Lavoie lives in northern British Columbia with her husband and two daughters. When she is not writing, she can be found working on her farm, kayaking on a lake, or snowshoeing in the forest.

Mandy Lawrence is a registered nurse, Christian speaker, and author of the award-winning book, *Wisdom from Wilbur: How My Dog Has Brought Me Closer to God*, and the novel *Replay*. Mandy and her husband Shane, along with their beloved weenie dog, Wilbur, live in North Carolina.

Cindy Legorreta is often asked where she gets story material. She says it can be found anywhere. Keenly observing what Walt Whitman called the "blab of the pave," Cindy is endlessly inspired. And when she moves to New Orleans, she looks forward to a new batch of flavors and a new locale!

Mary Lennox is a retired professional who worked in the field of finance for forty years. She has been taking a writing class since 2014 and has published short stories in books of anthologies. Mary loves to travel and plans trips for her extended family. She also loves to read and spend time with her husband, three grown children, and two granddaughters.

Bobbie Jensen Lippman is a prolific professional writer who lives in Seal Rock, OR with her robot named Waldo and her cat named Purrfect. Bobbie's work has been published nationally and internationally. She writes a human-interest column for the *Newport News-Times* in Oregon. E-mail her at bobbisbeat@aol.com.

In 2017, **Chris Lowe** lost her beautiful twenty-year-old son, Hudson, to suicide. Since then, she has made it her mission to speak out at high schools and to youth groups in hopes of inspiring young people to "fall forward," the title of Hudson's 2015 speech where he inspired his peers to never give up.

L.M. Lush is a freelance writer and adjunct college professor at Westchester Community College in New York where she teaches courses in Creative Writing and Music Appreciation. She enjoys playing the piano and cello and often hikes with her dogs, Sadie and Oreo. Learn more at LMLush.com.

Joyce Styron Madsen has done corporate and medical research and written children's stories and articles. She is an avid animal advocate, rescue dog mom, Humane Society volunteer, and handler for Lila Comfort Dog. She usually writes surrounded by her four former puppy mill dogs. E-mail her at joycestyron@sbcglobal.net.

Donna L. Marsh attended Tennessee Tech University and went on to a career in cable TV. She now lives in Nashville, where she writes, crafts, volunteers, watches the clouds, and occasionally strolls through cemeteries. She enjoys time with her sons and grandson and excitedly awaits the arrival of her second grandchild.

Amanda Mattox graduated summa cum laude from Cal Poly Pomona with a bachelor's degree in English and a minor in communication. She works at a local university as a writer and editor. She resides in Southern California with her cat, Dottie.

Ange May, an Engineering Technologist, traveler and nature lover, can normally be found enjoying the picturesque scenery surrounding her small mountain home. She only recently returned to her love of writing and wrote this story for her dad, in his loving memory.

Nicole Ann Rook McAlister has studied Journalism and pursues an avid interest in World Religion and Mythology. Nicole enjoys adventures in camping, sunrises on the beach, painting, crafting and all manner of such things. Several of her pieces have been on exhibit at the Whitesbog Art Gallery in Browns Mills, NJ.

Mary B. McGrath is a freelance writer based in Los Angeles, CA. Her work has appeared in a number of books, magazines, newspapers and on several websites. Beyond writing, she enjoys photography, jazz, travel and fine dining.

Kelli Miller, LCSW, MSW is a psychotherapist, radio host, and author. She is a co-host on LA Talk Radio and the author of *Thriving with ADHD for Kids* and *Professor Kelli's Guide to Finding a Husband*. Kelli lives with her husband, who she adores when he does the dishes, their two boys, and their pet whippet Moose.

Ferna Lary Mills lives in East Texas. Her greatest loves are her family, her church, writing, and making sleeping mats for the homeless from plastic bags. She is a published author and currently manages two pages on Facebook: "Rainbow Faith — Encouraging Words," and "Caring Hearts and Helping Hands," her mat ministry.

Diane Moore is an award-winning journalist whose works have appeared in several media. Diane and her husband Col. Patrick H. Moore USA (ret.) call San Antonio, TX home, and travel extensively throughout the U.S. and Europe to visit their six children and six grandchildren.

Angel Morgan, a Philadelphia native and current resident, is a self-published author of *A Maze In Love*, a compilation book of poetry.

Angel's passion for writing was reignited after enrolling in a community college English course in 2015. Since then, she's written essays, poems, short stories and blog articles.

Marya Morin is a freelance writer. Her stories and poems have appeared in publications such as *Woman's World* and *Hallmark*. Marya also penned a weekly humorous column for an online newsletter, and writes custom poetry on request. She lives in the country with her husband. E-mail her at Akushla514@hotmail.com.

Rachel Dunstan Muller is an author, storyteller, speaker and workshop facilitator. She and her family live on Vancouver Island, on the west coast of Canada. Learn more at www.racheldunstanmuller.com.

Jenn P. spends her days growing Japanese maple trees and flowers at her small-town home in Georgia. She has a passion for nature, writing, and being a mother to her two sons. She also enjoys crocheting and reading in her free time. She plans to pursue her love for the written word and write a novel.

Sister Josephine Palmeri, MPF, teaches at Villa Walsh Academy in Morristown, NJ. She has taught Spanish to teens for more than fifty years. She enjoys hiking, reading, writing, and singing. She has published two joke books, *Tales from the Barber Shop* and *More Tales from the Barber Shop & Pittston*.

Nancy Emmick Panko is a retired pediatric nurse turned writer with ten stories published in the *Chicken Soup for the Soul* series. She has also contributed to *Guideposts* and recently published her first novel, *Guiding Missal: Fifty Years. Three Generations of Military Men. One Spirited Prayer Book*. She loves to be on the water with her family.

Jenny Pavlovic, Ph.D. is the author of *8 State Hurricane Kate, The Not Without My Dog Resource & Record Book*, and many published stories. She lives in Wisconsin with dogs Chase and Cayenne and cat, Junipurr.

She loves to spend time with and listen to other creatures. Learn more at www.8statekate.net.

Amy Rovtar Payne lives on a hobby farm with her husband and an assortment of animals. She holds a degree in education, and is a certified horseback riding instructor. Amy enjoys competing in agility with her rescue dogs, working with her American mustang horses, and showing Rhinelander rabbits.

Vicky Webster Pealer is making her publishing debut in this book. She is a proud mother of two children, Cheyanne and Dalton. She works with the elderly, as both a Meals On Wheels driver and as a home health aide. She enjoys lunch dates with friends, laughing with co-workers, and spending time with her family.

Kristen Mai Pham is delighted to have found her true passion for writing in the second half of her life. This is her seventh published story. When she's not writing, she spends time with her adorable husband, Paul, and their imaginary corgis. Follow her on Instagram or e-mail her at kristenmaipham3@gmail.com.

Amanda JE Phillips lives in Michigan with her father, her husband, and her young daughter. She is a dollhouse miniature food artist and loves to paint portraits of people and their pets. She hopes to write children's books one day. E-mail her at miniaturemaker@gmail.com.

Sylvie Phillips has been a diaconal minister in the British Methodist Church for twenty-five years. A qualified counsellor, she has a Master of Arts in Mission from the University of Manchester and specialises in coaching for leadership. Widowed twice, she has recently become engaged to Robert, a local history author. She has one grown son, Michael.

Connie Kaseweter Pullen lives in rural Sandy, OR near her five children and several grandchildren. She earned her Bachelor of Arts degree at the University of Portland in 2006, with a double major in Psychology and Sociology. Connie enjoys writing, photography and exploring nature. E-mail her at MyGrandmaPullen@aol.com.

Sheila Quarles worked in sales until an accident resulted in a traumatic brain injury. Determined not to use medical drugs, she traveled for twenty years to study indigenous healing techniques. She became a Reiki Master and partnered with Kathy Morris to create a holistic healing center. E-mail her at innerjourneys@att.net.

Camille A. Regholec is a pastor and loves writing inspirational stories. She is a published author of various articles as well as a novel, a memoir and a children's picture book. She is finishing up a novel and a mystery. She and her husband, Gerold, live in New York and have four children, ten grandchildren and two great-grandchildren.

Janet L. Revino has earned her bachelor's and master's degrees in Fine Arts. Janet, her husband Augie, and their cat and dog live in Wisconsin, where she teaches drama at a Christian school. Janet is very active in their church and especially enjoys working in its ministry to senior citizens.

Mark Rickerby has contributed twenty-three stories to the *Chicken Soup for the Soul* series. He's the creator/head writer of an upcoming western TV series, co-author of his father's memoir *The Other Belfast*, and lyricist/singer of fifteen original songs for *Great Big World*, a music CD dedicated to his daughters, Marli and Emma. Learn more at www.markrickerby.com.

Rose Robertson received a Master's in Pastoral Studies from Loyola University in 2001. She and her husband have three married sons and four grandchildren; she enjoys gardening, reading, writing, and needlework. Rose works with children as a grief companion, and also with parents who have suffered the death of a child.

Tia Ruggiero is a Licensed Clinical Social Worker providing therapy to children and their families. She and her husband Jamie have four children, Dustin, EmilyAnn, Dominick, and Elias. Tia enjoys spending time with her family, reading, camping, writing, and working with children. She has plans to become a Christian author.

K.C. Runkel is a wife, mother, and writer living in her home state of Wyoming. She is the creative mind behind "The Rustic Hideaway"—a blog about faith, motherhood, and healthy living. When she is not writing, you can find her at the gym lifting heavy things, or spending time with her electrician husband and little boy.

Thomas Schonhardt received his Bachelor of Arts in 2011 from Truman State University. He is married to his wife Laura of three years and has two dogs. Thomas works as a Firefighter/EMT for the Columbia, Missouri Fire Department. E-mail him at TSchonhardt@gmail.com.

Beverly Hood Schultz attended Oklahoma State University and graduated in 1969 with a Bachelor of Arts in Spanish. A former teacher, she is retired and has five young grandsons. She enjoys writing and reading. She has published stories in a few magazines and newspapers in the past and is getting back to writing again.

Mary Bader Schwager has worn many hats throughout her long life, including that of award-winning painter, art teacher, respiratory therapist, craftswoman, docent, and bereavement group leader. At age ninety, she is still designing necklaces. She thanks her daughter, Nancy K. S. Hochman, for her help with this essay.

Susan Sellani-Hosage earned bachelor's and master's degrees from Misericordia University and a graduate certificate in Executive and Professional Coaching from the University of Texas at Dallas. She recently co-authored a vegan cookbook with her twin sister, Sandra. She resides in Pennsylvania with her husband, Stephen.

Elise Seyfried is Director of Spiritual Formation at Christ's Lutheran Church in Oreland, PA. She is the author of three books of humorous spiritual essays and many freelance articles. Elise is also a playwright and has written hundreds of skits and plays for churches.

Terri Sharp lives in Southeast Michigan and has three children and three cats who enjoy helping her write. Her first children's book, *Princess Joslyn and The Dragon*, was published this fall and she is working on the next one.

Mandi Smith began writing at age six and has yet to put down her pen. She was married for sixteen years before being widowed in 2012. She has found love again and shares a home in North Texas with her boyfriend Lonnie, dogs Honeybun and Twinkie, and Bruce the cat. She works in telecommunications but dreams of becoming a writer.

Misty McLaughlin Stantz received her Bachelor of Arts in Elementary Education from McNeese State University in 2005. She has three sons: Deacon, Tyson, and Weston. She currently teaches fifth grade and her husband Brent is an Assistant Principal.

Gary Stein co-founded an NYSE-member investment-banking firm. He was a strategy advisor to Lionsgate, Miramar and Seventh Generation and built a thirty-time Emmy-winning kids TV business. Gary is proud to be a mentor to several outstanding young women. He is a six-time contributor to the *Chicken Soup for the Soul* series.

A.L. Tompkins received a Bachelor of Science, with honours, from the University of Trent, and lives in Ontario, Canada. She has several pieces of short-fiction published, and enjoys reading and spoiling her dog.

Award-winning author **Susan Traugh** writes adult-living curricula for special needs teens from her home in San Diego, CA. She lives with her husband and adult children who were her inspiration for her curricula and YA novel, *The Edge of Brilliance*. Learn more at susantraugh.com.

Deirdre Twible-Kenny is a reading teacher who loves sharing the gift of books and stories with young children, including her own. In preparing to teach a writing workshop for students on memoir writing, Deirdre participated in a collegial workshop for teachers. Her story, "Full Circle," is the product of that workshop.

Miriam Van Scott is an author and photographer who works in print, television and online content. Her books include *Song of Old: An Advent Calendar for the Spirit*, *Candy Canes in Bethlehem* and the *Shakespeare Goes Pop!* series. Learn more at miriamvanscott.com.

Stephanie Schiano Wallace is a public school teacher in Lexington, KY. She enjoys spending time with her husband and two beautiful young children, reading, doing yoga, and being outdoors.

Denise Wasko retired in 2016 after spending thirty years in the Early Childhood Education field. She lives on acreage and enjoys raising alpacas. Recently she has written her first children's book, *Nana D's Alpacas* — a nonfiction story with actual photos and events in the life of her alpacas.

Dorann Weber is a freelance photographer for a New Jersey newspaper and contributor for Getty Images. Her photos have appeared on Hallmark cards and magazines. She has a newfound love for writing, especially for the *Chicken Soup for the Soul* series. She lives in Pine Barrens with her family. E-mail her at Dorann_weber@yahoo.com.

Dorothy Wills-Raftery is an award-winning book author, photojournalist, blogger, and dog radio show host. Inspired by her Epi-dog, she is a Purple Day for Epilepsy Ambassador and founded the FiveSibes #LiveGibStrong K-9 Epilepsy Awareness Campaign. She loves being a mom, grandmother, and "hu-mom" to five Siberian Huskies!

Nicki Wright received her Bachelor of Arts and went on to complete a bachelor of education and a Master's in Special Education. Nicki is currently teaching and has also created a business called The Wright Stuff Bath and Beauty Products. She enjoys watching her three children play sports and coaching soccer.

Fay A. Yoder and husband Richard share three grown children and six grandchildren. She was editor of *The New Republic* for eighteen years, and a high school Administrative Assistant for ten. Along with publishing the local historical society publication, she continues to freelance her writings.

Audrey Zelenski received her Bachelor of Arts degree in Creative Writing from California State University, San Bernardino in 2014. She and her husband, along with their two-year-old twin daughters, reside in Peoria, AZ. Audrey enjoys traveling, hiking, and working with animals. She plans to write novels.

Meet Amy Newmark

Amy Newmark is the bestselling author, editor-in-chief, and publisher of the *Chicken Soup for the Soul* book series. Since 2008, she has published more than 150 new books, most of them national bestsellers in the U.S. and Canada, more than doubling the number of Chicken Soup for the Soul titles in print today. She is also the author of *Simply Happy*, a crash course in Chicken Soup for the Soul advice and wisdom that is filled with easy-to-implement, practical tips for enjoying a better life.

Amy is credited with revitalizing the Chicken Soup for the Soul brand, which has been a publishing industry phenomenon since the first book came out in 1993. By compiling inspirational and aspirational true stories curated from ordinary people who have had extraordinary experiences, Amy has kept the twenty-six-year-old Chicken Soup for the Soul brand fresh and relevant.

Amy graduated *magna cum laude* from Harvard University where she majored in Portuguese and minored in French. She then embarked on a three-decade career as a Wall Street analyst, a hedge fund manager, and a corporate executive in the technology field. She is a Chartered Financial Analyst.

Her return to literary pursuits was inevitable, as her honors thesis in college involved traveling throughout Brazil's impoverished northeast region, collecting stories from regular people. She is delighted to have come full circle in her writing career — from collecting stories "from the people" in Brazil as a twenty-year-old to, three decades later, collecting stories "from the people" for Chicken Soup for the Soul.

When Amy and her husband Bill, the CEO of Chicken Soup for the Soul, are not working, they are visiting their four grown children and their first grandchild.

Follow Amy on Twitter @amynewmark. Listen to her free podcast — "Chicken Soup for the Soul with Amy Newmark" — on Apple Podcasts, Google Play, the Podcasts app on iPhone, or by using your favorite podcast app on other devices.

Thank You

We owe huge thanks to all of our contributors and fans. We were overwhelmed by the thousands of stories and poems you submitted about your miraculous experiences. Our Associate Publisher D'ette Corona, our Senior Editor Barbara LoMonaco, and our editors Ronelle Frankel, Laura Dean, and Crescent LoMonaco made sure they read every single one.

Susan Heim did the first round of editing, D'ette Corona chose the perfect quotations to put at the beginning of each story, and editor-in-chief Amy Newmark edited the stories and shaped the final manuscript.

As we finished our work, D'ette Corona continued to be Amy's right-hand woman in creating the final manuscript and working with all our wonderful writers. Barbara LoMonaco and Kristiana Pastir, along with Elaine Kimbler, jumped in at the end to proof, proof, proof. And, yes, there will always be typos anyway, so feel free to let us know about them at webmaster@chickensoupforthesoul.com, and we will correct them in future printings.

The whole publishing team deserves a hand, including Executive Assistant Mary Fisher, Senior Director of Marketing Maureen Peltier, Senior Director of Production Victor Cataldo, and our graphic designer Daniel Zaccari, who turned our manuscript into this beautiful book.

Sharing Happiness, Inspiration, and Hope

Real people sharing real stories, every day, all over the world. In 2007, *USA Today* named *Chicken Soup for the Soul* one of the five most memorable books in the last quarter-century. With over 100 million books sold to date in the U.S. and Canada alone, more than 250 titles in print, and translations into nearly fifty languages, "chicken soup for the soul®" is one of the world's best-known phrases.

Today, twenty-five years after we first began sharing happiness, inspiration and hope through our books, we continue to delight our readers with new titles, but have also evolved beyond the bookstore with super premium pet food, television shows, podcasts, positive journalism from aplus.com, movies and TV shows on the Popcornflix app, and licensed products, all revolving around true stories, as we continue "changing the world one story at a time®." Thanks for reading!

Share with Us

We all have had Chicken Soup for the Soul moments in our lives. If you would like to share your story or poem with millions of people around the world, go to chickensoup. com and click on "Submit Your Story." You may be able to help another reader and become a published author at the same time. Some of our past contributors have launched writing and speaking careers from the publication of their stories in our books!

We only accept story submissions via our website. They are no longer accepted via mail or fax. Visit our website, www.chickensoup. com, and click on Submit Your Story for our writing guidelines and a list of topics we are working on.

To contact us regarding other matters, please send us an e-mail through webmaster@chickensoupforthesoul.com, or fax or write us at:

Chicken Soup for the Soul
P.O. Box 700
Cos Cob, CT 06807-0700
Fax: 203-861-7194

One more note from your friends at Chicken Soup for the Soul: Occasionally, we receive an unsolicited book manuscript from one of our readers, and we would like to respectfully inform you that we do not accept unsolicited manuscripts, and we must discard the ones that appear.

Chicken Soup for the Soul

Angels and Miracles

101 Inspirational Stories about Hope, Answered Prayers, and Divine Intervention

Amy Newmark

Paperback: 978-1-61159-964-0

eBook: 978-1-61159-263-4

More amazing stories

Chicken Soup for the Soul

Miracles and More

101 Stories of Angels, Divine Intervention, Answered Prayers and Messages from Heaven

Amy Newmark

Paperback: 978-1-61159-975-6
eBook: 978-1-61159-275-7

of faith and hope

Paperback: 978-1-61159-987-9
eBook: 978-1-61159-287-0

Tales of family

Chicken Soup for the Soul

Grandparents

101 Stories of
Love, Laughs and
Lessons Across the
Generations

Amy Newmark

Paperback: 978-1-61159-986-2
eBook: 978-1-61159-286-3

love and wisdom

Chicken Soup Soul.

Life Lessons from the Dog

101 Stories About Our Canine Companions & What Matters Most

Amy Newmark

Royalties from this book go to
AMERICAN★HUMANE
FIRST TO SERVE™

Paperback: 978-1-61159-988-6
eBook: 978-1-61159-288-7

And the other family members

Chicken Soup for the Soul

101 Stories About Our Feline Friends and What Matters Most

Life Lessons from the Cat

Amy Newmark

Royalties from this book go to
AMERICAN·HUMANE
FIRST TO SERVE

Paperback: 978-1-61159-989-3
eBook: 978-1-61159-289-4

and the joy they share

Changing the world one story at a time®
www.chickensoup.com